CRIME AND CULTURE

Advances in Criminology

Series Editor: David Nelken

Titles in the Series

Crime and Culture

An Historical Perspective

Edited by

AMY GILMAN SREBNICK
RENÉ LÉVY

ASHGATE

Published by
Ashgate Publishing Limited
Gower House
Croft Road
Aldershot
Hants GU11 3HR
England

Ashgate Publishing Company
Suite 420
101 Cherry Street
Burlington, VT 05401-4405
USA

Ashgate website: http://www.ashgate.com

British Library Cataloguing in Publication Data
Crime and culture : an historical perspective. - (Advances
   in criminology)
   1. Crime in literature 2. Criminology - History 3. Discourse
   analysis, Narrative
   I. Srebnick, Amy Gilman II. Lévy, René, Dr
   364'.09

Library of Congress Cataloging-in-Publication Data
Crime and culture : an historical perspective / [edited by] Amy Gilman Srebnick and René
   Lévy.
      p. cm. -- (Advances in criminology)
   Includes index.
   ISBN 0-7546-2383-1
   1. Crime in literature. 2. Criminology. I. Srebnick, Amy Gilman. II. Lévy, René. III.
Series.

HV6249.C75 2005
364--dc22

2004024406

ISBN 0 7546 2383 1

Printed and bound in Great Britain by MPG Books Ltd, Bodmin, Cornwall

Contents

List of Tables, Figures, Maps and Graphs

List of Contributors

Pascal Bastien is Professor of History at the *Université du Québec à Montréal* (UQAM) (Canada). His research has focused on judiciary rituals in early modern France and he is currently preparing a book on public executions in eighteenth-century Paris. He has recently published 'Erreurs et miracles judiciaires dans la France d'Ancien Régime,' in Benoît Garnot (ed.), *L'erreur judiciaire de Jeanne d'Arc à Roland Agret* (Paris, 2004), and he is working (with Daniel Roche) on an annotated edition of the 'Journal d'événements' (1764-1789) of the Parisian bookseller, Siméon-Prosper Hardy.

Peter Becker is Professor at the European University Institute (Florence) and a historian of eighteenth, nineteenth, and twentieth-century Europe. He has published widely on the history of criminology as discourse and practice (recently *Verderbnis und Entartung. Eine Geschichte der Kriminologie des 19. Jahrhunderts als Diskurs und Praxis*, Göttingen, 2002) and is currently working on a book project on the history of administrative language and its reform in Europe and the United States.

Jean-Marc Berlière is Professor of Contemporary History at the University of Burgundy in Dijon (France). He has written widely on the history of the police in France. His books include: *Le préfet Lépine. Vers la naissance de la police moderne* (Paris, 1993), *Le monde des polices en France XIXème-XXème siècles* (Brussels, 1996), *Les policiers français sous l'Occupation* (Paris, 2001), *Le crime de Soleilland* (Paris, 2003), *Le sang des communistes* (Paris, 2004, with Frank Liaigre).

György Csepeli is Professor of Social Psychology at Eötvös Loránd University in Budapest and past president of the Hungarian Sociological Association. He is the author of many works including: *National Identity in Contemporary Hungary* (New York and Colorado, 1997); *Az antiszemita előítélet (Anti-Semitic Prejudice)* (Budapest, 1999 (2nd ed.)); *European Nations and Nationalism: Theoretical and Historical Perspectives* (Aldershot, 2000, coedited with H. Dekker, L. Hagendoorn and R. Farnen); and, coauthored with A. Örkény and M. Székelyi, *Grappling with National Identity: How Nations See Each Other in Central Europe* (Budapest, 2000).

Clive Emsley is Professor of History at the Open University (United Kingdom), where he is also co-director of the International Centre for Comparative Criminological Research. His research interests focus mainly on the history of crime and policing in Europe since the end of the eighteenth century. His publications include *Gendarmes and the State in Nineteenth-Century Europe* (Oxford, 1999) and *Crime and Society in England, 1750-1900* (London, 2004 (3rd edition)). He is currently completing a book on the English and violence since the late eighteenth century.

Mary Gibson is Professor of History at John Jay College and the Graduate Center, City University of New York. A specialist in Italian History, her books include: *Born to Crime: Cesare Lombroso and the Origins of Biological Criminology* (2002) and *Prostitution and the State in Italy, 1860-1915* (1986 and 1999). She is currently preparing, with Nicole Rafter, new translations of Lombroso's classic works, *Criminal Woman, the Prostitute, and the Normal Woman* (Durham, 2004) and *Criminal Man* (forthcoming).

René Lévy (co-editor) is director of research at the *Centre National de la Recherche Scientifique* (France). He has published on policing, on electronic monitoring, and on criminal justice history and is the editor (since 1997) of the IAHCCJ's journal, *Crime, Histoire & Sociétés/Crime, History & Societies* (Geneva, Droz). His work includes: *Du suspect au coupable: le travail de police judiciaire* (Geneva, Médecine & Hygiène, 1987); he has also co-edited (with Hartwig Zander), G. Rusche and O. Kirchheimer, *Peine et structure sociale* (Paris, 1994 [*Punishment and Social Structure*, New York, Columbia University Press, 1939]), and (with Xavier Rousseaux), *Le pénal dans tous ses États. Justice, États et sociétés en Europe (XIIème-XXème siècles)* (Bruxelles, 1997).

Mónika Mátay is Assistant Professor of History and Communications at the Eötvös Loránd University in Budapest. Her dissertation, 'Captured by the Dead', is an analysis of Hungarian Protestant wills in the eighteenth and nineteenth centuries. Her first book on nineteenth-century Hungarian divorce cases will be published in 2004.

Wilbur R. Miller is Professor of History at the State University of New York, Stony Brook and the author of *Cops and Bobbies: Police Authority in New York and London, 1830-1870* (Chicago, 1977, reprinted: 1998) and *Revenuers and Moonshiners: Enforcing Federal Liquor Law in the Mountain South, 1865-1900* (Chapel Hill, 1991).

Herbert Reinke teaches criminology at the Bergische Universität Wuppertal (Germany). His research interests cover long-term trends of crime and criminal justice in Germany and the development of the German police. He has edited: '...*nur für die Sicherheit da...?' Zur Geschichte der Polizei im 19. Und 20. Jahrhundert* (Frankfurt-am-Main, 1993), and (with G. Fürmetz and K. Weinhauer) *Nachkriegspolizei. Sicherheit und Ordnung in Ost- und Westdeutschland 1945-1969* (Hamburg, 2001).

Xavier Rousseaux is Associate Researcher at the Belgian FNRS, and Associate Professor at the Université Catholique de Louvain (Belgium). He specializes in the history of crime and justice and is the co-editor of several works including, *Le pénal dans tous ses États. Justice, États et sociétés en Europe, (XIIème-XXème siècles)* (with René Lévy), and *Révolutions et Justice pénale en Europe (1780-1830)* (with Marie-Sylvie Dupont-Bouchat and Christian Vael). He is currently working on the history of state formation and criminal justice in north-western Europe, Benelux, and France, 1750-1850.

Amy Gilman Srebnick (co-editor) is Professor of History at Montclair State University (United States). She writes on crime and culture, the city, and women in

United States history. She is the author of *The Mysterious Death of Mary Rogers: Sex and Culture in Nineteenth-Century New York* (New York, 1995, 1997), and co-editor of *The Mythmaking Frame of Mind: Social Imagination and American Culture* (Belmont (CA), 1992).

Allen Steinberg is Associate Professor of History at the University of Iowa (United States). He is the author of the prizewinning book, *The Transformation of Criminal Justice: Philadelphia 1820-1880* (Chapel Hill, 1989), and the forthcoming book, *The Lawmen Take New York: Murder, Politics and the Origins of the Penal State in Progressive New York*.

Introduction

Crime and Culture:
An Historical Perspective

The essays in this collection explore how the history of crime provides a way to study time, place, and culture. Using an international and interdisciplinary perspective to investigate the historical discourses of crime in Europe and the United States from the sixteenth to the late twentieth century, these original works provide new approaches to understanding the meaning of crime in modern western culture and underscore the new importance given to crime and criminal events in historical studies. Written by both well-known historians as well as younger scholars from France, England, the United States, Canada, Belgium, Hungary, Austria, and Germany, these essays reveal that there are important continuities in the history of crime and its representations in modern culture, despite particularities of time and place.

Scholarly interest in the history of crime has grown dramatically in recent years and because scholars associated with this work have relied on a broad social definition of crime, one that includes acts that are against the law as well as acts of social banditry and political rebellion, crime history has become a major aspect not only of social history, but also of cultural as well as legal studies. While the large volume of research in this area makes it difficult to categorize, several areas of investigation have tended to dominate the field: the study of crime, violence and punishment over time; the history of policing and state control; the history of the varieties of popular rebellion; and the history of criminology itself. In the last few years, work on sensational crimes and *causes célèbres* has become a significant part of this scholarship, providing a way of examining specific cultural moments or mentalities.[1]

The essays in this volume reflect new directions in the field: they stress the importance of an international perspective, interdisciplinarity (drawing especially upon history, sociology, anthropology, and legal studies), and openness to a wide range of theoretical perspectives. They illustrate how similar themes and topics cross national boundaries – the discourses of criminology, the realities of police corruption, the representations of crimes and criminals in popular media. Most importantly, however, the essays in this volume focus on the implications of a close reading (and sometimes

---

[1] Much of this work has been generated by the local and international conferences of the International Association for the History of Crime and Criminal Justice (IAHCCJ, founded in 1978; http://www.h-net.org/~iahccj/) and several groups that have been informally associated with it (in particular, the Social Science History Association in the US, and the European Social Science History Conference in Europe), as well as several other groups and journals, including the journal, *Crime, Histoire & Sociétés/Crime, History & Societies,* edited by René Lévy, and published in French and English by the IAHCCJ (Geneva, Librairie Droz).

a conscious or unconscious misreading) of texts and sources and they explore both representation and narrative as ways for understanding the complex social and power relationships and political implications that are the essence of crime history.

The authors included here analyze the texts not only for the information they yield, but also for the way they convey that information, for whom it was originally addressed, for what purpose it was intended, and how it was ultimately used. Consequently, they examine rhetoric, narrative, and even the politics of literary production (once the territory of literary critics and students of intellectual history) to inquire into the issues of popular rebellion, murder, and police corruption. The essays are concerned with at least two forms of texts: 1) the texts through which criminal events are made known, such as police records, trial narratives, newspapers, and novels; and 2) those which criminal events themselves produce, such as legislative documents and laws, as well as theories about the origins of crimes and criminals.

Some of the essays, such as those of Peter Becker, Mary Gibson and Herbert Reinke focus quite specifically on the discourses of criminology, discourses that both reflected and determined social and penal policy; others, such as those by René Lévy, Jean-Marc Berlière, Clive Emsley and Allen Steinberg focus specifically on the role of the police in very different contexts; still others by Xavier Rousseaux, Pascal Bastien, Mónika Mátay and György Csepeli, and Wilbur Miller examine the popular representations of crimes and criminals. Throughout all of these essays, the significance of crime is understood in its social context; the essays are concerned with how individuals, governments, and even cultures, project definitions of crime and criminality and how those definitions and their understood meanings in turn provide rationales for the policies of the state and the police. Another underlying theme concerns the significance of memory and the way the remembering of historical events is manipulated, sometimes deliberately, sometimes unconsciously, with the passage of time. And throughout all of these essays there is an ongoing concern with how the meaning of crimes and the definitions of what is criminal projects, reflects, and even transforms, power structures, politics, and the understanding of history itself.

These essays seek to forge an approach to the history of crime which is quite consciously grounded in both social history, with its traditional attention to issues of class, race, gender, and ethnicity, and cultural studies, with its attention to the interpretation of texts, the importance of cultural patterns, layers of meaning, and the significance of multiple discourses. As such, they explore an important new turn in the history of crime and justice studies, one that reflects the new attention in historical studies directed to cultural meanings, to the history of memory, to the importance of narrative, and especially to the value of applying literary approaches to texts and language in conjunction with more traditional forms of historical analysis.

*

Crime and Culture: An Historical Perspective addresses, and is organized around, several major topics in crime history. The initial section, 'Crime and the Construction of Historical Narrative,' sets the tone, with essays that explore how crime history engages with historical texts – trial narratives, police reports, sources of popular culture (newspapers, novels, etc.) to construct analyses of criminal events. Amy Gilman Srebnick's introductory essay examines the intimate connection between history and story as it emerges in reconstructions of crime. It includes a discussion of the fascination with the exploration of historical crimes in contemporary fiction, and a discussion of the implications of some contemporary theory for crime history; it concludes with the examination of one particular sensational crime in US history, the Gillette-Brown murder case of 1906, and its most important literary representation in Theodore Dreiser's 1925 novel, *An American Tragedy*.

The next section on 'Discourse and Narrative in Criminal Justice History' features the work of Peter Becker, Mary Gibson and Herbert Reinke, who focus on how representations of criminals defined the history of criminology and criminological science in Germany and Italy. Becker's essay focuses on the history of German criminology, specifically the texts produced by police, psychiatrists, prison wardens, anthropologists, and academics, from a Foucauldian perspective. This essay chronicles the narrative shift in this literature from early practitioners in the field to academics and 'experts' at the end of the nineteenth century. Ultimately, Becker concludes that two significant representations of criminals dominated late nineteenth-century criminology: 1) the notion of the criminal as a 'fallen man'; and 2) the notion of the criminal as a 'degenerate,' one who was beyond the reach of reformation. This dual notion of the criminal was, he argues, the product of social transformations associated with industrialization and the restructuring of the state at the end of the nineteenth century, and more specifically, with the shift from a liberal to an 'interventionist' state. Gibson shows how the Italian criminologist, Cesare Lombroso, a figure also discussed by Becker, created the field of 'Positivist Criminology' by codifying descriptive representations and statistical profiles, along with narrative accounts of criminals in order to define typologies of male and female offenders. Gibson describes a notorious female criminal as 'the old woman of vinegar,' a late eighteenth-century character believed to have helped several Palermo women murder their husbands with arsenic-laced vinegar; and also the prostitute and convicted murderer, Ernesta Bordoni. Working with the tools of cultural analysis, she shows how Lombroso and his disciples melded anatomical descriptions of such criminals (heavy wrinkles, for example) with narratives of their crimes to gain acceptance of their 'science' of criminal anthropology. Reinke looks at the work of one particular criminologist, Robert Heindl, to explore how his definitions of the 'professional criminal' were used during the Weimar, Nazi, and post-war periods in Germany. His argument shows surprising continuities of belief about criminal behavior and its origins over the course of the twentieth century.

The section, 'The Reconstruction of Events in Police and Criminal Justice History,' shows the mutability of interpretations of events involving the police, and how events can be reconstructed to serve immediate political needs and interests. This section includes four essays about the police in London, New York, and Paris, all of which use internal police documents as well as legislative records to develop arguments about the way internal police affairs were controlled and explained to defuse public criticism and, in some cases, to solidify, political power. Clive Emsley, in the first of these, discusses how widespread police corruption was transformed into a case of one man 'on the take.' This essay begins with a detailed discussion of a particular case, that of George Goddard, a former Station Sergeant of the Metropolitan Police sentenced (in 1929) at the Old Bailey to eighteen months hard labor. From here the essay broadens out to set the case in its context; it assesses other disciplinary cases in the Metropolitan Police and in Goddard's division which included the principle 'vice' district in London between the wars. The essay discusses how this and other cases were reported and the response of the Commissioner of the Police to press reports. In conclusion, the essay reflects on the consequences of the official and semi-official discourse for systemic problems within police forces such as London's Metropolitan Police when men are encouraged to unite and enjoy a strong *esprit de corps*, at the same time as confronting highly profitable vice. In the next essay, Allen Steinberg examines the Becker-Rosenthal murder case in Gilded Age New York to show how a case of murder and endemic police corruption were re-invented to serve the political agenda of reformist politicians. His paper challenges the traditional interpretation about the reform of criminal law enforcement in Progressive New York (and elsewhere) and, in light of the Becker-Rosenthal case, offers an alternative interpretation to show the growth of a new kind of pro-penal state conservatism that adopted many of the most unseemly and disturbing features that has sometimes been called American 'popular' justice. Steinberg's paper also draws some interesting parallels with Becker's on late nineteenth-century criminology.

In his detailed study of the Paris police, Jean-Marc Berlière reveals how the post World War II French government reinvented the Paris police of the Vichy period as agents of resistance. He compares and contrasts the different memories of these events: the official memories (those of the State, the Police, the unions), with those of the actors (police agents) and the victims (communists, Jews) and concludes with acknowledging the uncomfortable position of the historian called upon to tell it *like it was* in an era haunted by the *duty* to remember. René Lévy brings this section up to the modern period by tracing events that resulted in new laws in the 1990s about drug trafficking in France and by showing how those laws reflected a power struggle between ministries in the French government. Originating from a scandal involving illegal undercover actions by customs officers, these events illustrate the common tendency to change the law to match police practices rather than the reverse. In this case, however, the Ministry of Justice successfully bargained an amnesty for the sued officers in exchange for increased control on undercover operations by police and customs agencies. Unfortunately, the courts enforced the new laws in a way that considerably weakened these new safeguards.

The final section, 'Representations of Crimes and Criminals,' focuses on issues of cultural, political, and literary representation in the history of crime, and illustrates how both crimes and criminals assume complex meanings within different historical and interpretive frameworks. This section includes two essays on the late eighteenth century: the first, by Pascal Bastien, discusses the different representations of a sensational murder in late eighteenth-century Paris; the second, by Xavier Rousseaux, considers *lieu de mémoire* and the different interpretations of a revolt by Belgian peasants against the French Republic. Bastien, writing about the execution of Antoine-François Derues, explores how the public discourse about the crime can be used to understand the dialogues of power and the use of penal rhetoric in the decades before the French Revolution. Using an array of previously unavailable documents, Rousseaux shows how the understanding of the revolt in the former Austrian Netherlands and the Principality of Liège, annexed by the French in 1798, became inseparable from the context in which the memory of the events themselves were produced. Thus, the revolt was alternately understood as a 'rebel uprising,' the

Belgian Vendée, the *Boerenkrijg,* or the *Kleppelkrick,* depending on the region and its political constructs. These essays about France and Belgium are followed by an innovative piece by the Hungarian team of Mónika Mátay and György Csepeli that explores the changing conceptions of a remarkably enduring figure, the Hungarian *betyár* or highwayman, from the early nineteenth to the late twentieth century. Mátay and Csepeli follow the history of this illusive character and his various representations, placing them in their historical contexts. And finally, Wilbur Miller's essay, 'From Cap Collier to Nick Carter,' examines the changing figure of the detective in the very popular 'Dime' novels of the late nineteenth-century United States. His exploration of works featuring characters like 'Nick Carter, the Young Detective' or 'Old Sleuth,' discusses the nature of the audience for these popular thrillers and shows how these stories reflect a changing economy and society, as well as changing perceptions of detectives, the city, and even of criminality itself.

*

Acknowledgments

The essays in this volume were derived from a series of papers presented at the conference, 'Crime and Culture: Texts and Contexts,' held in Florence (Italy) in May 2001, sponsored by the *International Association for the History of Crime and Criminal Justice* (IAHCCJ), and supported by the *Fondation des Treilles* (Paris, France), and the *Centre de recherches sociologiques sur le droit et les institutions pénales* (CESDIP, Guyancourt, France), with the help of the *Fondation de la Maison des Sciences de l'Homme* (Paris, France), the Department of History and Civilization of the *European University Institute* (Florence, Italy), and the *Centro di Studi CISL* (Florence, Italy). We particularly wish to thank Maurice Aymard, Peter Becker, and Clive Emsley for their help in organizing this conference, and Isabelle Passegué, Bessie Leconte, Walter Srebnick, and Lisa Hacken for their help in preparing this volume. The intellectual spirit of the 2001 conference in Florence, and the conversations it generated about the history of crime discourse, provided the basis for this collection. As a result, this volume has really been an international effort and we are grateful to friends and colleagues on both sides of the Atlantic for making it possible.

Amy Gilman Srebnick
René Lévy

PART I
CRIME AND THE CONSTRUCTION
OF HISTORICAL NARRATIVE

Chapter 1

Does the Representation
Fit the Crime?
Some Thoughts on Writing Crime History
as Cultural Text[1]

Amy Gilman Srebnick

In the past ten years scholarly work on the history of crime has focused on several related topics: the history of specific, even celebrated, criminal events and their cultural meaning, the changing perceptions of crime and criminals over time, the relationship between crime and the development of mass culture. In American studies much of this work has focused on the nineteenth century, particularly on murders or presumed murders, and on crimes set in metropolitan cities. These studies have used crime history not as an end in itself, but as a window into issues and themes in the history of society, culture, and politics.[2]

Interestingly, in U.S. history, at least, many of these works were not originally intended as studies either in the history of crime or of criminology. Unlike notable work in English and Continental history, they were not self-consciously about long-term trends in the history of crime or punishment, about policing or even social control; rarely were they intended as explorations of changing attitudes about social polity. Indeed, with the exception of works that focused on issues of slavery, race, and Southern history, they studied the history of culture and explored issues such as the history of sexuality and gender, the history of urban culture, or even the transformations of literary forms. And while the possibilities of this new connection were exciting for historians like myself, who unexpectedly found themselves attached to a new (for us) sub-discipline of the history of crime and justice, it was also clear

---

[1] I wish to thank Carole Turbin, Bill Miller, and especially Walter Srebnick for reading earlier versions of this essay.

[2] In U.S. history relevant works include: Daniel Cohen, *Pillars of Salt: The Transformation of American Crime Literature, 1674-1860*, New York, 1992; Patricia Cline Cohen, *The Murder of Helen Jewett: the Life and Death of a Prostitute in New York*, New York, 1998; Karen Halttunen, *Murder Most Foul: The Killer and the American Gothic Imagination*, Cambridge, 1998; Paul Johnson and Sean Wilentz, *The Kingdom of Matthias: The Story of Sex and Salvation in 19th-Century America*, New York, 1994; Simon Shama, *Dead Certainties (Unwanted Speculations)*, New York, 1991; Amy Gilman Srebnick, *The Mysterious Death of Mary Rogers: Sex and Culture in Nineteenth-Century New York*, New York, 1995; Andrea Tucher, *Forth and Scum: Truth, Beauty, Goodness, and the Ax Murder in America's First Mass Medium*, Chapel Hill, 1998.

that our approach was somewhat different from the already established work in the history of crime that tended to focus on police history, crime rates, and criminology.[3]

Whether this latest scholarship focused on specific events, on the construction of the criminal, or on the genesis of particular patterns of legal or criminal behavior, it shared several working assumptions which gave it definition: 1) It accepted the notion that crimes, as well as criminals, were essentially social and historical constructs; 2) It depended for evidence and analysis on the close reading of texts (usually, but not necessarily literary texts, including police reports, depositions and trial narratives as well as newspaper accounts and ephemeral literature); 3) It adopted many of the techniques of more traditional literary analysis, taking what the theorist and historian Dominick LaCapra has identified as a 'literary turn' in order to understand these same texts; 4) It often regarded what had previously been seen as literary topics (the development of genres and forms of representation – the newspaper, the execution sermon, the sentimental novel) as both historical and literary constructs; and 5) It employed several assumptions of cultural theory and analysis: the reciprocity of high and low cultural forms, the importance of discourse, and the moveable wall between imaginative works and non *belles lettres*, language-based texts; it acknowledged the importance of ideology and power; and it was concerned with ideology and the modes of cultural production. In these cultural areas it drew quite consciously from the works of Walter Benjamin, Michel Foucault, and Raymond Williams. In a sense, these new works in 'crime' and cultural history (produced on both sides of the Atlantic) were the historian's (postmodern) version of what literary scholars had defined rather awkwardly as the 'New Historicism.'[4]

Because this kind of historical analysis depended so essentially upon the interpretation of texts, it is not surprising that theoretical questions about the use of narrative – the reliability of narrative accounts and the interpretation of texts generally – also made so many of us particularly sensitive to the debates over truth and objectivity that were simultaneously raging within the profession; here I am referring to what Peter Novick, drawing upon questions raised most provocatively by Hayden White, defined several years ago as the 'Objectivity Question.'[5] The proble-

---

3   Other recent work in U.S. history specifically defined as crime history include: Eric Monkkonen, *Murder in New York City*, Berkeley, 2001, and Roger Lane, *Murder in America: A History*, Columbus, 1997.

4   In English History one of the first to treat crime and culture with a 'literary turn' was Judy Walkowitz in *City of Dreadful Delight: Narratives of Sexual Danger in Late-Victorian London*, Chicago, 1992. Several more recent studies in English History have treated crime from a broad cultural perspective, most notably Victor Gatrell's *The Hanging Tree: Execution and the English People 1770-1868*, Oxford, 1994, which investigates the problem of social and cultural sensibility (and the history of emotions) in the wake of England's 'Bloody Penal Code.' For an excellent discussion of historical analysis and literary studies in English literature see: Martin Wiener, 'Treating 'Historical' Sources as Literary Texts: Literary Historicism and Modern British History,' *Journal of Modern History*, 1998, 70, pp. 619-638.

5   Peter Novick: *That Nobel Dream: The Objectivity Question and the American Historical Profession*, Cambridge, 1988; Hayden White, 'The Fictions of Factual Representation,' and other essays in *The Tropics of Discourse: Essays in Cultural Criticism*, Baltimore, 1985 (1978), and *The Content of the Form: Narrative Discourse and Historical Representation*, Baltimore, 1987. The literature on

matics of deciphering point of view and subjectivity in archival sources and of accounting for polyphonic voices and interpretations was, from the start, critical to our work. Moreover, the process of writing crime history, of creating our own narratives about crimes and criminal events, raised certain unusual historiographic questions.

Seen from this perspective, the history of crime became increasingly bound to a set of theoretical and methodological questions about narrative history that are at the center of the already widely acknowledged debates over historical method and interpretation. Three recent publications, A.S. Byatt's, *On Histories and Stories*, Dominick LaCapra's, *History and Reading*, and Carlo Ginsburg's *Rhetoric, Narrative and Proof*, address, from different perspectives, the two interrelated issues in historical studies that I have already alluded to: 1) the nature of historical truth and its adjunct – 'the objectivity question,' and 2) the interpretation of sources by the application of methods of literary analysis and theory (these two issues are quite obviously related since both implicitly are concerned with the reading of historical texts and the ways in which we, as historians, arrive at our conclusions about the past). And, since these two conjoined issues are at the heart of the focus of this collection of essays, I would like to address some of this recent work, and suggest how the perspectives of Byatt, LaCapra and Ginsburg help to raise and illuminate questions about writing the history of crime. My purpose here is not to summarize the recent discussions about either the relationship of literary and cultural theory to historical analysis, or the currently very intense and, I think, quite complex debates about the objectivity of historical narrative and analysis, but rather to problematize these issues more specifically in terms of writing crime history. My hope here is simply to open the door a crack, and then, by briefly examining a celebrated case in U.S. history, to suggest the relevance of this recent work to understanding how representations of crimes in historical studies serve as prisms for understanding past cultures.[6]

On Reading, Narrative, and History

A.S. Byatt's essays, *On Histories and Stories*, address the connection between history and literature from the perspective of a fiction writer and literary critic. In this collection Byatt explores the way fiction writers use historical events, and even 'real' historical individuals, as the subjects of contemporary fiction. At issue here is not the use of history in fiction in the traditional sense – as devices to provide setting and detail for fictive or imaginative tales – but rather a much more self-conscious use of the historical event or individual, or even the historical moment, as vehicles for fictive narratives. Byatt's specific subject is the recent explosion in historical novels – the

---

this topic is extensive; for a good summary of some of these debates see Robert F. Berkhofer, Jr., *Beyond the Great Story: History as Text and Discourse*, Cambridge, 1995.

6   A.S. Byatt, *On Histories and Stories: Selected Essays*, Cambridge, 2000; Dominick LaCapra, *History and Reading: Tocqueville, Foucault, French Studies*, Toronto, 2000; and Carlo Ginsburg, *History, Rhetoric, and Proof: The Menahem Stern Jerusalem Lectures*, Hannover-London, 1999. An even more recent work on this subject is: Mark C. Carnes, (ed.), *Novel/History: Historians and Novelists Confront America's Past (And Each Other)*, New York, 2001.

works of Graham Swift, Pat Barker, or Peter Ackroyd, to name just a few in English letters.

Byatt, who has written many novels with specific and dense historical detail, is also a biographer who approaches historical subjects with great care – hence she approaches the relationship between history (and histories) and stories with knowledge and respect for the issues. As she notes at the outset, the 'renaissance of the historical novel has coincided with a complex self-consciousness about the writing of history itself.'[7] Referring to the contemporary discussions inspired by Hayden White and others about narrative, subjectivity, and modes of interpretation in historical studies, Byatt is particularly sensitive not only to the multiple uses of history and historical events as subjects for imaginative writing, but also to the uses of the past more generally. Why, she asks, is there this 'renaissance,' in historical novels? She answers this question in several ways: 1) it is a response to the simple power, what she calls the 'narrative energy,' of the past; 2) it stems from a desire to recreate the histories and, presumably, actual narratives of those on the social margins – slaves, for example, as in Toni Morrison's *Beloved*, a novel about infanticide; and 3) in the case of war novels, it indicates the ways in which wars, in particular, make possible the subtle manipulation of biological or linear time and allow either for the exploration of the self as an essential modernist theme, or for the investigation of the fragmentation of that same self in a post-modern context.[8]

Byatt takes this issue a step further because she is also curious about what she identifies as the 'slippage between personal histories and social or national histories,' and how both novelists and historians have chosen to meld history and fiction.[9] Norman Mailer's *Armies of the Night* – a book divided into the two sections 'History as a Novel' and 'The Novel as History' – is still one of the classic examples of this genre. More recently, Pat Barker's *Regeneration* trilogy about World War I illustrates this phenomenon quite clearly: Barker uses the 'real' characters of the poet Siegfried Sasoon and the psychologist W.H.R. Rivers in her novel *Regeneration*, but she has them interact with a purely 'fictive' character, Billy Prior.[10] The historian Simon Schama uses the real and the imagined freely in *Dead Certainties*, a work about the celebrated murder of George Parkman at Harvard University in 1849. And a host of other recent works do the same, for example, Alexandra LaPierre's *Artemesia*, a new novel about art, crime (rape), and law in Renaissance Italy, or the works of Thomas Pynchon, as well as many other well researched works of fiction. Even Michael Frayn's play, *Copenhagen,* set off a series of debates about his interpretation of the famous 1941 meeting between Neils Bohr and Werner Heisenberg.[11] All of these works are extremely well

---

7   Byatt, *On Histories and Stories*, p. 9.
8   This latter issue, the problem of cognitive disjuncture offered by wars or catastrophic events is similarly addressed in LaCapra's exploration of the historical writing of Tocqueville and Foucault; the former writing in the shadow of the French Revolution, the latter in the shadow of the Nazi holocaust and World War II.
9   See especially Byatt's chapter, 'True Stories and the Facts in Fiction,' *On Histories and Stories*, pp. 91-122.
10   Barker, *Regeneration; The Eye in the Door; The Ghost Road;* Byatt, *On Histories and Stories*, p. 30.
11   Simon Schama, *Dead Certainties (Unwarranted Speculations)*, New York, 1991. Alexandra Lapierre's *Artemesia, A Novel*, New York, 1998, contains extensive scholarly notes; Michael Frayn's *Copenhagen* (1998) contains a lengthy historiographic essay in the American edition,

researched, many cite their sources, and some even include historiographic and bibliographic essays. In short, their authors all attempt, like good historians, to represent the past, and all the works are intentionally mimetic in their artistic renderings. Comparing her research method to that of a traditional historian, Byatt speaks of how, when working on a project, she immerses herself, sometimes over a period of years, 'in a disparate set of texts.'[12] Taking Byatt's discussion under consideration, the historian might ask not what the differences are between the historian and the novelist – a debate that goes back to Aristotle's *Poetics* – that is not the point; but rather how the forms of the novel, particularly the contemporary novel with its multiple points of view, its concern with the relationship between narrator and subject, its validation of subjective responses to historical events, and its lack of linearity, might help the historian to understand and even to write about the past. In other words, how does the novel, or rather the new construction of the historical novel, offer useful models for the historian struggling with representations and narrative?

*

In a recent volume of essays, *History and Reading*, the historian Dominick LaCapra addresses similar issues of subjectivity, evidence, narrative, and interpretation. Like Byatt, LaCapra argues that wars are particularly important as markers of shifts in modes of historical interpretation and he explores two central texts to develop his argument: Tocqueville's *The Old Regime and the French Revolution* (1856), produced, he argues, in the wake of the French Revolution, and Foucault's, *History of Madness* (1961), written against the backdrop of World War II. But LaCapra is really concerned with the inverse of Byatt's interest in how imaginative writers read the past and employ it in fictive narrative: His quest is to explore how historians quite literally *read* texts and other forms of signification. Like Byatt, he begins by briefly noting the extent of current debates about objectivity and literary theory, and he investigates how the traditional paradigm of research, in which the historian reads for evidence, is no longer sufficient. 'There is a sense,' he writes, 'in which placing language, or more generally, signification, in the foreground of attention and having it apply self-reflexively to the practice of the historian creates a crisis or at least a minor trauma in historiography.'[13] 'The current problem in historiography,' he continues, is 'to conjoin both reading and writing' and to 'attempt to determine what range of practices combines in an acceptable manner a revised understanding of research and modes of reading and writing (or, more generally), practices of signification.'[14] A rethinking of the process of historical writing and analysis would thus necessarily involve alternative notions of objectivity as well as attention to the 'referential dimensions' of the individual assertions of both historians and the sources themselves. LaCapra sets forth five models by which historians read their sources, and ultimately argues for the usefulness of Bakhtin's dialogic approach, which, he suggests, refers in a 'dual fashion

---

New York, 2000. The latter was the subject of a lively exchange in *The New York Review of Books*, 8 February 2001, 28 March and 11 April 2002.

[12]   Byatt, *On Histories and Stories*, p. 107.

[13]   LaCapra, *History and Reading*, p. 24.

[14]   *Ibid.*, p. 27.

both to the mutually challenging or contemporary interplay of forces in language and to the comparable interaction between social agents in various specific historical contexts.'[15] In other words, he pleads for attention to the relational aspect of historical sources, as well as attention to language, point of view, and even the role of transference, in the psychoanalytic sense, in the sources themselves and in the interpretation of those sources.

LaCapra's concern with the voicing in narrative texts, their inherent subjectivity, and with the question of how historians *read* sources has special resonance for crime history. LaCapra's work on historiography, which in recent years has been essentially about the relationship between the observer and the observed, and about the engagement of narrator and subject, suggests some additional issues for us to consider. Many years ago he wrote *Madame Bovary on Trial*, which analyzed the testimony used to prosecute Flaubert in 1857 (for an 'outrage to public morality and religion').[16] But more recently LaCapra, still concerned with subjectivity in historical sources and in the construction of historical narrative itself, has moved his attention to the issue of trauma in historical interpretation. In this regard he has been part of a larger conversation involving historians such as Saul Friedlander, Geoffrey Hartman, and others that has been prompted, in particular, by reference to the historiography of the Holocaust.[17]

For a long time I have been acutely aware that researching and writing about crime, particularly certain crimes like murder, infanticide, or rape, raise particular issues for the historian. Indeed, since I first began working on the history of crime, I have been struck by the degree of personal anguish within the sources and also by the difficulty of maintaining critical distance and a perspective appropriate for an analytic treatment. But it was not until I began reading some of this recent work on the Nazi Holocaust that I began to think about the problem in a more theoretical and useful way. Indeed, reference to trauma, its significance and interpretation, is particularly relevant to crime history, perhaps in a different way and in a smaller frame than, say, writing about the role of trauma in connection with war or holocaust, but useful nevertheless. The servant girl who is the victim of a rape, the slave woman accused of infanticide, even the murderer himself, comes to the police, the court, or even the gallows, in a heightened emotional state. A range of subjective issues affects how these events are reported and understood. How they are told, how they are framed, and ultimately constructed, even in official documentation, is often in the context of extreme emotion. That these emotions are themselves historically reconstructed and determined by available language, or even by conventionally formulated crime reports, raises particular problems of reading and interpretation. Transference, moreover, is of great importance here, operating at all levels of the historical process. It is an issue for the historian who encounters and interprets the evidence, as well as for the early reporters who originally chronicled the event.

The historian faced with recounting and interpreting these issues encounters questions not only about trauma and the interpretation of 'testimony,' but also about

---

15   LaCapra, *History and Reading*, p. 65.
16   Dominick LaCapra, *Madame Bovary on Trial*, Ithaca, 1982.
17   Saul Friedlander, *When Memory Comes*, New York, 1979 (1978); Geoffrey H. Hartman, (ed.), *Holocaust Remembrance: The Shape of Memory*, Oxford, 1994.

the reliability of memory – the memory of the accused, the accuser, of the witnesses, etc. Writers on the Nazi Holocaust from Primo Levi on have noted the significance of memory loss, both individual and collective, as well as the importance of silences in the texts as mechanisms for contending with catastrophe and horror. How, I wonder, do the silences and distortions of memory pertain to crime testimony and to the historical analysis of traumatic crimes and criminal events? And, faced with writing the history of such events, we are always contending with questions about voicing, subjectivity (again), and multivocality. Where, for example is the 'voice' of the victim, the accused, or the accuser? Whose voice does the historian echo and how is a multivocal interpretation expressed within the traditional boundaries of the discipline? The 'middle voice' that LaCapra and others have constructed, the 'in-between' voice of undecideability and the ambivalence of clear-cut positions, provides a useful analytic tool.[18]

*

A third recent publication, Carlo Ginsburg's *History, Rhetoric, and Proof: The Menahem Stern Jerusalem Lectures* continues these explorations about narrative and historical truth. But for Ginsburg, whose focus, like LaCapra's, is really about reading, the dichotomy between narrative and historical truth, or as he refers to it, between rhetoric and proof is, most profoundly, an artificial one. Rhetoric, in its classic forms, he reminds us, was based on proof, and indeed *all* accounts based on language (and presumably also those that are not) are composed of metaphors, tropes, metonymies and synecdoches and thus require analysis and interpretation. Furthermore, narratives can be multivocal; they can, as Edward Said and others remind us reflect a multiplicity of narrative points of view or perspectives. But – and this is Ginsburg's central point – they can also, albeit with some difficulty, 'be known.' In other words, to accept the legitimacy of an analytic (in the sense of literary analysis) approach to historical sources is not to assume that all history is *simply* narrative construction or that it is equal to fictive representation in its final form. It is *not* to accept a flimsy relativism or assume the absolute equality of different perspectives. Rather, it is to urge involvement in a much more critical process of analytic engagement, one that utilizes the techniques and complexities of literary analysis – including attention to silences, narrative strategies and narrative perspective – in the service of historical understanding. To argue this, Ginsburg explores a range of (historical) narratives, including the works of Thucydides and Aristotle and Nietzsche; he analyzes an imaginative narrative, Flaubert's *Sentimental Education*, and he offers an interpretation of a late seventeenth-century historical document.[19]

Ultimately, Ginsburg brings us to a point of complexity. Citing Walter Benjamin, he reminds us that 'one has to learn to read the evidence against the grain, against the intentions of those who had produced it.' 'Only in this way,' he argues, 'will it be possible to take into account, against the tendency of the relativists to ignore the one

---

[18] Dominick LaCapra, *Writing History, Writing Trauma*, Baltimore, 2001, p. 20.
[19] Ginsburg's understanding of the dialogic text is somewhat different from LaCapra's and closer, I think, to that originally understood by Bakhtin. See Ginsburg, *History, Rhetoric, and Proof*, p. 77.

or the other, power relationships as well as what is irreducible to them.'[20] Ginsburg continues this discussion, asserting that narrative models intervene in historiographical labors 'at every stage of the research, creating both roadblocks and possibilities.'[21]

In his essay 'Alien Voices, the Dialogic Element in Early Modern Jesuit Historiography,' included in the collection *History, Rhetoric and Proof*, Ginsburg 'reads' the 1700 text of a Jesuit, Charles LeGobien, about a late seventeenth-century revolt against the Spanish in the Mariana Islands near the Philippines. The arrest and imprisonment of indigenous men on the island who were accused of the murder of a young Spaniard prompted the revolt. In the essay Ginsburg interprets what he calls 'the harangue' of the rebel leader, as reported by the Jesuit, LeGobien. Through an artful interpretation of the text, Ginsburg, using Bakhtin's notion of dialogic or polyphonic texts (those that express multiple viewpoints or voices rather than one singular perspective), argues that the specific text under study reflects the voice of LeGobien himself, rather that of its assumed author (the rebel leader), despite the fact that the text so clearly showed the political perspective of the rebels themselves. It is a conclusion that Ginsburg arrives at not only from his own understanding of the importance of context, but rather from his close analysis of language and rhetoric, to determine the 'authenticity' of the text under discussion. His point is simply this: texts, he reminds us, 'have leaks,' and through the leaks something unexpected arises, something 'akin to knowledge,' if not necessarily truth.

And while Ginsburg warns historians about the dangers of an overly facile relativism in understanding history, he also dismisses the simplistic idea that sources offer an immediate access to reality or even to one face of reality. 'Sources,' he reminds us, 'are neither open windows, as the positivists believe, nor fences constructing vision, as the skeptics hold: if anything, we could compare them to a distorting mirror. The analysis of the specific distortion of a very specific source… implies a constructive element.' But construction, he reminds us, 'is not incompatible with proof; the projection of desire, without which there is no research, is not incompatible with the refutations inflicted by the principle of reality. Knowledge (even historical knowledge) is possible.'[22]

Reading Crime

What are the connections between the issues raised by Byatt, LaCapra, and Ginsburg on reading, narrative, and the history of crime? A.S. Byatt ponders the question: why are novelists drawn to history? Historians might wonder why we are drawn to narrative. Crime historians, in particular, often contend with narrative and issues of narrativity: the narratives contained *within* the sources themselves – a victim's chronicle of events, a witness's description, an accuser's deposition; the social and political narratives, both explicit and implicit constructed *about* those crimes – the

---

[20] Walter Benjamin, 'Ueber den Begriff der Geschichte,' in R. Tiedemann and H. Schweppenhauser, (ed.), *Gesammelte Schriften*, vol. I, tome 2, Frankfurt/Main, 1978, p. 697, in *Ginsburg, History, Rhetoric, and Proof*, p. 24.

[21] *Ibid.*, p. 25.

[22] *Ibid.*

prosecutor's case, the newspaper; and finally, the historian's narrative itself. The first two, narratives that are subsumed within sources and the constructions or representations of crimes in contemporary accounts, both speak directly to the problems of reading, interpretation, voicing, and even transference raised by both Ginsburg and LaCapra. They also refer to the two largest topics addressed by the essays in this collection: 1) the interpretation of texts; and 2) the social, historical and cultural meaning of the representations of crimes and criminals. The third issue, that of the construction of historical narratives, raises somewhat different, if related, problems.

At every level of analysis there are multiple tellings of events. Often too, the original documents are fragmented and non linear; indeed the imposition of a narrative, a major aspect of the historian's craft, tends to impose linearity over what may not be sequential or linear events. Natalie Davis's account in *The Return of Martin Guerre* is a classic example of a crime narrative in which the silences, multiple voices, and differentiated meanings are all critical to any synthetic understanding of the case and its historical significance. A new work, *The Hanging of Ephraim Wheeler: A Story of Rape, Incest, and Justice in Early America,* studies a case of incest, a capital crime in early nineteenth-century Massachusetts, from the perspective of all of the important participants. Here the authors, a psychologist and an historian, give voices in their narrative to several of the participants in an attempt to express multivocality and disparate points of view.[23]

Celebrated cases illustrate Byatt's points even more specifically because they offer us windows into the ways in which historical events become culturally iconic. Indeed, celebrated cases are almost by definition cases where the representation becomes more important than the case itself. My own work on the death of Mary Rogers, a young woman whose body was found floating in the Hudson River near New York City in 1841, speaks to the problem of celebrated cases very specifically. Rogers's death was chronicled in a variety of printed forms: the new penny press, the dime novel, as well as in pamphlet and ephemeral literature. But it received its most expressive treatment from Edgar Allan Poe who used the case as the basis for one of his seminal detective stories: 'The Mystery of Marie Roget.' Because the case happened at a moment of critical cultural disjuncture, it served its contemporaries, as well as those who have chronicled it since in both fiction and non fiction, in similar ways: it enabled an exploration of a variety of issues – sex, abortion, a new urban culture, as well as changing assumptions about gender and class. The nineteenth-century narratives in particular were competing narratives, reflecting a range of political and ideological perspectives on a single event. And, whether fiction or nonfiction, all of the accounts not only reinvented Rogers herself in a variety of ways, they also imposed linear reconstructions and order to the events. That is, they created a tale that began with Mary's arrival in New York and ended with her 'tragic death.' It was, of course, what happened in the middle that was important, and this remained

---

23   Natalie Davis, *The Return of Marin Guerre*, Cambridge (Mass.), 1983; Irene Quenzler Brown and Richard D. Brown, *The Hanging of Ephraim Wheeler: A Story of Rape, Incest, and Justice in Early America*, Cambridge (Mass.), 2003. For a discussion of narrativity in historical sources see also Natalie Davis, *Fiction in the Archive: Pardon Tales and Their Tellers in Sixteenth Century France*, Stanford, 1987.

purely conjecture. But herein also lay an endless array of narrative about the city with its dangers and pleasures, its odd cast of urban characters, and the many versions of Mary's own life. Poe, the highly imaginative fiction writer who was presumably *not* bound by real events, was, in the end, the one most tied to them; he attempted to 'solve' the crime through the newspaper sources alone. Ironically, as if to prove the 'truthfulness' of artistic representation, Poe told the story of Rogers that came closest to the 'real.' His critical and artistic distance provided him with the wide angle lens that explored the contextual cultural issues that made the case both interesting and important.[24] Poe's version replaced what the writer Tim O'Brien calls 'happening truth' with 'story truth' and, as O'Brien reminds us in his collected stories about the U.S. in Vietnam, *The Things They Carried*, 'story-truth is sometimes truer than happening-truth.'[25]

Reading *An American Tragedy*

Another celebrated case, that of Chester Gillette, who was convicted and sentenced to death for murder of 'his castaway lover,' Grace Brown, in upstate New York in 1906 illustrates quite dramatically how a murder became a sensational event and how it was represented in contemporary accounts, as well as in subsequent versions in fiction and film. Because the case served as the basis for Theodore Dreiser's epic 1925 novel, *An American Tragedy*, it offers a good example of the way a notorious case was understood and reinvented by a writer who was both a veteran journalist and a celebrated novelist.[26]

The 'real' events or 'happening truths' took place in upstate New York State where Gillette, then twenty-three years old and working as a foreman at his uncle's skirt

---

[24] See Amy Gilman Srebnick, *The Mysterious Death of Mary Rogers: Sex and Culture in Nineteenth Century New York*, New York, 1995. Edgar Allan Poe understood the relationship between close textual reading and meaningful analysis. Writing in the early nineteenth century, he tried to write what we now term 'true crime' – work that straddled the boundaries between reportage and fiction. Reading and interpreting texts, especially the newspapers that not only reported, but also purported to solve crimes, preoccupied Poe. His argument, like that of his English contemporary and fellow aesthete and sleuth, Thomas DeQuincey, was that criminal events were essentially about legibility – they had to be read; solving crimes, on the other hand, was an act of interpretation that the detective, or a reader, engaged in only after the initial 'reading' had taken place. 'Reading' the available texts required, for Poe, intense engagement with both text and context to discover the clues that lay, often unexpectedly, within them.

[25] Tim O'Brien, *The Things They Carried*, New York, 1979, p. 203.

[26] References to Dreiser's novel are from *An American Tragedy*, New York, 2003 (1925). The relationship between Dreiser's novel and the case is explored in Richard Lingeman, *Theodore Dreiser: An American Journey, 1908-1945*, New York, 1990, esp. pp. 223-266, and Shelly Fisher Fishkin, *From Fact to Fiction: Journalism and Imaginative Writing in America*, Baltimore (Maryland), 1985, esp. pp. 117-122. A dramatic version, adapted by Patrick Kearney, was presented on Broadway in 1926. Two film versions were based on the novel: *An American Tragedy* (1931), directed by Josef von Sternberg (after a plan to use Sergei Eisenstein fell apart in Hollywood), was set in Vienna; and *A Place in the Sun* (1951), directed and produced by George Stevens.

factory in Cortland NY, became romantically involved with Grace 'Billy' Brown, a twenty year old factory worker and the daughter of a local farmer. At the time of her death Brown, already several months pregnant with Gillette's child, had left the factory and returned to live with her family. In early June, and perhaps, as the prosecution charged, in anticipation of marriage, she traveled with Gillette to a resort area in the Adirondack Mountains where they rowed a boat onto Big Moose Lake; it was an outing that ended with Brown's death and Gillette's disappearance. After their abandoned boat was discovered, searches were ordered, the lake dragged, and Brown's bruised body recovered. Gillette was soon discovered in the area, arrested, and charged with her murder.[27] At the time of the arrest, Gillette acknowledged Brown's death but claimed to the arresting officer that it was the result of an accident. The case, which rapidly hit the press, was tried for three weeks the following November in the local courthouse in the small rural town of Herkimer, New York. Gillette was convicted of murder in the first degree on the fifth ballot (one juryman held out) and was sentenced to death in the electric chair. The defense appealed in a lengthy brief that stressed the admission of controversial evidence, but the verdict was upheld and on 30 March 1908 Gillette was electrocuted.[28]

The prosecution maintained that Gillette had taken Brown out onto the lake with the intention of killing her and that he struck her before she fell into the water; the defense contended that Brown, 'desperate over [her] situation jumped into the lake thereby committing suicide.'[29] Although several doctors testified that Brown was beaten before she went into the water, the autopsy was seriously bungled and the admitted evidence in the case remained circumstantial. Among the important pieces of admissible evidence included in the trial were a cache of Brown's letters taken from Gillette's desk and a glass jar containing the preserved fetus that was taken from Brown's body at the autopsy.

The prosecution's case was based on an interesting interpretation of Gillette's motivation: it claimed that Gillette killed Brown, not only because of her pregnancy, but, more importantly, because his relationship interfered with his social aspirations. The state maintained that Gillette had seduced Brown but refused to marry her and it argued that he had 'largely screened this association [with Brown] from observation [and that] in public [he] sought the society of young ladies belonging to what would be regarded as a more pretentious social grade than that to which decedent belonged.'[30] At the trial the prosecuting attorney argued that Gillette's 'uncle's position had admitted Gillette to a different sphere of society from that in which the factory girl moved [and, in time,] the girl became a burden to him in his love affairs with other girls who did not have to work for a living...'[31] As evidence of this the prosecution used Brown's letters, which they claimed served as evidence of her affection for and trust and 'faith' in him. 'They were,' said the more authoritative and generally less

---

27 People of the State of New York v. Chester Gillette, Case Vol. 1, folios 2-10, pp. 418-427.
28 See the Appellant's Points of Counsel before the Court of Appeals, People v. Gillette, Points of Counsel.
29 *The World*, Nov. 29, 1908 contained coverage of this aspect of the trial.
30 The People of the State of New York, Respondent, v. Chester Gillette, Appellant, 191, NY 107, p. 111.
31 *New York Times*, Nov. 18, 1906.

sensational *New York Times*, 'full of pleadings and fears, and yet faith in the young man.' The letters, which might just have easily been used by the defense, taken together with the display of intended 'wedding clothes' and the fetus, elicited an enormous emotional response during the trial and, predictably, moved the jury as well as the crowd.[32]

The defense, contending that Brown was despondent, introduced as witnesses several factory workers who testified that Brown had intimated to them that 'they would never see her again,' and that she 'wished she was dead and would never see the sun rise again.' And Gillette, testifying in his own defense, claimed that Brown 'stood up in the boat and threw herself over into the lake' after a discussion in which he said that he intended to 'inform her father about her pregnancy.'[33] Gillette's explanation of events was weak; he equivocated on whether or not he had struck Brown, and under oath he acknowledged that he had lied when he had claimed (to the arresting officer) that the boat had tipped over causing her accidental death. He also testified that although he was able to swim, he had not tried to reach Brown once she was in the water. Gillette's testimony, taken together with his unapologetic behavior and his passive physical demeanor, did little to engage the sympathy of the jury. Combined with the sensational evidence, his manner was instrumental in securing the final verdict and sentence. The prosecution's case was also buttressed by the emotionally charged attendance of Brown's parents and siblings.[34]

From the outset, the case and the subsequent trial were public events: hundreds of people came into the area, many attended or tried to attend the emotionally charged trial, while others simply visited the town and the attendant sites relevant to the case. So intense was the activity around the trial that at the time of sentencing local authorities, fearing an outbreak of violence (particularly against the defendant), ordered out the local militia.[35] It is easy to understand why the case inspired such interest, having all of the elements of a celebrated case: romance, sex, betrayal and murder. But as Dreiser understood, the real significance of the case resided not only in its inherent personal drama but also in ways more subtle and more important. The case raised issues that were emblematic of transformations in American life in the first years of the twentieth century – the rise of the factory and the presence of a large female labor force, the transformation of class and community in the 'new' factory towns, the changing patterns of leisure, courtship and sexual behavior.

Local and national papers covered the case and the trial in great detail. Their accounts unfolded dramatic and highly speculative narratives of the case and especially about Gillette. Papers like the sensational New York *World*, which covered the case extensively, often accompanied their news stories with elaborate illustrations and photographs of Brown and Gillette (both of whom were extremely attractive), as well as with visual narratives of the events and the court proceedings. A front page story in one Sunday edition of *The World* featured the banner headline: 'MURDERED GIRL AND MAN ACCUSED OF KILLING HER, AND COURSE THEY TOOK

---

32   *New York Times*, Nov. 21, 1906.
33   *New York Times*, Nov. 29, 1906.
34   Gillette's mother, a Protestant evangelist from the Midwest, arrived with press credentials in time to hear the sentence.
35   *World*, Dec. 3, 1906.

TO LAKE WHERE SHE WAS DROWNED.' It featured sketched portraits of Brown and Gillette placed around a map depicting Gillette's journey after the presumed drowning. A scenic postcard of Big Moose Lake completed the composite image; underneath read the caption 'shows where Grace Brown's Body was found.'[36]

By 1906 the press, which had begun using sensational crimes to market newspapers as early as the 1830s, had developed the use of true crime narratives as a major and completely integrated element of the news. Papers like *The World* provided a steady diet of murders and sensational events to their readers; indeed this case vied for front-page space with several other crimes, including the very dramatic murder in New York City of the prominent architect and socialite, Stanford White. The Gillette case, like the story of White's murder, involved a love triangle of sorts, but it was particularly compelling because the participants, like the paper's readers, were so 'ordinary.' Moreover, the setting and the circumstances evoked familiar aspects of contemporary American culture: a 'cast off' and despondent pregnant young factory girl from a local and poor farm family; her beau, a poor but socially ambitious city boy; public discussion of pregnancy and abortion; and finally, a mysterious murder on a summer lake. The newspaper accounts, however, hardly needed to embellish the crime – the narratives introduced at the trial, along with the sensational evidence, were sufficient to hold public attention.

Whether expressed in the trial itself, in the prosecutorial and defense arguments made on appeal, in the newspaper versions, or in Dreiser's later fictional account, the case raises several significant interpretive issues. In particular, the perspectives addressed earlier in this essay in the discussion of Byatt, LaCapra, and Ginsburg, become particularly relevant: the importance of narrative, of close reading – not only of the evidence but also of the nuanced voices of the participants – and of sensitivity to both psychological and sociological dimensions. Finally, in analyzing this case from an historical perspective, the 'silences' in the texts may be just as significant as that which was explicit and overt.

Grace Brown's letters, for example, give us unusual access to the emotional life of the victim. They tell of her profound ties to community and family, of her deep sense of fear about her potential loss of respectability for herself and her child if Gillette were to abandon her, and most importantly, they chronicle her deteriorating relationship with Gillette. Indeed, the letters that were admitted at the trial testify that she was more anguished by what she understood as the alienation of Gillette's affections than she was by her pregnancy. Articulate, even at times eloquent, Brown's letters detail not only her personal dilemma, but also provide a portrait of a young woman caught between several cultures (that of farm and that of factory) and of the impending clash between a modern, individualist culture and one still bound to family and town. LaCapra's cautionary words about understanding trauma, about the nuances of subjective content and about the role of transference – to the jury, to the press, to the reader – take on full meaning here. Brown's own words pull the historian into the charged arena of subjectivity and human feeling.

For the historian writing the history of the Gillette case, the sources are rich and revealing; they tell several compelling narratives of turn-of the-century social life, of the transformation of sexual mores, of habits of leisure, and changing patterns of

---

[36] *World*, July 22, 1906.

work. They also tell much about the press, about the transmission of information and about the relationship between private life and public culture. Here were many narratives: that of the victim, that of the defendant, as well as that of their families and communities. But here also are narratives of social and economic mobility and of distinct differences in the lives and expectations of men and women. 'Happening truth' here was multilayered and reinvented in a series of melodramatic media accounts that transformed the *tragedy*, as Dreiser would name it, into a morality tale of innocence, guilt, sexual transgression, and the ultimate crime of murder.

The compelling quality of these underlying themes was recognized by Theodore Dreiser, an already established writer and able chronicler of turn-of-the-century American culture. Dreiser, who had written devastating critiques of American materialism and its attendant social values in his novels *Sister Carrie* and *The Financier*, was clearly drawn to the issues raised by the Gillette/Brown case. And because of the epic quality of his novel, with its detailed recounting of events and its elaborate psychological portraits, Dreiser's fictional recapitulation of the events became the metanarrative of the case, influencing and infusing all subsequent treatments. Much of this can be attributed to Dreiser's able pen, but Dreiser, working with 'real events,' embarked on his novel with the tools and curiosity of any good historian (echoes of Byatt's words here). Dreiser was, of course, also a 'contemporary' observer of the events; he was working as a journalist when the case first broke in 1906. But it was not until several years later, with some degree of hindsight, and in anticipation of writing a fictional treatment, that he embarked in 1920 on a research journey to the area of the crime.

Between 1906 and 1925, the date of publication, the world at large, as well as the world of America, had changed rather dramatically. The war years did not have the devastating impact that they would have on European culture and social mores, but they were transformative nevertheless. And so Dreiser began his quest to understand the case in earnest in the context of post-war twenties culture: it was a journey that took him not only to the scene of the crime and trial in upstate New York, but in an attempt to understand the psychological portrait of a murderer, to a series of conversations with Freud's American translator and disciple, the psychoanalyst, Dr. Abraham A. Brill.[37]

In working as a newspaper reporter, Dreiser had apparently long been fascinated by the frequent number of murder cases involving young, unmarried, pregnant, women.[38] At one point, writes one critic, 'he is said to have noted that such crimes appeared almost annually from 1895 to 1935.' Years later Dreiser wrote about observing 'a certain type of crime in the United States [that] seemed to spring from the fact that almost every young person was possessed of (...) growing ambition to be somebody financially and socially.' He went on to say that there were many types of

---

[37] Fishkin, *From fact...*, p. 116 and Lingeman, *Theodore Dreiser...*, p. 223 note that Brill had worked as a prison psychiatrist and served as Dreiser's advisor on criminal matters.

[38] Fishkin, *From fact...*, p. 92. Fishkin notes that Dreiser had collected clippings 'about young men who murdered (usually pregnant sweethearts) for social and economic advancement (...) there is evidence that Dreiser was familiar with at least ten murders of this sort (...) at one point he claimed that he knew of one crime of this nature that had taken place nearly every year between 1895 and 1935,' p. 114.

murder for money, one of which was that suggested by the case of Gillette and Brown; it was the story of 'the young ambitious lover of some poorer girl, who in the earlier state of affairs had been attractive enough to satisfy him both in the matter of love and her social station.' 'But 'nearly always,' he continued, 'with the passing of time and the growth of experience on the part of the youth, a more attractive girl with money or position appeared and he quickly discovered that he could no longer care for his first love.' According to Dreiser, what 'produced this particular type of crime (…) was the fact that it was not always possible to drop the first girl. What usually stood in the way was pregnancy, plus the genuine affection for the girl herself for her love, plus also her determination to hold him…'[39]

But it was in an attempt to understand a deeper psychological motivation that Dreiser sought the advice of his contemporary, Abraham G. Brill. No doubt these conversations helped Dreiser to delineate the detailed interior monologues of his central character in the *Tragedy*, monologues which reveal the protagonist and presumed murderer, Chester Griffith (a thinly disguised fictive version of Chester Gillette) to be a typical Dreiser character: a shallow person, with little moral sense and a strong, almost pathological, attachment to social advancement and the acquisition of material possessions.

But Dreiser was apparently as fascinated by Brill's 'stories,' that is the narratives of the psychoanalyst's case studies *à la* Freud, as he was by the theory behind them. And, as if in acknowledgment to the power of stories, he inscribed his copy of the novel to Brill with a reference to their 'Thousand and One Nights.'[40] The reference to the *Arabian Nights* was, however, more than a play on words: Dreiser had read the *Nights* as a boy, had reread them in 1918, and would incorporate them in the *Tragedy*. The Aladdin tale in particular, which tells of how a poor boy with magic power wins the Sultan's daughter, figures prominently not only as a central motif in the novel, where it serves as a means of understanding the motivations of the protagonist, but Aladdin himself is also specifically alluded to at the moment when Griffith makes his decision to murder his former lover, Roberta Alden (Grace Brown), in order to enable him to shun his dreary future and pursue his imagined freer, easier, and richer life. In one of the most chilling and compelling chapters of the novel, a genie appears to Griffith and engages him in a prolonged conversation in which he tells him that 'the plan' is in his 'hands' and he 'can arrange it as [he] will.' 'And how easy!' The genie continues, saying: 'So many boats upsetting every summer – the occupants of them drowning, because in most cases they cannot swim. And will it ever be known whether the man who was with Roberta Alden… could swim? And of all deaths, drowning is the easiest – no noise – no outcry – perhaps the accidental bow of an oar – the side of a boat. And then silence! Freedom… What is wrong with it? Where is the flaw?'[41]

If Dreiser turned to legend and the power of stories to move his character, he also turned to the original documents in the case: Grace Brown's letters, Gillette's testimony, the prosecutor's narrative, the extensive newspaper accounts are all

---

[39] Theodore Dreiser, 'I Find the Real American Tragedy,' *Mystery Magazine*, 2, Feb., 1935, pp. 9-11, reprinted in *Theodore Dreiser, A Selection of Uncollected Prose*, Detroit, 1977, p. 291, and in Fishkin, p. 113.

[40] Lingeman, *Theodore Dreiser…*, p. 223.

[41] *Ibid.*, pp. 243-244; Dreiser, *Tragedy*, pp. 534-535.

incorporated into his narrative. And, with a couple of notable exceptions, Dreiser stayed remarkably close to the detail of the case. Perhaps most significantly, Dreiser evaded the issue of ultimate culpability for the deed, if not ultimate guilt or responsibility. It remains unclear in the novel, just as it did in the case itself, whether Alden/Brown was struck by Griffiths/Gillette, whether she succumbed in a struggle that resulted in a fall, or whether she did in fact jump into the lake in an act of suicide, receiving a blow on the head as she fell.

Characteristically, Dreiser uses these events to chronicle the interplay of powerful historical and social forces, especially the forces of sex and money that he believed defined 1920s American culture. Played out against the tentative morality of American social life, these forces, in Dreiser's imagination, became harbingers of profound human loss and, ultimately, of 'tragedy' and violent death. But in the final analysis, Dreiser has written not the historical novel; rather he has written the novel as history. The title of the novel, with its homage to nineteenth-century references to sensational murders, speaks directly to the larger historical meaning of the event. For, as Dreiser explored in great detail, this was an *American* tragedy; it was defined by particular social, political, and personal landscapes, by typically *American* characters defined by their petty materialism, their narrow yearnings, desires, and social ambitions, and by the way these were acted out against the fragility of human feelings and affections.[42] But, above all, the *tragedy* referred to what Dreiser saw as a supreme crisis in American morality and values. This crisis is, no doubt, what Dreiser saw as tragic, as tragic as the events of the original case itself.

Conclusion

Ultimately, all narrative accounts, whether historical or fictional, impose a synthetic order over events that are *inherently* disordered and culturally disjunctive. Perhaps this raises one of the most salient issues in writing crime history: since crime is perhaps the ultimate disordering of the rationalized structures by which society tries to legitimize the dominant culture, our attempts to explore it, to understand the many ways crime is defined, legislated against, and even narrativized, gets to the core of those essential social constructs. Crime *history*, in its own way, revises the traditional narratives about social order, behavior, and personal and collective deviance. But whether the narratives are imaginative or real, or even deliberately reconstructed to distort the truth, we are all, in the final analysis, faced with working though the meaning of narrative accounts, with interpreting the representations they inspired, with contextualizing them and, finally, with endowing them with historical understanding and meaning. It would seem then that historians, especially historians of crime, are drawn to the narratives or stories contained within their sources for the same reasons as novelists: the narratives open a window to another world, reveal another *mentalité*, and introduce us into another subjective realm. They expose us not only to a range of experiences, but to the meaning of those experiences, in both the felt and the

---

[42]   Murder cases were routinely referred to as 'tragedies' with specific geographic references. The Roger's case was identified as the 'New York Tragedy,' the Lizzie Borden case as the 'Fall River Tragedy,' etc.

cognitive sense for others. For historians of crime these stories illuminate the critical disjuncture of a cultural moment, as they simultaneously attempt to rectify the challenge to cultural stasis provided by giving events a linear, or ordered, narrative. And since those accounts – those stories contained within sources – provided a mechanism for controlling the events described, our function is to both deconstruct the original ordering of events, and reconstruct it (with new meaning and interpretation attached) as coherently and richly as possible.

My point in introducing Dreiser and his novel into this discussion is to make the argument about the continuities between historical writing and fiction, which, either because it deliberately seeks to answer some historical question, or because it does so inadvertently, offers an approach to historical interpretation and knowledge, particularly in reference to celebrated criminal events. 'Happening truth' and 'story truth' obviously both offer ways of accessing and understanding the composite dimensions of significant criminal events. Both rely on narrative as a way of accessing and then interpreting historical events; both impose an order on events that are otherwise discursive and even perhaps chaotic; both impose narrative as a way of rendering the horrific knowable and manageable. Fiction, like any good art, is not a substitute for historical knowledge. But for the historian bound by the rules of evidence, fictive interpretations, particularly those offered by the likes of Dreiser, Poe or even Byatt, offer rich constructions of the past, and sometimes they provide the nuance, depth, and complexity that historians dream about.

PART II
DISCOURSE AND NARRATIVE
IN THE HISTORY
OF CRIMINOLOGY

Chapter 2

Criminological Language and Prose from the Late Eighteenth to the Early Twentieth Centuries

Peter Becker

This chapter analyzes German criminological writing from a structuralist perspective. Using Foucault's concept of discursive practice,[1] I will look at criminological texts as documents that reveal the wider 'political' relations between crime, criminals, and the institutions of crime prevention and detection. I am particularly interested in the various ways in which the logic of criminological writing (episteme) and the logic of crime control (theoretical reasoning and institutionalized strategies) interacted. Given the complexity of the interrelation between criminological reasoning on the one hand and practices of crime detection and prevention on the other, I presume that this interaction can be described neither as a mere reception/implementation of theory by practitioners nor as a theoretical legitimization of given practices of exclusion, stigmatization, and coercion.

My approach is structuralist; it reconstructs the figuration of various elements: political (mode of governance), institutional (organization of crime control), epistemic (the production of criminological knowledge), rhetorical (language games in the scholarly and practical domain authorized to deal with crime and criminals), and social (changing practices as objects of discourse). This analysis compares two different figurations over time: the first one dominating discourse and practice of criminology and crime control until the 1860s, the second one dominating thinking, writing, and performance of scholars and practitioners from the 1870s onwards.[2]

To present my case for a new approach toward criminology as discursive practice, I will proceed in five steps. First, I outline briefly the conceptual framework and its implications for understanding criminological writing of the nineteenth century. Second, I begin the comparative approach to criminology as discursive practice by looking at authors and their institutional positions. Third, I continue the

---

[1]   Michel Foucault, *Archäologie des Wissens*, London, 1972, p. 178ff; *cf.* also Marie-Christine Leps, *Apprehending the Criminal. The Production of Deviance in Nineteenth-Century Discourse*, Durham, 1992, p. 8ff; David Garland, *Punishment and Modern Society. A Study in Social Theory*, Oxford, 1990, p. 131ff; David Garland, *Punishment and Welfare. A History of Penal Strategies*, Aldershot, 1987, p. 10ff.

[2]   This argument draws on my book length study on the history of criminology: Peter Becker, *Verderbnis und Entartung. Zur Geschichte der Kriminologie des 19. Jahrhunderts als Diskurs und Praxis*, Göttingen, 2002.

reconstruction of these discursive practices by looking at criminals as the 'objects' of criminological writing. Fourth, I focus on the rules of formation of criminological arguments, *i.e.* the narratives and the language (registers) employed by criminologists. Fifth, I conclude this reflection on criminology as discursive practice by asking for the political, social, and discursive 'forces' which were instrumental in the transformation of the discursive practice of criminology in the second half of the nineteenth century.

Criminology as Discursive Practice

The term *criminology* is used here in a rather 'open' way: It refers to every systematic and methodical reflection on crime, its causes, and possible remedies. In order to provide a firm basis for the selection of writings, which I have grouped together under the heading of *criminology*, I have decided to use the authors' focus on criminals as the defining element.[3] Criminologists appear therefore under various disguises: they were police detectives and magistrates, prison chaplains and philanthropists, statisticians and hygienists, but also psychiatrists and phrenologists, penal law experts and anthropologists. They produced an enormous amount of text during the nineteenth century – about 2,500 books and pamphlets in German.[4] Their writings vary as to the style and narrative employed, but they have one feature in common: they are all interdiscursive; they incorporate evidence from many different sources, including works of fiction. In addition to this published material, there is a large quantity of unpublished texts: these include numerous memoranda and reports that are accessible in the archives of the police and the ministry of the Interior.

This rather 'open' concept of criminology goes beyond a mere history of discipline or ideas[5] and systematically integrates several sites of the production of criminological knowledge into my analytical framework. One important site, which is frequently overlooked in the history of criminology, is occupied by penal institutions – also a point very dear to Foucault. In the prison system, observation, classification, and re-education produced not necessarily reformed prisoners but always an enormous amount of dossiers in which the 'criminal' was reconstructed as a function within a moral, psychological, social, and economic field.[6]

If we leave the guidance of Foucault and venture into other institutional settings within the penal system, we find a massive contribution to criminological knowledge produced by members of the police and other legal institutions. The increasing

---

3   *Cf.* Günther Kaiser, *Kriminologie. Einführung in die Grundlagen*, Heidelberg, 7th edition, 1985, p. 1.

4   Hans-Heinrich Huelke, Hans Etzler, *Verbrechen, Polizei, Prozesse. Ein Verzeichnis von Büchern und Kleineren Schriften in Deutscher Sprache*, Wiesbaden, 1959; *cf.* also Peter Becker, 'Randgruppen im Blickfeld der Polizei. Ein Versuch über die Perspektivität des 'Praktischen Blicks',' *Archiv für Sozialgeschichte*, 1992, 32, p. 296ff; Peter Becker, *Verderbnis und Entartung...*, p. 14ff.

5   *Cf.* Foucault, *The Archeology of Knowledge...*, p. 135ff.

6   Michel Foucault, *Surveiller et punir. Naissance de la prison*, Paris, 1975, p. 251ff; Michel Foucault, *Histoire de la sexualité. Tome 1: La volonté de savoir*, Paris, 1976, p. 188ff; François Ewald, 'Norms, Discipline, and the Law,' in Robert Post (ed.), *Law and the Order of Culture*, Berkeley, 1991, p. 154.

awareness of magistrates and police detectives about the importance of biographical and ethnographic data on criminals resulted in extensive data collections in these fields. These collections were used extensively by practitioners within police and legal institutions for crime detection, but also for a systematic reflection on the criminal, his background, his socialization, and his activities. These investigations into the logic of the criminal underworld contributed to an emerging specialized discourse on crime, criminals, and crime prevention in the first half of the century. Therefore, we have to include the publications by practitioners in the field of criminological research and writing.[7]

Criminologists are thus *men* who can legitimately claim some authority to speak about crime and, especially, about criminals. As I will argue in this chapter, the grounds on which this legitimization was based, differed. In order to profile more sharply the criminological towards the common-sense and/or fictional knowledge, I would like to state briefly that criminologists were identifiable by their specialized *gaze* on their evidence. This specialization was gained either through experience (exposure in the sense of participatory observation) or through superior observational and analytical skills (as deployed in the laboratory). As long as 'experience' was the main criteria (the *practical gaze*),[8] expertise was not exclusively defined by a specific institutional affiliation. At the end of the eighteenth century, even Johann Ulrich Schöll, a theologian, and Friedrich Schiller, a poet, could claim authority for their representations of criminals.[9]

Comprising all these writings – from theologians, magistrates, psychiatrists, and criminal anthropologists – under the same heading requires a specific analytical approach towards the history of criminology. Looking at criminology as discursive practice requires a conceptual framework, which intends to contribute neither to the genealogy of a well established discipline, nor to the history of the concepts of crime and criminals. The criminologists' reflections on criminals, on their characteristics, on the causes for their existence, and on the strategies to prevent or combat crime, are rather seen as a function of the social, political, institutional, and epistemic setting.

---

[7]   Peter Becker, 'Von der Biographie zur Genealogie. Zur Vorgeschichte der Kriminologie als Wissenschaft und Diskursive Praxis,' in Hans Erich Bödeker, *et al.*, (eds.), *Wissenschaft als Kulturelle Praxis, 1750-1900*, Göttingen, 1999, p. 339ff; Peter Becker, 'Strategien der Ausgrenzung, Disziplinierung und Wissensproduktion: überlegungen zur Geschichte der Kriminologie,' *Geschichte und Gesellschaft*, 2004, 30, p. 399ff.

[8]   The practitioners described their expertise as *praktischer Blick* (practical gaze) and used thus the same concept as medical experts of the late eighteenth and early nineteenth centuries, when they reflected on the epistemological basis of their diagnosis: Becker, 'Randgruppen...'; *cf.* also Wolfgang Eich, *Medizinische Semiotik. Ein Beitrag zur Geschichte des Zeichenbegriffs in der Medizin*, Freiburg/Breisgau, 1986; Michel Foucault, *Naissance de la clinique. Une archéologie du regard médical*, Paris, 1963, 5ème éd., p. 111ff; Barbara Maria Stafford, *Body Criticism. Imaging the Unseen in Enlightenment Art and Medicine*, Cambridge (Mass.), 1991, p. XVII.

[9]   F.Ch.B. Avé-Lallemant, *Das Deutsche Gaunerthum in seiner social-politischen, literarischen und linguistischen ausbildung zu seinem heutigen Bestande*, Leipzig, 1858, 1, lauded in his bibliographical survey of literature on the criminal underworld the book of J.U. Schöll, *Abriß des Jauner und Bettelwesens in Schwaben nach Akten und andern sichern Quellen*, Stuttgart, 1793, and referred to the novel of Friedrich Schiller, 'Der Verbrecher aus verlorener Ehre. Eine wahre Geschichte,' in *Edited works in 5 vols. Vol. 4: Gütersloh*, 1786, pp. 13-36.

The work of the police and penitentiary, the obsession with work and authenticity, the credibility of officials based on their *objective distance*, the shaping the criminal figure as the negative mirror image of the idealized citizen, and finally the relation between anthropological ideas and the forms of governance, altogether defined the structural pattern of criminology as discursive practice. The complex pattern of structural links between the criminological discourse and state, politics, and civil society was subject to change. The analysis of its transformation offers insights into historical processes far beyond the narrow confines of a history of criminology.[10]

When we look at Foucault's remarks on discourse analysis, my research strategy can be easily located within his methodological reasoning outlined in the *Archaeology of Knowledge*. There, he distinguishes three different types of relations between objects and discourses: primary – or 'real' – relations, linking crime rates with socioeconomic structures; secondary – or 'reflective' – relations, focusing on contemporary reflections on crime rates; tertiary – or 'discursive' – relations as the set of structural conditions which assign a particular space to discourses and practices.[11] In his own research agenda regarding the history of criminal policy and criminology, Foucault restricts himself more to the discussion of primary and secondary relations. He failed to develop a convincing outline of the tertiary, discursive, relations for the history of criminology. My brief outline of a history of criminology as discursive practice, which is based on a more comprehensive study, tries to cover the space left void by Foucault by looking more closely at the 'tertiary relations' structuring criminological discourse.[12]

The empirical basis of this study is provided by the analysis of criminological writings produced mainly by German-speaking authors. Even though I will quote a limited number of examples, I will rely on an extensive collection of published and unpublished texts. The unpublished material is collected from four different archives with substantial collections from police departments and their supervising authorities: Berlin, Lübeck, Hannover and Vienna. Towards the late nineteenth century, criminological research and police practices became part of a European, if not global,

---

10 Peter Becker, 'The Standardized Gaze: The Standardization of the Search Warrant in the 19th Century,' in Jane Caplan and John Torpey, (eds), *Documenting Individual Identity. The Development of State Practices in the Modern World*, Princeton, 2001, p. 197ff; M.Ch. Leps, *Apprehending the Criminal...*, p. 8ff.

11 Foucault, *The Archeology of Knowledge...*, p. 45ff.

12 This is not intended to reverse Foucault's shift in perspective towards a 'social history of practices', but to reflect critically on the influence of an emerging social science approach towards social problems on institutional strategies of preventing and fighting crime. On Foucault's shift in perspective *cf.* Ulrich Brieler, 'Foucaults Geschichte,' in GG 24, 1998, p. 261ff. My reflection will not just provide a critique of *Discipline and Punish*, but contribute toward a new history of criminology as discursive practice: focusing on issues of disciplines and power, I offer an approach to criminology as discourse practice: I offer an approach to criminology as discourse that differs from the one Foucault employs, who focused entirely on issues of disciplines and power. For a critique on Foucault from this perspective *cf.* Thomas Lemke, *Eine Kritik der politischen Vernunft. Foucaults Analyse der modernen Gouvernementalität*, Berlin, 1997, pp. 46-50. For a convincing reflection on linguistically oriented approaches to discourse analysis *cf.* Peter Schöttler, 'Historians and Discourse Analysis,' *History Workshop Journal*, 1989, 27, pp. 37-65.

discourse; for this time period, I have looked more systematically at non-German materials.

In terms of research strategies, I have started with a deconstruction of the notion of *criminals*. I have then related the various constructions of criminals to their discursive and inter-discursive contexts – anthropological ideas, ethnographic and medical style of writing, etc. Further, I have established a structural pattern by linking these representations to the institutional practices of police, penitentiaries, and courts. Finally, I have integrated as much information as possible to describe the structural pattern of criminological discourse and its transformation.[13]

Within the time period under study, two major transformations within criminology as discursive practice took place.[14] The first one, the change from a pre-modern to a modern penal system is well described by Foucault's and other authors' analyses of the penal apparatus.[15] I will therefore not focus on it but rather concentrate on the transformation that occurred during the second half of the nineteenth century, which is ignored in Foucault's argument. Even though this discontinuity did not radically change the legal and penal institutions, it did redefine the criminal as object of study, shifted the authority to produce knowledge about criminals from practitioners to medical and anthropological scholars, and reorganized criminological narratives.

Subjects

Criminological discourse was heterogeneous. Its subjects, the authors, presented their reflections on and solutions for the crime problem from many different perspectives. Looking closely at the production of knowledge about deviants in the first half of the nineteenth century, we are confronted with much more variety than Foucault considers. We find the first statisticians such as J.G. Hoffmann (1821) and G. Mayr (1865); philanthropists such as J.H. Wichern (1902 [1849]) from Hamburg; phrenologists such as J. Attomyr (1842); forensic psychiatrists such as J.B. Friedreich (1842) and J.Ch.A. Heinroth (1833); penal law experts such as P.J.A. Feuerbach (1808-1811) and K.J.A. Mittermaier (1832, 1850); as well as an impressive number of magistrates and police experts such as J.F.K. Merker (1818), F.Ch.B. Avé-Lallemant (1858), and F. Eberhardt (1828).[16]

---

13   *Cf.* Becker, *Verderbnis und Entartung...*
14   My concept of discontinuity is derived from Foucault, not from French epistemological authors. This concept refers thus not to the difference between scholarly and everyday observation, but rather to the ruptures within discursive formations. *Cf.* Lemke, *Eine Kritik der Politischen Vernunft...*, p. 41ff.
15   Foucault, *Surveiller et punir...*, p. 75ff.
16   J.G. Hoffmann, *Beitraege zur Statistik des preußischen Staates aus amtlichen Nachrichten, von dem statistischen Büreau zu Berlin bearb*, Berlin, 1821; G. Mayr, *Statistik der Bettler und Vaganten im Königreiche Bayern*, München, 1865; Johann Hinrich Wichern, 'Die Innere Mission der deutschen evangelischen Kirche. Eine Denkschrift an die deutsche Nation,' in Johann Hinrich Wichern, *Prinzipielles zur Inneren Mission*, Hamburg, 1902 (1849), pp. 261-490; Joseph Attomyr, *Theorie der Verbrechen auf Grundsätze der Phrenologie basiert*, Leipzig, 1842; Johann Baptist Friedreich, *System der gerichtlichen Psychologie*, Regensburg, 2nd ed., 1842; Johann Christian August Heinroth, *Grundzüge der Criminal-Psychologie; oder, Die Theorie des Bösen in ihrer*

In quantitative terms, the contribution of magistrates and police experts was the most significant. In monographs and articles in specialized periodicals these authors contributed to an ever growing knowledge about criminals, their social, psychological, and moral 'constitution,' and about the peculiarities of the criminal world. Many of these publications were circulated only among the practitioners themselves, sometimes – as in the case of police gazettes – explicitly reserved for official usage.

In practitioners' contributions to the criminological discourse the link between institutional practice and the discursive construction of the figure of the criminal is obvious. But even in the writings of psychiatrists, statisticians, and phrenologists, we can identify quite a strong link between their logic of argumentation and existing practices of adjudication. This link was particularly strong in their expert opinion regarding the evaluation and classification of criminals and in their contributions to debates about the revision of the penal law. Even though some of these authors were critical of existing penal and police procedures, they criticized them from *within* – that is, on the basis of shared anthropological premises.[17]

In the first half of the nineteenth century, criminological authors gained their authority from their personal experience with criminals, whom they questioned as magistrates, examined as forensic experts, observed as police detectives, or tried to reform as prison officials and philanthropists. In their writings as well as in their functions within the penal system, the authors claimed to have an *experienced* and at the same time *practical gaze*, which privileged their observations and representations. The *practical gaze* was considered to be based on expertise gained through a systematic and reasoned analysis of bodies, habits, and living conditions. It was based on experience and could not be systematically taught but only acquired in some kind of apprenticeship.[18]

The *practical gaze* of magistrates and police detectives was of crucial importance in detecting the *fake* appearances of professional criminals who disguised themselves as the bourgeois during the first half of the nineteenth century.[19] This ability to question bogus appearances lent authority to the experts' readings of events and habitus – especially within penal and police procedures. The claim for expertise became more explicit in those circumstances, when decisions on proper strategies were contested.

Anwendung auf die Criminal-Rechtspflege, Berlin, 1833; Paul Johann Anselm Feuerbach, *Merkwürdige Criminal-Rechtsfälle*, Gießen, 2 vols., 1808-1811; Karl Joseph Anton Mittermaier, *Das deutsche Strafverfahren in der Fortbildung durch Gerichts-Gebrauch und Partikular-Gesetzbücher und in genauer Vergleichung mit dem englischen und französischen Straf-Prozesse*, Heidelberg, 2 vols., 1832; Karl Joseph Anton Mittermaier, *Der neueste Zustand der Gefängnisseinrichtungen in England und englische Erfahrungen über Einzelhaft*, Heidelberg, 1850; J.F.K. Merker, *Handbuch für Polizey-Beamte im ausübenden Dienste*, Erfurt, 1818; Avé-Lallemant, *Das Deutsche Gaunerthum…*; Friedrich Eberhardt, *Polizeiliche Nachrichten von Gaunern, Dieben und Landstreichern nebst deren Personal-Beschreibungen. Ein Hülfsbuch für Polizei- und Criminal-Beamte, Gensd'armen, Feldjäger und Gerichtsdiener*, Coburg, 1828.

17 *Cf.* Becker, *Verderbnis und Entartung…*, chap. 1-4.
18 *Cf.* Ludwig Hugo Franz von Jagemann, *Handbuch der gerichtlichen Untersuchungskunde (Bd. 1)*, Frankfurt/Main, 1838, p. 305; G. Zimmermann, *Die Deutsche Polizei im Neunzehnten Jahrhundert*, Hannover, 1849, vol. 3, p. 1241.
19 Peter Becker, 'Kriminelle Identitäten im 19. Jahrhundert. Neue Entwicklungen in der Historischen Kriminalitätsforschung,' *Historische Anthropologie*, 1994, 2, p. 160ff.

This was the case in the frequent controversies between magistrates and psychiatrists over insanity pleas (and the assertion that criminals were thus less responsible for their acts), or in the controversy between the vice squad and philanthropists over the tolerance of entertainment for working-class youth.[20]

Towards the end of the nineteenth century, the criminological gaze was completely different. The authority of speaking about criminals shifted from practitioners to academics, or at least to medically trained practitioners in penal institutions. Psychiatrists such as Kurella (1893) and physicians such as Baer (1893) used their expertise and experience to challenge the existing legal system from a medical vantage point. They were joined by anthropologists and, to some extent, by penal law experts such as Franz von Liszt (1905),[21] who tried to invoke *scientific* knowledge in their lobbying efforts for a complete overhauling of the penal law. The authority of these criminological experts was based on a superior theoretical framework for the understanding of crime and criminals as a social and political problem, which promised to overcome the shortcomings associated with the existing system of penal law.[22]

The shift from practitioners to medical experts as the authority regarding crime and criminals was linked to a wider trend in restructuring political and social discourses, which are usually described under the headings of *medicalization* and, more aptly, *scientification of the social (Verwissenschaftlichung des Sozialen).*[23]

While practitioners gained their expertise mostly through verbal interactions with their objects, criminologists subjected their objects of curiosity to an instrument-based form of examination. The bodies, psyches, and experiences of criminals were no longer seen as utterances within an (unequal) exchange, but rather as data, which gained its meanings within the conceptual framework of criminal anthropology or criminal sociology.[24]

---

[20] *Cf.* Becker, *Verderbnis und Entartung...*, pp. 86ff and 169ff.

[21] Hans Kurella, *Naturgeschichte des Verbrechers. Grundzüge der criminellen Anthropologie und Criminalpsychologie. Für Gerichtsärzte, Psychiater, Juristen und Verwaltungsbeamte*, Stuttgart, 1893; Abraham Adolf Baer, *Der Verbrecher in anthropologischer Beziehung*, Leipzig, 1893; Franz von Liszt, *Strafrechtliche Aufsätze und Vorträge*, Berlin, Vol. 1: 1875-1891; Vol. 2: 1892-1904.

[22] *Cf.* Peter Strasser, *Verbrechermenschen. Zur Kriminalwissenschaftlichen Erzeugung des Bösen*, Frankfurt/Main, 1984; Renzo Villa, *Il Deviante e i suoi segni. Lombroso e la nascita dell'antropologia criminale*, Milano, 1985; Laurent Mucchielli, (ed.), *Histoire de la criminologie française*, Paris, 1994; Bondio M. Gadebusch, *Die Rezeption der kriminalanthropologischen Theorien von Cesare Lombroso in Deutschland von 1880-1914*, Husum, 1995; Martine Kaluszynski, *La République à l'épreuve du crime. La construction du crime comme objet politique, 1880-1920*, Paris, 2002; Richard Wetzell, *Inventing the Criminal. A History of German Criminology, 1880-1945*, Chapel Hill, 2000.

[23] Lutz Raphael, 'Die Verwissenschaftlichung des Sozialen als Methodische und Konzeptuelle Herausforderung für eine Sozialgeschichte des 20. Jahrhunderts,' *Geschichte und Gesellschaft*, 1996, 22, pp. 168 and 173ff; *cf.* also M.J. Shapiro, *Language and Political Understanding. The Politics of Discursive Practices*, New Haven, 1981, p. 160.

[24] Cesare Lombroso, *Der Verbrecher in anthropologischer, ärztlicher und juristischer Beziehung*, Hamburg, 1887, vol. 1, p. 293; *cf.* also Mary Gibson, 'On the insensitivity of women: Science and the woman question in liberal Italy, 1890-1910,' *Journal of Women's History*, 1990, 2, pp. 11-41; Philippe Artières, *Le livre des vies coupables. Autobiographies de criminels (1896-1909)*, Paris, 2000.

Within this new setting, criminals lost their status as subjects. A similar trend can be seen also within criminal investigation techniques. The introduction of refined technologies for the reading of the crime scene and the remains of the criminal deed contributed to lessening the importance of the statements of suspects, victims, and witnesses, whose depositions were subjected to an increasing amount of criticism.[25]

Even though the approach to criminals changed radically in the late nineteenth century, the criminological gaze still remained a *practical* one. Practical experience with the usage of measurement tools, psychometric instruments, and clinical data remained of crucial importance for the production of reliable classifications.[26] This praxeological dimension of criminological research was one of Lombroso's main arguments against the compilation of large data sets. Large data sets are only useful, Lombroso argued, if they are based on observations that can be made even by unskilled personnel. As soon as the analytical framework required the registration of evidence that was more complicated to assess, such as the psychological character or the form of the skull, the building of large data sets was considered impossible. Under these conditions, a limited number of observations from *competent men* was more valuable than large data sets compiled by incompetent clerks.[27]

Objects

Nineteenth-century criminological writers focused on a heterogeneous group of criminal types. We find robbers and swindlers, vagabonds and alcoholics, pimps and gamblers, professional thieves and passionate murderers, hopeless degenerates and promising sons from good families. Women appear as well, but they are only considered as moral threats to upright males, as supporters of deviant males, or as victims of the blood lust of degenerate males.[28] These figures were sketched in different ways depending on the analytical interest and the institutional position of the author. Until the 1860s-1870s criminological authors wrote under the spell of a strong normative tone: they acknowledged that different representations of criminals existed; they understood these differences, however, as the result of the limited capacities of their practical gaze. Their ultimate dream was the reconstruction of the only 'real' and true representation of the criminal. Only towards the end of the century, criminologists became more aware of the benefits of a multi-facetted representation of criminals. Similar to a cubist painting, their figure of the criminal was consciously fragmented.

Criminologists were closely linked to the practices and objectives of criminal policy and law enforcement. They were unable to ignore systematically the significant

---

25   Hans Gross, *Handbuch für Untersuchungsrichter*, München, 1913, 6th ed., p. 76; *cf.* also Becker, *Verderbnis und Entartung...*, p. 348ff.

26   David G. Horn, 'Making criminologists: Tools, techniques and the production of scientific authority,' in Peter Becker and Richard Wetzell, (eds.), *Criminals and their Scientists: The History of Criminology in International Perspective*, New York, 2004, *in print.*

27   Lombroso, *Der Verbrecher in anthropologischer...*, p. XIX.

28   *Cf.* Becker, *Verderbnis und Entartung...*, p. 205ff; M. Tatar, *Lustmord. Sexual murder in Weimar Germany*, Princeton, 1995.

criminal activities of their times. In their writings they focused, nevertheless, on a limited spectrum of crimes and painted figures of criminals that were 'paradigmatic' of a specific formation of the criminological discourse. In the first half of the nineteenth century, the main emphasis was on property crimes and on professional thieves called *Gauner*. Until the mid-century, property offenses, including arson, were discussed in about 60 per cent of all books and pamphlets dealing with crime, criminals, and the penal system. Only in the last quarter of the century, violent and sexual crimes took the lead in more than 50 per cent of all criminological writings.[29] At that time, violent and sexual offenses were instrumental in understanding the threat posed by the spread of degeneration: the criminal assumed a pale face, a weak volition, and a degenerate physical and psychological constitution.[30]

Table 2.1 Criminological publications by crime types

	1801-1825	1826-1850	1851-1875	1876-1900
Property	59%	37%	37%	35%
Violence	22%	38%	40%	26%
Sexuality	5%	13%	17%	28%
Other	14%	12%	6%	11%
Total	**90**	**195**	**228**	**285**

Gauner and degenerates as criminal figures were shaped by criminological reasoning; they differed not simply with regard to the specific types of crimes they committed. The field of ascription depended on two contrary constructions of criminal identity. The *Gauner* was basically the figure of the volitional wrongdoer – an individual who decided to use his intellectual, social, and physical potential to the detriment of bourgeois society. He was seen as a strong character, but not strong enough to subdue his sensual inclinations or the fantasies that led him astray. The *Gauner* was no born offender. He was presented as having the same potential for a respectable life as his fellow citizens. In his case, an interplay between deviant tendencies and environmental stimuli led him toward a criminal career. The *Gauner* was a fallen man.[31]

The figure of the *Gauner* provided ample evidence for a critical evaluation of society and for the call for new police strategies. On the first level, *i.e.* the link between the criminal figure and social critique, the main emphasis was on the identification of those social practices and environments where men's lives frequently took a wrong turn. Liquor stores, brothels, and gambling houses were presented as the main sites of moral deprivation.[32] But also theaters, the yellow press, and juveniles'

---

29 See table 1.
30 This analysis is based on the bibliography compiled by Huelke and Etzler, *Verbrechen, Polizei, Prozesse...*
31 A systematic reflection on the philosophical basis and legal implications of this mode of representation can be found in Becker, *Verderbnis und Entartung...*, chap. 1.
32 J.F.K. Merker, *Hauptquellen der Verbrechen gegen die Eigenthums-Sicherheit in Berlin, mit Hindeutung auf die Möglichkeit der Verminderung Derselben*, Berlin, 1839, p. 146ff; *cf.* also Dirk Blasius,

exposure to indecency were major concerns.[33] In order to prevent the *fall* of respectable men, criminologists proposed interventionist measures and bemoaned any traces of liberal policies.

On the second level, *i.e.* the link between the *Gauner* and police techniques, the authors were mainly concerned with the problem of identification.[34] To combat professional criminals, seen as the main threat to bourgeois society, they had to be first identified as such. For this purpose police departments, registration offices (Meldeämter), and police gazettes established an increasingly tight communication network and efficient methods of registration to trace the biographies of the *Gauner*.[35] The Berlin police expert *Thiele* found a very fitting expression for this preoccupation: 'Only the biography characterizes the *Gauner*.'[36] Moreover, police experts and magistrates tried to develop a specific *semiotics* to penetrate the phony appearance of crooks. Part of this theory was based on a belief in the existence of a criminal counter-society with specific modes of communication and peculiar lifestyles, which were detectable upon close observation of physiognomies and habits.

Just as the *Gauner* himself was portrayed as the negative representation of the respectable citizen, so too was his social environment described as the negative mirror image of the bourgeois world. Families, associations, a division of labor, maternal love, and specific forms of communication were present. However, the meaning of these institutions was the inversion of their counterparts in the bourgeois world.[37] Maternal love was positive for respectable families, but it had detrimental effects in the underworld as it contributed to strengthening the social ties of crooks.[38] The *semiotics* of deviance tried to make use of these insights and look for links to the underworld: familiarity with the thieves' cant, frequent contacts with other members of the underworld, and specific habits were all signs of a possible membership in the underworld.[39]

Bürgerliche Gesellschaft und Kriminalität. Zur Sozialgeschichte Preußens im Vormärz, Göttingen, 1976, p. 56ff.

[33] H.A. Frégier, *Des classes dangereuses de la population dans les grandes villes et des moyens de les rendre meilleures*, Bruxelles, 1840, p. 184; S.E. Huppé, *Das Sociale Deficit von Berlin in seinen Hauptbestandteilen*, Berlin, 1870, p. 22; Central-Ausschuß, *Die öffentliche Sittenlosigkeit mit besonderer Beziehung auf Berlin, Hamburg und die anderen großen Städte des nördlichen und mittleren Deutschlands. Petition und Denkschrift des Central-Ausschuß für die innere Mission der deutschen evangelischen Kirche an den Reichstag des norddeutschen Bundes*, Berlin, 1869, p. 15ff.

[34] Becker, *The Standardized Gaze...*, p. 145ff.

[35] G. Zimmermann, *Wesen, Geschichte, Literatur, Characterische Thätigkeiten und Organisation der modernen Polizei. Ein Leitfaden für Polizisten und Juristen*, Hannover, 1852, p. 36ff; *cf.* also Dirk Riesener, *Polizei und Politische Kultur im 19. Jahrhundert. Die Polizeidirektion Hannover und die Politische öffentlichkeit im Königreich Hannover*, Hannover, 1996, p. 68ff; Wolfgang Siemann, 'Deutschlands Ruhe, Sicherheit und Ordnung,' *Die Anfänge der politischen Polizei, 1806-1866*, Tübingen, 1985, p. 207ff.

[36] A.F. Thiele, *Die jüdischen Gauner in Deutschland, ihre Taktik, ihre Eigenthümlichkeiten und ihre Sprache*, Berlin, 1842, vol. 1, 2nd ed., p. IIIff.

[37] Becker, 'Kriminelle Identitäten im 19. Jahrhundert...,' p. 150ff.

[38] Schöll, *Abriß des Jauner...*, pp. 245 and 322; *cf.* also Thiele, *Die jüdischen Gauner in Deutschland...*, p. 99.

[39] Avé-Lallemant, *Das deutsche Gaunerthum...*, 2, p. 51ff; F.A. Wennmohs, *Ueber Gauner und über das zweckmäßigste, vielmehr einzige Mittel zur Vertilgung dieses Uebels. 1: Schilderung des Gauners nach*

The degenerate male of the late nineteenth century was quite a different figure. He was a weak personality, incapable of social integration. Because of his lack of carnal inhibition,[40] the degenerate was feared to be capable of every gruesome crime. Degenerates were extremely dangerous, but they were at the same time not deemed responsible for their aggression.[41] Owing to social pressures and negative familial influences, degenerates could never fully develop into mature people. Their exculpation for wrongdoings was more than matched by society's strong claim for protection against the threat posed by them.[42]

The criminologists of the late nineteenth century, writing as psychiatrists, anthropologists, and penal law experts, reconstructed the criminal type with the same objectives in mind as their predecessors. They used their representation of the criminal as the starting point for launching a systematic social critique: Alcohol abuse, venereal disease, the excessive burden placed on weak individuals by urban environments, and the detrimental effects of life in urban ghettos – these were the social problems, which criminologists identified as the main reasons for the very existence and spread of degeneration within society.[43]

While biographies defined *Gauner*, genealogies characterized degenerates. Every degenerate was believed to have hereditary taints that could be traced back to his ancestors. This genealogical approach is very well captured by Foucault's apt phrase that bourgeois society has its inverted nobility: the blood full of stains with ancestors' epilepsy, hysteria, cancer, health problems, or any other forms of obvious deviations from the normative, healthy body.[44] The genealogical approach to criminal identity posed problems for the penal system, however, because degenerates could not easily be held responsible for their criminal acts; they were to be 'sacrificed' for the good of society.[45]

Narratives

When reading criminological texts of the nineteenth century, one is immediately struck by the difference in the organization of the narrative depending on the time of the publication. Statistics, tables with anthropometric measures, and illustrations are important rhetoric devices in the late nineteenth century. For present-day readers, the

---

seiner Menge und Schädlichkeit, in seinem Betriebe, nach seinem Aeußern und als Inquisiten, Güstrow, 1823, pp. 31 and 320ff.

[40] *Cf.* Roger Smith, *Inhibition. History and Meaning in the Sciences of Mind and Brain*, Berkeley, 1992, p. 27ff.

[41] K.J. Kley, *Die Kriminalpolizei. Vol. 1: Verbrecherkunde und Strafrecht mit Kommentar zum Strafgesetzbuch und zur Strafprozessordnung*, Hamburg, 1929, 3rd ed., p. 76; *cf.* also F. Nietzsche, *Menschliches, Allzumenschliches. Ein Buch für freie Geister*, München, 1988 (1878), 1, p. 66.

[42] K. Wilmanns, *Zur Psychopathologie des Landstreichers. Eine klinische Studie*, Leipzig, 1906, p. 418; *cf.* also Daniel Pick, *Faces of Degeneration. A European Disorder, c.1848-c.1918*, Cambridge, 1989, pp. 6 and 20ff; Strasser, *Verbrechermenschen...*, p. 91.

[43] Degeneration theory as an 'ultimate signifier of pathology' was appropriate for conceptualizing these fears: Pick, *Faces of Degeneration...*, p. 8.

[44] Foucault, *Histoire de la sexualité...*, p. 164ff.

[45] Kley, *Die Kriminalpolizei...*, p. 76.

numerous photographs of the physiognomy of criminals and their tattooed body parts are particularly remarkable. In the first half of the nineteenth century, illustrations and tables are a rather rare commodity in criminological writings; text dominates. It is striking how much emphasis was placed on lengthy quotations in thieves' cant. Authors such as Avé-Lallement[46] risked making their argument almost illegible to the non-initiated in order to prove their familiarity with this secret form of communication.

Criminological narratives also differ with regard to the representation of the criminals.[47] These differences are, however, obfuscated by the continuity of themes, *i.e.* the importance of consumption, sexuality, and work habits in the descriptions of criminals throughout the nineteenth century. A closer look at the meanings given to these stigmatized practices reveals the differences in the construction of the criminal. These distinctions were strongly related to differing concepts of *normality*.[48] The criminal was constructed in stereotypical terms and in opposition to an idealized image of the ordinary citizen. The focus on the *Gesinnung*, *i.e.* on the moral-ethical character, during the Vormärz-period strongly influenced the construction of one specific criminal type. Similarly, an emphasis on sanity and fitness left lasting traces on another criminal type.

To understand the logic of the criminological discourse and its transformations, we have to look therefore at *Menschenbilder*, *i.e.* the anthropological premises, which guided the binary constructions of criminals and respectful citizens. The consideration of anthropological premises within the analytical framework provides a conceptual tool for the integration of knowledge, language, and social practices in state and society.[49]

Anthropological ideas determined the linguistic resources available for the classification and representation of men, their habits, and their activities; these schemes of classifications influenced the observations and reflections of criminologists, physicians, anthropologists, and philanthropists as well as penal law experts' discussion on criminal liability. The same ideas were of fundamental importance to the construction of criminals in literature, newspapers, and pulp fiction. Anthropological ideas provided thus a cultural framework in which the observations and strategies of practitioners were endowed with meaning but subjected them, at the same time, to external critique.

---

46 Avé-Lallement, *Das deutsche Gaunerthum...*
47 The studies of Richard J. Evans (*Rituals of Retribution. Capital Punishment in Germany, 1600-1987*, London, 1996), Martin Wiener (*Reconstructing the Criminal. Culture, Law, and Policy in England, 1830-1914*, Cambridge, 1990), Pick (*Faces of Degeneration...*), and Robert A. Nye (*Crime, Madness, and Politics in Modern France. The Medical Concept of National Decline*, Princeton, 1984) reconstruct, from different perspectives, the complex interrelationship between politics, social and cultural practices, and the conceptualization of deviance and normality.
48 *Cf.* Peter Becker, 'Der Verbrecher zwischen Dämonisierung und Normalisierung. Überlegungen zur Kriminologie des 19. Jahrhunderts,' *Wiener Zeitschrift zur Geschichte der Neuzeit*, 2004, 4, pp. 53-78.
49 *Cf.* Achim Barsch and Peter M. Hejl, 'Zur Verweltlichung und Pluralisierung des Menschenbildes im 19. Jahrhundert: Einleitung,' in Achim Barsch and Peter M. Hejl, (eds.), *Menschenbilder. Zur Pluralisierung der Vorstellung von der menschlichen Natur (1850-1914)*, Frankfurt/Main, 2000, p. 11ff.

To understand fully the implications of these anthropological premises, one has to look beyond the classification schemes employed in criminological writings. It is also important to take the narrative dimension into account, which was used to represent the moral or physical degradation that led to criminal careers. A systematic deconstruction of the criminological texts reveals two different master narratives structuring the argumentation.[50]

In my reflections on the subjects and objects of the criminological discourse of the nineteenth century, these two master narratives have been already briefly mentioned. The first master narrative represented the criminal as *fallen man,* whose sensual lust, excessive fantasy, and lack of discipline sent him into the criminal underworld and/or the insanity asylums.[51] The basic assumption behind this master narrative was that every individual was capable of structuring his life according to moral-ethical principles. This assumption was at the core of the liberal notion of social and political integration. Police and penal law were thus understood as the bulwarks only toward those individuals who consciously denied integration into bourgeois society.[52]

The second master narrative was based on the concept of degeneration instead of a moral-ethical outlook on life. Criminals were seen as the unfortunate outcome of an impeded individual evolution, which prevented them from fully developing their social, intellectual, volitional, and physical potential as human beings.[53] Impeded men were considered to be too weak for the demands of modern society. They had to be protected from their own outbursts of violence and from evil influences and misguided choices; at the same time, society had to be protected from them. This protection referred to two different aspects. First, they had to be isolated so that they could not harm other citizens. Second, they had to be prevented from procreating in order not to contribute to the quickly spreading degeneration.[54]

These two master narratives were neither theoretical nor individual constructions. They belonged to the commonsense knowledge about criminals and helped to organize evidence and theoretical positions about criminal careers into a widely accepted narration. Moreover, master narratives were instrumental in guiding the development and implementation of bureaucratic practices for the prevention and control of crime.

Conclusion: On Transformation

The transformation of criminology as discursive practice in the last decades of the nineteenth century was no mere reflection of the changes that took place in the social

---

[50] In both cases, criminologists ascribed an identity to criminals, which was constructed as 'narrative identity.' P. Ricœur, *Temps et récit. 3: Le temps raconté,* Paris, 1985, esp. p. 354ff.

[51] *Cf.* Becker, *Verderbnis und Entatung...,* p. 35ff.

[52] The truly virtuous citizen needed common sense 'Gemeinsinn' (*Vierhaus*), in order to use his liberties in a responsible manner: Rudolf Vierhaus, *"Wir nennen's Gemeinsinn"* (We call it public spirit) Republic and Republicanism in the German Political Discussion of the 19th Century,' in Jürgen Heideking and James Henretta, (eds.), *Republicanism and Liberalism in America and the German States,* Cambridge, 2002, p. 21ff.

[53] Becker, *Verderbnis und Entartung...,* p. 255ff.

[54] R. Heindl, *Der Berufsvebrecher,* Berlin, 1926, 6th ed., p. 328ff.

and economic setting. The process of industrialization, urbanization, and the emergence of ghettos in cities such as Berlin have to be considered as important contexts for this shifting discursive practice. Observations about the negative impacts of social changes on the fitness of military recruits, as well as the threat of socialism's seductiveness upon the uneducated masses, further influenced the conceptual framework of criminologists. Of equal importance was the failure of existing practices of crime prevention and crime control. Publicly available statistics on crime and recidivism painted a dark picture of an avalanche of criminals who could neither be reformed nor deterred by the existing institutional framework.

At the same time, the success of Darwinism and the increasing importance of degeneration theory provided the anthropological basis for a new understanding of men. The legal and penal apparatus could be exculpated on the grounds of these new anthropological premises: the natural born criminal could neither be deterred nor reformed. For the criminologists of the second half of the nineteenth century, these insights demanded a systematic restructuring of the penal apparatus, in which liberal notions of self and society had to give way to a new interventionist state practice, directed and guided by the superior reason of medical experts. Deviance assumed a new character: it was no longer perceived as a normative problem, that is, as unethical behavior to be eliminated. Now, criminologists understood deviance increasingly as a specific kind of normality, which posed a threat to state and society and had to be contained as well as regulated.

The transformation of the criminological discourse is therefore closely related to the restructuring of state and society in the second half of the nineteenth century. The shift from a liberal to an interventionist state, the medicalization and scientification of social, economic, and even – to some extent – of political problems were part of the same transformation.

Chapter 3

Science and Narrative in Italian Criminology, 1880-1920

Mary Gibson

In 1893 Cesare Lombroso published *Criminal Woman, the Prostitute and the Normal Woman*, his companion piece to *Criminal Man* and the founding text in the criminology of women. True to the principles of his internationally-renowned theory of criminal anthropology, he detailed the many physical anomalies that distinguished the female born criminal from the 'normal' woman. One of these was an excess of 'exaggerated wrinkles,' and he supported this conclusion with both quantitative and qualitative data.[1] The former were organized into a table comparing 158 normal women with 70 female criminals in terms of the severity of wrinkles on eight different parts of their faces. Although his statistics showed that female offenders were 'in general' no more wrinkled than normal women, his table did identify certain types of wrinkles as more frequent among older criminal women: vertical wrinkles on the forehead, creases on the cheeks, lines around the lips, and crow's feet at the edges of the eyes.[2]

Lombroso complemented this rather ambiguous statistical evidence with the story of a female murderer from the late eighteenth century, who was still remembered by the Italian public. Commonly referred to as 'the old woman of vinegar,' she had helped a series of women from the popular neighborhoods of Palermo kill their husbands with a type of 'vinegar' made with arsenic and commonly sold to treat the heads of children for lice. She was memorialized by a bust in the Museum of Palermo, a photograph of which is included in *Criminal Woman*. According to Lombroso, 'This bust, with its virile angularity and especially the extraordinary wealth of wrinkles that mark her ancient demonic grin, is enough by itself to prove that this woman was born for evil.'[3] By recalling this notorious example, Lombroso was able to end his short section on wrinkles with a clear verdict that immorality is written on the body of born criminals.[4]

---

[1] Cesare Lombroso and Guglielmo Ferrero, *La donna delinquente, la prostituta e la donna normale*, Turin, 1893, p. 321. Nicole Rafter and Mary Gibson have recently completed a new translation of this classic work on female criminology entitled *Criminal Woman, the Prostitute and the Normal Woman*, Durham (NC), 2004.

[2] *Ibid.*

[3] *Ibid.*

[4] Giovanna Fiume has written a fascinating micro-history of this case, in which she contrasts the popular belief that the old woman was using magic with learned legal opinion that her victims died of poison. See *La vecchia dell'aceto: Un processo per veneficio nella Palermo di fine Settecento*, Palermo, 1990.

Such a conclusion seems dubious and contrived to modern scholars, especially in light of Lombroso's general intellectual project. Lombroso and his followers claimed to have revolutionized the study of crime, replacing abstract philosophical analysis with scientific proofs. Their so-called 'positivist criminology' was to be based on material facts that could be measured and counted. Like other scientists, they promised to eschew prejudices in favor of objective investigation of the causes of crime.[5]

From this perspective, Lombroso's discussion of the relationship of wrinkles to female crime seems less than scientific. Although appearing objective, his table falls short in several ways. He offers no explanation of how he chose his two samples of women, besides mentioning that urban workers and peasants comprised the 'normal' group. As he himself admits, the data show no overall difference between the two groups. He thus turns to a more specific comparison by type of wrinkle and age. But because he starts with only 70 female offenders, the numbers resulting from this cross-tabulation are statistically insignificant. That he concludes with a sensational case of a wrinkled murderess seems an act of desperation to save his hypothesis. This strategy is unconvincing in scientific terms, because one case does not prove a general law.

But can we read the story of the 'old woman of vinegar' in another way than simply as an example of bad science? Lombroso's chapter on wrinkles in criminal woman was not an exception, but exemplified the mode of argumentation employed by Italian criminal anthropologists in general. Throughout their writings are combined statistical data – often displayed in tables, charts, and maps – with a variety of narrative examples drawn from myths, literature, history, proverbs, and current news. Lombroso's fondness for drawing evidence from so many sources may have come partly from his Italian educational background, where he was steeped in the classics and humanities. Furthermore, as his biographer Renzo Villa has pointed out, the most formative intellectual influence on Lombroso came not from the scientist Charles Darwin but from the linguist, Paolo Marzolo.[6] From Marzolo, Lombroso learned to correlate the stages of language with the progress of civilization. Throughout his life, he retained a vivid interest in speech as a sign of biological evolution, recording examples of 'savage' speech and criminal jargon.

In her analysis of the 'production' of criminological discourse, Marie-Christine Leps has recently suggested another reason for the surprising presence of stories in scientific texts, including those of Lombroso. For her, 'narratives did not represent passing aberrations in otherwise rigorously scientific texts,' but 'they intervened whenever dogmatic or enthymematical discourse could no longer reason what had to be demonstrated.'[7] In other words, when positivist criminologists ran out of statistical

---

5   For an analysis of the Italian positivist school of criminology, including its views on women, see Mary Gibson, *Born to Crime: Cesare Lombroso and the Origins of Biological Criminology*, Westport (CT), 2002; Daniel Pick, *Faces of Degeneration*, Cambridge, 1989; Delia Frigessi, *Cesare Lombroso*, Torino, 2003; Renzo Villa, *Il deviante e i suoi segni: Lombroso e la nascita dell'antropologia criminale*, Milano, 1985.

6   Villa, *Il deviante e i suoi segni...*, p. 91.

7   Marie-Christine Leps, *Apprehending the Criminal: The Production of Deviance in Nineteenth-Century Discourse*, Durham, 1992, p. 56.

evidence to prove their theories, '*short stories* would take over and function as the *direct manifestation of reality*.'[8] Using the technique of analogy, criminologists drew examples from botany, biology, paleontology, archeology, linguistics, and history and reduced them to equivalent, self-evident facts. The truth of notions like 'criminal man,' therefore, lay not in scientific proof but from intertextuality, that is, the appearance of corresponding 'facts' and 'stories' in a series of different texts.

I would like to explore further the hypothesis that the presence of stories in the works of Italian criminal anthropologists did not simply represent scientific weakness, but served a larger purpose. This line of enquiry is inspired by the new cultural history, which is interested less in what a text means than how it works.[9] From this perspective, internal inconsistencies in a text are less important than its ability to persuade. Indeed, by combining different types of seemingly incompatible evidence, Lombroso potentially strengthened his argument and broadened his circle of converts to the idea that wrinkles were a sign of evolutionary atavism. The statistical table would most impress those readers with a scientific bent while the story would persuade others less able to follow abstract or mathematical reasoning.

The new cultural history also suggests that texts are not simply a pale reflection of social life or, in Marxist terms, a passive aspect of the superstructure. As Sarah Maza explained in a recent review essay on 'Stories in History,' 'culture is not just reflective, it is also, and above all, performative.'[10] Although narratives do follow accepted scripts and often derive their power from embodying conventional wisdom, they are also active agents in the process of social change. As Foucault has shown, the new discourses of the nineteenth century about deviance and sexuality did not reflect an objective reality, but acted to constitute those very concepts. From this point of view, even the Lombrosian theories that seem most silly today, like that on the correlation between wrinkles and crime, deserve scrutiny as types of 'knowledge' that produced 'power.'

Because culture is performative, historians have begun to pay particular attention to the writers and the readers of different types of narratives. Roger Chartier has reminded us of the inherent tension between these two groups: writers try to control the meaning of their texts, but readers bring diverse experiences and expectations that often subvert this meaning.[11] Thus it is most fruitful to view Italian criminal anthropology as a discourse marked not by unity but fragmentation. Authors like Lombroso did not themselves produce unified texts, but employed a variety of proofs, like statistics and stories, that appealed to different groups in their audience. How did their readers interpret these texts, especially when, in Chartier's phrase, 'reading is a creative practice?'[12] Could criminologists impose a unified meaning on their disparate data

---

8   *Ibid.*
9   A phrase of the literary critic Fredric Jameson, quoted in Lynn Hunt's 'Introduction' to her edited volume entitled *The New Cultural History*, Berkeley-Los Angeles, 1989, p. 15.
10   Sarah Maza, 'Stories in History: Cultural Narratives in Recent Works in European History,' *American Historical Review*, Dec. 1996, p. 1501.
11   Robert Chartier, 'Texts, Printing, Readings,' in Lynn Hunt, (ed.), *The New Cultural History*, Berkeley, pp. 156-157.
12   *Ibid.*, p. 156.

40   *Crime and Culture: An Historical Perspective*

once their texts were in the hands of various 'interpretive communities' of readers, each with their own needs and interests?[13]

This essay will explore these themes in relation to a certain type of cultural production typical of Italian criminal anthropology, that of the vulgarized or popularized text. From the publication of the first edition of *Criminal Man* in 1876, Lombroso set the tone for a movement that consciously sought publicity, even at the risk of sensationalism. He and his followers delighted in regaling their students and the press with tales about their ability to walk unannounced into any prison and guess the crime of each inmate based simply on his/her physical features.[14] Labeled 'the master,' Lombroso forged a new field that claimed to be a science but inspired almost religious zeal from its adherents.[15] As part of their task of spreading the positivist gospel to the masses, criminal anthropologists were indefatigable in giving lectures and writing articles for popular audiences.

Such an endeavor was refreshingly democratic in a country prone to intellectual elitism and academic stuffiness. The impulse to break out of the ivory tower had political roots, both in the Lombroso's ardent support of the liberal *risorgimento*, the Italian movement for unification, and the later adherence of most criminal anthropologists to the socialist party.[16] But it posed a challenge to a movement purporting to be constructing the first rigorous science to examine the etiology of crime. How could Lombroso and his followers produce a discourse that was at the same time scientific and popular? I will suggest some answers to this question by examining three positivist texts that were written specifically for a larger audience: an article by Lombroso published in *Nuova Antologia*, a magazine with wide circulation among the educated classes; an article written by Guglielmo Ferrero, published in a volume analyzing famous trials; and a lecture by Salvatore Ottolenghi to a class of police cadets, which was reprinted in the journal of the national police academy.

The first example is an article entitled 'The Last Brigand,' published in 1902 by Lombroso in *Nuova Antologia*. The article marked the capture of Giuseppe Musolino, a 'celebrated brigand' from Calabria who had evaded capture for years.[17] Opening his article with the words that 'everyone knows' the details of the arrest, Lombroso indicates that he has purposely chosen a sensational case. He holds his readers' attention by ridiculing the government for having had to spend one million lire and employ over 1,000 soldiers and policemen to bring the brigand into custody. Recasting the capture as a farce, he describes Musolino's defeat as coming not from the security forces, but rather from the wires used to train grape vines, which prevented his quick retreat from a vineyard where he was finally captured. The tone of the first few paragraphs, therefore, is one of sarcasm that seems to favor the brigand over the state.

---

13   Phrase coined by Chartier, 'Texts, Printing, Readings,' p. 158.
14   For example, Enrico Ferri, Lombroso's most famous follower and author of *Criminal Sociology*, made such a claim. See Gibson, *Born to Crime...*, p. 35.
15   On the establishment of criminology as an academic field and a science, see Christian Debuyst, Françoise Digneffe, Jean-Michel Labadie, and Alvaro P. Pires, *Histoire des savoirs sur le crime et la peine*, Brussels, 1995.
16   For an overview of the *Risorgimento*, the Italian movement for unification, see Spencer di Scala, *Italy: From Revolution to Republic, 1700 to the present*, Boulder (Col.), 4th edition, 2004.
17   Cesare Lombroso, 'L'ultimo brigante,' *Nuova Antologia*, 1st Feb. 1902, p. 508.

As the article becomes more didactic, however, Lombroso undercuts his earlier sympathy for Musolino by pronouncing him to be a born criminal with physical and psychological anomalies. As was often the case, Lombroso had not collected this evidence himself, but relied on photographs and the observations of other criminal anthropologists. Nevertheless, he authoritatively listed the signs of anatomical degeneration in the brigand: a receding forehead, protruding eyebrows, and an asymmetrical face. Even more damning were his psychological anomalies including 'an instinct for killing and revenge.'[18] After attempting homicide twenty-four times, often successfully, Musolino felt no remorse. Instead, he exhibited a 'diseased sense of vanity,' eagerly awaited publicity in the press, claimed to be protected by a special saint, compared himself to the Count of Montecristo, and predicted that he would be elected to Parliament.[19]

At the root of such impulsive and egocentric behavior was epilepsy, which was 'the basis of born criminality,' according to the latest edition of Lombroso's seminal work, *Criminal Man*.[20] That Musolino had purportedly suffered episodes of epilepsy since the age of twelve was consonant with his family history. His uncle and three cousins were criminals, another cousin and three sisters epileptic, his grandfather and uncle 'apoplectic,' and his father suffered 'dizziness, which constitutes the embryonic form of epilepsy.'[21] In short, the brigand was 'a born delinquent by heredity' marked by the 'contradictory character' typical of epileptics: 'now excessively agitated and verbose, later silent and stupid like an idiot...; now suspicious [and] diffident, later childishly trustful; and intermittently alternating a beastly blood-thirsty ferocity with a certain affability.'[22] Lombroso explained Musolino's strange behavior by biological determinism, which had distributed a germ of degeneracy throughout his entire family.

In the second part of his analysis, Lombroso returns to his earlier tone of admiration for Musolino, declaring him to have 'extraordinary intelligence.'[23] Only in this way could he explain the bandit's rapid promotion to the position of *capo* (head) of the local mafia, his genius for evading capture for so many years, and even his ability to compose verses that were 'not worse than those of many little poets in Italy.'[24] He noted that Musolino enjoyed widespread sympathy among the rural poor, who 'considered vendetta to be a right and even a duty,' especially against the rich and powerful.[25] Lombroso also admired his sense of proportion in meting out 'barbarous justice' and his refusal to stoop to petty crimes like theft.[26] Such reservations led Lombroso to admit at one point in the article that perhaps Musolino did not represent

---

[18] *Ibid.*, p. 509.

[19] *Ibid.*, p. 510.

[20] *Ibid.*, p. 509. Lombroso's most famous book, *L'uomo delinquente* (*Criminal Man*), went through five editions between 1876 and 1896-1897. In the fourth edition (1889), Lombroso introduced epilepsy as the equivalent of atavism in causing inborn criminality.

[21] *Ibid.*

[22] *Ibid.*, pp. 509-510.

[23] *Ibid.*, p. 510.

[24] *Ibid.*, p. 511. Lombroso uses the word 'mafia' in reference to Musolino's Calabrian gang, although its use is generally limited to Sicily.

[25] *Ibid.*, p. 512.

[26] *Ibid.*, p. 509.

'the complete criminal type,' but fell halfway between a criminaloid and a born criminal.[27]

Lombroso suggested two other factors that had shaped Musolino's criminal nature – social environment and race. Consonant with his socialist sympathies, Lombroso outlined the extreme poverty and illiteracy of Calabria, partly the fault of the state, which led to high rates of crime and sympathy for outlaws. Of more importance for explaining Musolino himself was race, and Lombroso assumed that his readers understood the racial peculiarities of the South. For example, Musolino was long-headed with a protruding jaw, normal for 'this regional type' but inferior to northern physique.[28] He easily committed homicide because it 'is not considered so serious a crime as in other parts of the country.'[29] That Calabrians were marked by a 'really inferior stage of moral development' was attributable to their racial origins, which included 'semi-savage colonies of Albanians and Greeks.'[30]

Lombroso carefully crafted his article to appeal to the educated, but generally non-academic, readers of *Nuova Antologia*. The most widely-circulated magazine of its type (comparable to the *New Yorker*), *Nuova Antologia* included articles on politics, science, and art. To popularize the theory of criminal anthropology, Lombroso turned one sensational case into a narrative. He interwove seamlessly his own 'scientific' analysis with an account of Musolino's life, family, and community. His conclusion that the brigand was a born criminal, or at least a criminaloid, seemed to emerge naturally from the 'facts' of his biography in a way that was easier to grasp than tables with statistics. Lombroso made no attempt to put this case in a wider context or offer any objective proof that Musolino was representative of a larger group, whether of bandits, criminals, or Southerners. But his mode of story-telling assumed that this famous figure symbolized larger issues.

Despite the seeming simplicity of the tale, however, Lombroso's text lacked unity. Alternating between disdain for Musolino's atavistic heredity and admiration for his daring, the tone of the article is inconsistent. Lombroso offered contradictory explanations for Musolino's behavior: on the one hand he blamed innate physical factors like epilepsy and race while on the other he decried the deplorable economic and social conditions in Calabria. This ambiguity in tone and message, however, may not have confused readers but rather attracted groups of varying political opinions into the orbit of criminal anthropology. Lulled by the promise that science under-girded Lombroso's conclusions, conservatives could read them as sanctioning biological determinism while liberals and socialists could focus on his environmental analysis.

The second example of a text intended to popularize criminal anthropology comes from a volume entitled *World of Crime*, published in 1893. Part of a series edited by three of Lombroso's followers – Guglielmo Ferrero, Augusto Bianchi, and Scipio Sighele – this volume recounted the proceedings of famous criminal trials and then offered the reader a *perizia*, or 'scientific' analysis of the evidence. We will look at the

---

[27]   *Ibid.*, p. 508.
[28]   *Ibid.*, p. 508.
[29]   *Ibid.*
[30]   *Ibid.*, p. 513.

case of the murderess Ernesta Bordoni as retold by Ferrero, who, as the co-author of the *Criminal Woman*, had an expertise in female crime.

In Ferrero's version of the story, Bordoni was a prostitute who was fortunate enough to work outside the system of legalized brothels. Stating that she came from an impoverished neighborhood of Bologna 'crowded with hovels that seemed almost to be mud huts of savages,' Ferrero hinted at her atavistic origins.[31] While admitting that Bordoni was 'one of the most admired seamstresses of the quarter of Porta San Vitale,' he predicted that she would have ended up in a squalid brothel if she had escaped criminal indictment.[32] Accused of killing her ex-boyfriend with a kitchen knife on March 1, 1891, Bordoni claimed that she had acted in self-defense. Zannino, the boyfriend, had insisted that she resume their relationship and, when she refused, hit her several times. Some witnesses to the incident threw doubt on Bordoni's version, claiming that she was initially quite friendly to Zannino but later initiated the violence after shouting 'You villain, I'll kill you.'[33] Her actions seemed premeditated, since she had borrowed an especially sharp knife from a neighbor before going to meet Zannino. Furthermore, the prosecution argued that she had been instigated by her half-brother, Rodolfo Ferri, because of an incestuous love he harbored for her. Found guilty of murder but without premeditation, Bordoni received a relatively light sentence of four years' imprisonment. Her half-brother Ferri got a much heavier punishment of fifteen years, since he was held to be the instigator of the episode.

In his perizia, Ferrero pronounced the verdict 'very strange;' it seemed illogical to label Bordoni's action spontaneous and unpremeditated if it had been instigated by her half-brother.[34] But Ferrero mentioned this inconsistency only in passing, reserving the bulk of his article for analyzing the physical and psychological deficiencies of Bordoni. From her photograph, he identified two anomalies: 'a low forehead and small head in relation to her body; and an elongated face, which I would call almost horsy, without any expression whatsoever.'[35] Psychologically Bordoni was morally insane, since she lacked modesty, the second most important virtue for women after motherhood. Her act of homicide could not be excused as a defense of her honor, since she lacked the innocence of a renaissance Juliet. Neither could it be explained as a 'crime of love' since Bordoni had testified that she had never loved anyone. Identifying these last words as 'the confession of a real moral idiot,' Ferrero labeled her violence as 'a crime of hate' motivated by 'one of those intense, blind, and irrational hatreds' typical of born criminals, epileptics, and hysterics.[36] This type of hatred needed no external stimulus, but could arise automatically from a 'morbid incitement of the psychic centers' and expand to such exaggerated intensity that it exploded into violence.[37] According to Ferrero, normal people had the mental power

---

[31] Guglielmo Ferrero, Augusto G. Bianchi, and Scipio Sighele, *Il mondo criminale italiano*, Milano, 1893, p. 86.

[32] *Ibid.*, p. 87.

[33] *Ibid.*, p 89.

[34] *Ibid.*, p. 104.

[35] *Ibid.*, p. xi.

[36] *Ibid.*, pp. 95 and 97.

[37] *Ibid.*, p. 98.

to block or redirect this nervous energy, but Bordoni's lack of emotional restraint recalled the behavior of children, primitives, and even wild animals.

The influence of Lombroso on this analysis would be clear even without Ferrero's explicit acknowledgment of 'the profundity of the theory of Lombroso.' Ferrero diagnosed Bordoni in Lombrosian terms, tracing the roots of her perversity to moral insanity, atavism, epilepsy, and disease. What distinguished Ferrero's analysis of Bordoni from positivist case studies of men was its emphasis on her sexuality. Because Bordoni had 'a string of romantic intrigues, and not all of them platonic' by the age of eighteen, Ferrero pronounced her morally insane.[38] On the other hand, her lover, Zannini, was 'basically an honest worker' despite his affair with Bordoni.[39] Although Bordoni was known in her neighborhood as an excellent seamstress, Ferrero asserted that she was also a *grisette*, a part-time prostitute. And he concluded that if she had been instigated by her half-brother, only a sexual relation like that of incest could explain such submission.

The purpose of Ferrero's article was in many ways similar to that of Lombroso's in *Nuova Antologia*. The authors of both essays presented sensational cases in narrative form. The readers of *The World of Crime*, like the *Nuova Antologia*, were educated and middle class, able to afford such publications. They were sophisticated enough to be offered a 'scientific analysis,' although a 'soft' one based on stories rather than a 'hard' one based on statistics. Both articles were didactic and sought to diffuse the language and terminology of criminal anthropology to an audience outside of academic circles. While Lombroso wove his analysis into his story, Ferrero apparently adopted the more rigorous method of telling the unadorned story and only then offering criminological analysis. He carefully prepared the reader for his 'scientific' conclusions, however, by sprinkling his story with phrases like 'mud huts of savages' that were only thinly veiled metaphors for atavism.

In contrast with Lombroso, Ferrero presented a more unified narrative. The only ambiguity in his analysis related to the underlying cause of Bordoni's anomalies, which he attributed variously to atavism, disease (degeneracy), moral insanity, and epilepsy. His lack of clarity echoed Lombroso, who had gradually expanded his definition of the born criminal to include all of these categories as equivalent causes of deviancy. But for the most part Ferrero was unrelentingly direct in his diagnosis of Bordoni as physically and emotionally perverse. Her criminal act, like her life in general, was rooted in sexual behavior more typical of 'savages' than civilized Europeans. He showed no admiration, as Lombroso had for Musolino, of any of her traits.

Ferrero's unremitting condemnation of Bordoni implies that Italian society faced a widespread eruption of violent crime by women. Yet, as Ann-Louise Shapiro has pointed out in her study of Parisian trials in the same period, 'the very fact that contemporaries wrote extensively about the problem of the female criminal in the absence of statistically important criminal behavior by women seems to point to 'female criminality' as a code that condensed, and thus obscured, other concerns.'[40] In the case of Bordoni, crime is a code for the growing threat of unrestrained female

---

[38] *Ibid.*, p. 92.
[39] *Ibid.*, p. 91.
[40] Ann-Louise Shapiro, *Breaking the Codes: Female Criminality in Fin-de-Siècle Paris*, Stanford, 1996, p. 4. On women's crime rates in Italy, see Gibson, *Born to Crime…*, pp. 55-60.

sexuality – and perhaps freedom in general – which positivist criminologists like Ferrero diagnosed as pathological. The reductionism with which criminal anthropology traced female criminality to sexual deviancy remained one of their strongest legacies to future criminology.

The third text comes from the *Bulletin of the School of Scientific Policing*, a journal published by the staff of the national training institute for administrators in the Public Security force (PS) and distributed to police officials, prison wardens, and magistrates throughout the nation.[41] Entitled 'A violent convicted thief with hysterical-epilepsy and tuberculosis,' the article was included in the section of the *Bulletin* entitled 'Criminology Clinic.' It began with a transcription of a lesson given by the director of the School, Salvatore Ottolenghi, before a class of 100 students. Ottolenghi, a disciple of Lombroso, put criminal anthropology into practice by bringing the thief from his prison cell to the classroom and giving him a physical and psychological examination. Giovanni Falco, the author of the article and a junior instructor, then interpreted the 'facts' elicited from the body and mind of the thief in terms of criminal anthropological theory. Thus, the class literally exemplified the well-known positivist adage to study the criminal not the crime.

This article was more complex than the other two because it combines the voices of several participants in this drama: those of the prisoner, his wife, police, prison administrators, magistrates, asylum officials, and criminal anthropologists. Conflict arose not only between the story of the thief and authorities, but also among different institutions within the criminal justice system. Considered 'sincere' by Ottolenghi and Falco, the thief related his life in terms that conform to official records: he had been sent to a reformatory at the age of seven; worked periodically as a butcher, upholsterer, and street vendor of fruit; been interned in a mental hospital eleven times; and been arrested fifteen times for theft, assault, and resisting authority. Under questioning by Ottolenghi about his morality, he admitted to getting drunk almost every day and having had lovers before his marriage. However, he contested the assertion of his wife and her family that he was insane, accusing them of vindictiveness rather than concern for his health. He also denied having assaulted police without provocation, claiming that they were 'insolent' and 'always had it out for him.'[42]

According to the 'direct examination' by Ottolenghi, the thirty-three year old thief was emaciated with 'mild signs of degeneration' of the head including facial asymmetry, a detached right ear, and widely-separated cheekbones; he also exhibited deep cavities around his collar-bone.[43] Of more interest to Ottolenghi were the scars on his left forearm and chest from 'self-mutilation.'[44] According to the prisoner, whose words were recorded verbatim in the article, he had wounded himself while interned in an insane asylum. He also had scratches all over his body from a struggle with police during his most recent arrest; his wife had called the police after a quarrel, during which he had stripped himself naked. Ottolenghi also noted the physical

---

41   The Public Security Force (PS) was one of Italy's two major police forces with responsibility for policing cities. The other force, the *Carabinieri*, patrolled the countryside but eventually also took up urban duties.

42   *Ibid.*, p. 239.

43   *Bolletino della Scuola di Polizia Scientifica*, 1916, p. 237.

44   *Ibid.*, p. 238.

symptoms of an advanced case of tuberculosis, considered a sign of degeneracy by positivist criminologists.

The question of the thief's mental state created tension between police, magistrates, and officials of the insane asylum. According to his police file, which filled three volumes, the thief was a threat to society, having been arrested almost yearly. But these arrests were often contested by other authorities. When sent to the Mental Hospital of Santa Maria della Pietà for being 'unbalanced,' prison doctors routinely labeled him a malingerer and released him for lack of pyschopathic symptoms. As an alternative, police repeatedly put him on the list of habitual criminals subject to special surveillance (*ammonizione* or *vigilanza speciale*). Such orders were often rescinded by judges, however, who believed that such close scrutiny by police only increased his mental instability.

Falco took into account both Ottolenghi's 'direct examination' of the prisoner and these other 'indirect' sources for his criminological diagnosis of the thief. Consonant with the positivist emphasis on heredity, Falco noted that both his father and sister had been interned in an insane asylum. From childhood, the thief had been impulsive and violent, attacking police, his cellmates in prison, and even himself. In short, he was a 'habitual thief, with a congenital inclination toward crime and a tendency for violence against the authorities.'[45] Dangerous to society, he was not insane enough to be permanently committed to an asylum. Therefore, police would have to submit him to 'rational surveillance' that would not provoke psychotic behavior. His advanced case of tuberculosis might succeed where the criminal justice system had failed by weakening his body and therefore his ability to threaten society.

More interesting than Falco's conclusions were the multiple readings afforded by the text. Containing voices of many different parties, the reader could easily find support for a variety of diagnoses. Unlike the first two examples, this article more rigorously separated and documented the different sources of information, so that it contained a series of parallel narratives. Such richness and ambiguity may have arisen from its purpose as a semi-professional text. Ottolenghi's lesson was directed toward students who already had law degrees and were preparing to enter the elite, administrative ranks of the Public Security forces. Expected to imbibe the methods of forensic examination, these future police administrators would adopt the mission of spreading criminal anthropology throughout the Italian peninsula. Therefore, Ottolenghi and Falco loosened their control over the narrative by refusing to edit the 'facts' to make a single and consistent story. They also allowed the possibly subversive voice of the prisoner himself to speak directly to the class, and through Falco's transcription, to all readers of the *Bulletin*.

In conclusion, these three texts illustrate the value of narrative for Italian criminal anthropologists in their crusade to spread their 'scientific' theory, whether to the next generation of students or to the public at large. By focusing on individual, sensational cases, Lombroso and his followers easily piqued the interest of their readers and slipped in didactic lessons that probably went unnoticed. These narratives were also easily digestible because they drew on what Chartier has called 'preknowledge' and Leps labels 'preconstructs' shared by scientists and their audience.[46] Positivist crimi-

---

45   *Ibid.*, p. 249.
46   Chartier, Texts, Printing, Readings, p. 165; Leps, *Apprehending the Criminal...*, p. 11.

nologists, therefore, never had to prove certain assumptions that all educated readers brought to the texts. For example, common wisdom held that 'savages' were less evolved than Europeans, that women were irrational and impulsive, and that physical features reflected moral character. Such widely-held notions made positivist analysis easier to grasp and, in a circular manner, the prestige of science reinforced their seeming validity. This circularity of power/knowledge helps to explain why Lombroso and his colleagues became celebrities in Italian society.

It would be wrong, however, to see the adoption of narrative by criminal anthropologists as simply an artificial ruse to win converts. As I mentioned above, Lombroso was a student of linguistics and brought a fascination with proverbs, myths, and history into his new school of criminology. Furthermore, he was a physician and psychiatrist, trained to study the symptoms of his patients. Therefore, the criminal case study, where he classified and interpreted the various signs of physical and mental deviancy, was consistent with his academic training. A tension runs throughout positivist criminology between this intense focus on peculiarities of the individual criminal and the attempt to quantify rates of anomalies in mathematical tables. The first exemplifies what Carlo Ginzburg has called the 'semiotic paradigm' that proceeds through 'the analysis of specific cases which [can] be reconstructed only through traces, symptoms, and clues.'[47] For Ginzburg, this is the only appropriate method for the human sciences, including medicine and history, 'in which the object is the study of individual cases, situations, and documents, precisely *because they are individual.*'[48] He contrasts the semiotic paradigm to that of Galilean science, which assumes 'quantification and the repetition of phenomena' that is found only among inanimate objects.[49] From this perspective, criminal anthropology was on more solid methodological ground when telling stories than when proposing abstract laws based on statistical evidence. Narrative, therefore, might be seen not as a weakness marring the texts of Lombroso and his followers, but rather as their strength. While failing as science, the texts of Italian criminal anthropology merit further study as narratives.

---

[47]   Carlo Ginzburg, 'Clues: Roots of an Evidential Paradigm,' *Clues, Myths and the Historical Method*, Baltimore, 1989 (orig.: 1979 in Italian), p. 104.

[48]   *Ibid.*, p. 106.

[49]   *Ibid.*

Chapter 4

'Robert Heindl's *Berufsverbrecher*': Police Perceptions of Crime and Criminals and Structures of Crime Control in Germany during the First Half of the Twentieth Century

Herbert Reinke

Introduction: Robert Heindl's *Berufsverbrecher*

Crime and the police, especially the *Kriminalpolizei* and its detectives, became popular topics in the media in Germany during the Weimar Republic years. Thrilling homicide cases excited the readers of the newspapers and made the detectives who handled prominent homicide cases public figures. Many detectives started writing themselves, taking their readers into the tracks of criminals.[1]

Most of these detective writers produced popular mixtures of facts and fiction, but one author, Robert Heindl, became highly popular because he dealt with facts only – or, to be more precise – what he considered the 'facts.' In 1926 Robert Heindl published a voluminous study on the *Berufsverbrecher*, the habitual and/or professional criminal.[2] This book had tremendous impact and success in the 1920s: It was re-printed seven times in three years and – according to the author – received hundreds of reviews in the national and international press. The success of Robert Heindl's book on the *Berufsverbrecher* is evidence that the author was more than just a detective writer: By the mid-1920s, Robert Heindl, who had successfully introduced innovations into the German *Kriminalpolizei*, had already made a reputation for himself as a criminological author and as an influential expert in police matters.

Who was Robert Heindl? Born in 1883, Heindl had already started to build himself a career as a man of innovative criminological thinking (in issues of contemporary criminological standards) when he was a university student of criminal

---

1   Ernst Engelbrecht, *In den Spuren des Verbrechertums. Ein Streifzug durch das großstädtische Verbrechertum und seine Schlupfwinkel*, Berlin, 1931; Birgit Kreutzahler, *Das Bild des Verbrechers in Romanen der Weimarer Republik. Eine Untersuchung vor dem Hintergrund anderer gesellschaftlicher Verbrecherbilder und gesellschaftlicher Grundzüge der Weimarer Republik*, Frankfurt/Main, 1987; Patrick Wagner, *Volksgemeinschaft ohne Verbrecher. Konzeptionen und Praxis der Kriminalpolizei in der Zeit der Weimarer Republik und des Nationalsozialismus*, Hamburg, 1996.

2   Robert Heindl, *Der Berufsverbrecher. Ein Beitrag zur Strafrechtsreform*, Berlin, 1926.

law. In 1902, when he was only a nineteen-year old student,[3] Heindl published a memorandum that proposed the introduction of fingerprinting as an identification technique. Heindl sent this proposal to the police headquarters of a number of major German cities. Only one year later, the police of Dresden, Berlin and Hamburg had introduced fingerprinting. In 1909 Heindl became responsible for the implementation of the identification service of the Bavarian state police, and that same year he began travelling to explore penal colonies in East Asia and Australia. This travel was intended to investigate whether the transportation of convicted criminals to overseas penal institutions could be an option for improving penal strategy, one that might be adopted by the German criminal justice system. Robert Heindl published the experiences of his journey in 1913, under the title *Meine Reise zu den Strafkolonien* (My Journey to the Penal Colonies), and in it he argued against using penal colonies as an aspect (and as an improvement) of the German criminal justice system.[4] At this time he had been head of the Dresden *Kriminalpolizei* for two years, and he used this position to propose further innovations, such as the creation of an identification and data service for the *Kriminalpolizei* on the national level; additionally, from 1917, he had edited one of the leading German language criminological journals. In 1919, he left the police service to start a new career at the counterespionage department of the German Foreign Office. But this new career did not end his multi-faceted reputation as a criminologist and as an expert in police matters: In 1922, he drafted a national law on the implementation and the institutionalization of a *Reichskriminalpolizeiamt* (a national office for the *Kriminalpolizei*, intended to increase the efficiency of the criminal police); additionally, Robert Heindl became a leading member in the influential *Kriminalpolizeiliche Kommission*. In 1933, at the age of fifty, he was forced to retire by the Nazi government, which distrusted Robert Heindl for a number of reasons. After the war, the Americans reengaged him (among other experts) to rebuild the police in Bavaria, and, until 1949, Heindl directed the identification office of the Bavarian state *Kriminalpolizei*. Robert Heindl died in 1958.[5]

What made Robert Heindl's text on the *Berufsverbrecher* an influential work? Its impact was largely based on the author's abilities to place his arguments at the center of a number of police discourses: Heindl summarized the experiences and practices of the contemporary police, as well as the ways the police organized these experiences and practices into data files and collections, photographic albums, fingerprint collections, etc. In other words, Heindl's book reflected police practice, already in place for some time, but not previously made explicit in a focused and specific way by any other German-speaking author.[6] But Heindl went further: He not only summarized contemporary police practices, he also pretended to have detected the *Ureigenschaften*, the very basic principles of crime and criminal motivation. Heindl understood these *Ureigenschaften* as being inscribed in individual characteristics that distinguished *Gelegenheitsverbrecher* from *Berufsverbrecher*. From his point of view,

3   Rüdiger Herren, 'Robert Heindl. Der Mann, der Deutschland die Daktyloskopie brachte,' *Kriminalistik*, 1972, pp. 570-572.
4   Robert Heindl, *Meine Reise zu den Strafkolonien*, Berlin, 1913.
5   Herren, *Robert Heindl...*
6   Wagner, *Volksgemeinschaft ohne Verbrecher...*; Patrick Wagner, *Hitlers Kriminalisten. Die deutsche Kriminalpolizei und der Nationalsozialismus*, München, 2002.

Gelegenheitsverbrecher were those criminals who committed casual crimes from time to time, whereas *Berufsverbecher* were those criminals who committed crimes in a sort of habitual *and* professional way and as a professional career. A translation of Heindl's term *Berufsverbrecher* comes close to the notion of the 'professional criminal,' implying not only the aspect of professionalization (in the strict Anglo-American sense of the term), but also implying the characterization of criminal activities as 'work,' as well as a task that required skills, technical competences, and, above all, specialization. To distinguish *Gelegenheitsverbrecher* from *Berufsverbrecher* was not really that new at the time Heindl proposed it, nor was it greatly original. In the German-speaking context, in the decades around the middle of the nineteenth century, experts among the German police personnel had put forward similar views about the criminal population in the German-speaking countries.[7] The discourse of penal reform, which had started in Germany shortly before the turn of the twentieth century, argued along similar lines.[8] But due to his reputation and his 'good writing,' Heindl's arguments became highly influential in the arena of German-speaking criminal and penal policy, and especially among the senior ranks of the German *Kriminalpolizei*. In his bestseller he argued that the number of *Berufsverbrecher* had grown considerably since the decades before the First World War, and that the most serious crime problem resulted from this group of *Berufsverbrecher*, and consequently, that fighting these *Berufsverbrecher* would tackle the contemporary crime problem at its very center. On the basis of a recounting of some German criminal statistics and also the extrapolations of experiences that Heindl had made while working as the head of the Dresden *Kriminalpolizei*, as well as some good guessing, he estimated that some 8,500 *Berufsverbrecher* could be seen as the core group of the criminal class in the Weimar Republic of Germany.[9] Although a number of critics, including experts from the senior ranks of the *Kriminalpolizei* questioned some of the basic assumptions of Heindl's distinctions, finding them too simple, many officers saw them as matching their professional experiences and read them as 'ideal-type' representations of their work.

The Development of the *Kriminalpolizei*

How did the practice and activities described in Heindl's text look to the Weimar Republic *Kriminalpolizei* officers, and how did they compare to their actual police work and professional backgrounds? Most of the background information, the police's perceptions of crime and criminals, investigation techniques, control structures and strategies, had already been developed before the First World War and had not changed significantly during the Weimar Republic years. During most of this period the *Kriminalpolizei* in Prussia was largely identical to the Berlin branch of this police, which was quantitatively and qualitatively the largest single *Kriminalpolizei*, not only in Prussia, but in all of Germany. Shortly before the First World War almost 14 per cent of the personnel of the Berlin police belonged to this department. In 1931, among the

---

7   Peter Becker, *Verderbnis und Entartung. Eine Geschichte der Kriminologie des 19. Jahrhunderts als Diskurs und Praxis*, Göttingen, 2002.

8   Richard F. Wetzell, *Inventing the Criminal. A History of German Criminology*, Chapel Hill, 2000.

9   Heindl, *Der Berufsverbrecher*...

approximately 7,000 men in the ranks of the Prussian State *Kriminalpolizei*, more than 2,000 belonged to the Berlin branch of this state police. But the Berlin *Kriminalpolizei* was more than just the largest *Kriminalpolizei* apparatus in the country, it was technically the most elaborate as well, and thus also served as a sort of model organization for most of the other *Kriminalpolizeien* in Germany.

The Berlin *Kriminalpolizei* had attained this first rank position only gradually during the second half of the nineteenth century. In the years after 1870, the *Kriminalpolizei* were to a large extent institutionally separated from the rest of the general apparatus at the Berlin police headquarters, as well as increasingly internally specialized.[10] The *Kriminalpolizei* had started during the middle of the nineteenth century as a police branch whose work had been based primarily on 'intuitive observation and detection.'[11] It was not until the 1870s that the first attempts to professionalize the police personnel, and to elaborate and standardize their work patterns and organization, gained ground. These patterns increasingly included elaborate approaches to forms of documentation and the registration of specific categories of crime and criminals. These efforts can be understood as the police's response to specific urban developments in late nineteenth-century Germany, among them, in particular, the growth of big cities.[12] Berlin, for example, as the most outstanding example of these big cities, with its growing concentration of commerce and manufacturing activities provided increased (in the terms of modern criminology) 'opportunity structures,' referring to opportunities to steal and trade stolen goods.[13] For the *Kriminalpolizei*, the alarming growth of property crime rates and, even more threatening, the growing professionalization and specialization of perpetrators, were a direct outcome of urban developments. The answers of the *Kriminalpolizei* to these patterns consisted of developing and elaborating a card and index system for documenting and identifying property crimes, thereby focusing on those recidivistic

---

[10]   Albrecht Funk, *Polizei und Rechtsstaat. Die Entwicklung des staatlichen Gewaltmonopols in Preußen 1848-1918*, Frankfurt/Main, 1986.

[11]   Wagner, *Volksgemeinschaft ohne Verbrecher...*; Th. Roth, *Die Kölner Kriminalpolizei im Dritten Reich, vornehmlich unter dem Gesichtspunkt der vorbeugenden Verbrechensbekämpfung*, Bonn, 1998 (unpublished MA-thesis.)

[12]   Funk, *Polizei und Rechtsstaat...*

[13]   Wagner, *Volksgemeinschaft ohne Verbrecher...* Before the First World War, the collection of data on property crimes (Diebstahlssammlung), included 1. Einbruchsdiebstähle in Wohnungen, 2. Einbruchsdiebstähle in Wohnungen und Kontoren, 3. Einbruchsdiebstähle in Läden, 4. Boden- und Kellerdiebstähle, 5. Einbruchsdiebstähle in Neubauten, Buden und Kirchen, 6. Handwagen und Fahrraddiebstähle, 7. Kollidiebstähle, 8. Schaukastendiebstähle, 9. Paletotdiebstähle, 10. Marktdiebstähle, Diebstähle aus Fleischerwagen, 11. Korridordiebstähle, 12. Schlafstellendiebstähle, 13. Diebstähle beim Beischlaf, 14. Diebstähle auf Bahnhöfen, 15. Diebstähle gegen Kinder auf der Straße, 16. Taschendiebstähle, 17. Ladendiebstähle, 18. Abhängediebstähle und Fledderei. This collection more or less mirrored urban, small and middle sized commerce and trade, but it went further, by including very specialized perpetrators as well. The file 'bicycle theft' included those specialists who took stolen bicycles apart, rebuilding new ones from the parts, in order to sell unidentifiable bikes (Herbert Reinke, "Großstadtpolizei'. Städtische Ordnung und Sicherheit und die Polizei in der Zeit des Deutschen Kaiserreiches,' in Martin Dinges and Fritz Sack, (eds.), *Unsichere Großstädte. Vom Mittelalter bis zur Postmoderne*, Konstanz, 2000, pp. 217-239).

perpetrators who primarily committed property crimes. For contemporary police experts recidivism in this field was seen as having significant technical characteristics. For example, the way burglaries were carried out, the tools used, the traces left, etc., were interpreted as the characteristics of persistent and repetitive criminals. Robert Heindl labelled these characteristics the *modus operandi* of specific perpetrators, and he identified the technical persistence of criminal acts as *Perseveranz*, a term he phrased.[14]

Although, in the debates, many police experts, penalists, and other members of the German criminal justice system, pointed out the weak points of Heindl's concepts, these recidivistic perpetrators were usually seen as being at the core of Germany's crime problem. Critics saw Heindl's arguments as resembling a closed circle that led to the overenforcement of a specific group of perpetrators. With the existence of an enormous number of *modus operandi* files and information, detectives organized investigations more or less along the lines laid out by these files, adding new data to them, using the files again the next time, etc. Contemporary experts even criticized the *Berufsverbrecher* as a self-fulfilling prophecy. But the concept appealed to many detectives for other reasons as well; to some extent the ideas about *modus operandi* and the so-called *Perseveranz*, which functioned as a *Leitmotiv* in the whole debate, were comparable to approaches in (modern) medicine. Symptoms were interpreted as an indicator of a deeper problem. In the case of the criminals dealt with by the *Kriminalpolizei*, fingerprints were understood to indicate the perpetrator and the traces of his tools (like those he used to get a safe out of the wall), as indicating the *modus operandi* and the *Perseveranz*. But for the *Kriminalpolizei*, interpreting symptoms or traces like this meant not only the use of an interpretative rationale of identification or detection, but also something 'more.' Robert Heindl provided the *Überbau* for this 'more'; his ideas about the *modus operandi* of criminals and about the *Perseveranz* of criminal acts, were interpreted not just as useful assumptions guiding the investigations of the *Kriminalpolizei*, but were also turned into a kind of sociology of a criminal group, the *Berufsverbrecher*, and beyond this group, as an interpretation of the criminal class in general.

The internal structure and the organization of responsibilities of the *Kriminalpolizei* at Berlin headquarters matched these generalized police perceptions of the crime problem in Germany. At the turn of the twentieth century, when the departments dealing with property crimes became increasingly differentiated according to the growing variety of such crimes, homicide cases were not yet dealt with by a separate department. The homicide department was created years later. By that time, the number of sub-departments at the Berlin *Kriminalpolizei* headquarters dealing with property crimes had increased again.[15] In 1930 the Berlin *Kriminalpolizei* headquarters held approximately 130 file systems, one of which contained data on about 50,000 individuals. According to the principle of *modus operandi*, these files differentiated 47 different types of crime, 70% of them property crimes. In addition, by that time, the Berlin police headquarters possessed more than half a million sheets of ten-finger-prints.[16]

---

[14]   Heindl, *Der Berufsverbrecher...*
[15]   Reinke, 'Großstadtpolizei'...
[16]   Wagner, *Volksgemeinschaft ohne Verbrecher...*

The *Berufsverbrecher* during the Nazi Period: The Career of a Concept

Robert Heindl's *Berufsverbrecher* met a receptive professional public, not only because of the author's abilities to pinpoint and synthesize the everyday practices and work of the *Kriminalpolizei*, but also because of his proposals for a permanent incapacitation of the *Berufsverbrecher*. In many of his writings, Heindl argued for specific forms of indefinite detentions of the *Berufsverbecher*. He meant this as a strategy for the definite solution of the crime problem in Germany. Heindl's proposals were not that new, they mirrored an ongoing discourse among experts in other European countries and in North America, but in Germany they had only been discussed in the context of the discourse of penal reform since the turn of the century.[17] Since then, proposals for the permanent detention of specific categories of criminals had been an ongoing part of the German penal reform discussion and had found their way into a number of drafts for a new penal law code.[18] But Robert Heindl went further: During the Weimar Republic years, he enhanced a debate among the senior ranks of the *Kriminalpolizei*, men who saw themselves increasingly – due to the expertise they ascribed themselves – as having the overall competence to judge whether or not a professional criminal should be held and/or sent into indefinite, preventive detention. However, during the 1920s, the penal reform movement did not succeed in introducing a permanent detention into a reformed penal law code, nor did the *Kriminalpolizei* succeed in gaining powers far beyond the 'ordinary' competences of the police.[19] These proposals for more police powers, which were discussed among the *Kriminalpolizei* experts, included far reaching consequences for the German criminal justice system. One of these proposals, labelled as a proposal for a reform of criminal justice procedures, argued for a reduction of the statuary rights of persons under suspicion in favor of an increase in the police's powers to deal with them; another one argued for a change of the position of the *Kriminalpolizei* within the institutional settings of the German criminal justice system. Traditionally, German detectives investigating a crime were *Hilfsbeamte der Staatsanwaltschaft*, auxiliary officials of the public prosecutor, but they wanted to be more; the *Kriminalpolizisten* wanted to be independent of the orders of the public prosecutor and wanted powers in their own right.[20]

Quite soon after the seizure of power by the Nazis at the end of January 1933, many of the demands of the experts among the ranks of the senior officers of the *Kriminalpolizei* became reality. Before 1933, the discussion about preventive detention strategies was – as already mentioned – not limited only to German police officers and German criminologists. But after the Nazi seizure of power (although not immediately), the reality of these strategies became something that went significantly beyond the limits of the *Rechtsstaat*, the rule of law: Preventive detention became used by the police increasingly without any legal restraint and was applied to categories of people beyond the rather limited category of *Berufsverbrecher*.

---

17 Wetzell, *Inventing the Criminal*...
18 Herbert Reinke and Melanie Becker, 'Kriminalpolitik in der Weimarer Republik,' in Hans-Jürgen Lange, (ed.), *Kriminalpolitik*, Wiesbaden, 2004, *in print*.
19 Heindl, *Der Berufsverbrecher*...
20 Wagner, *Volksgemeinschaft ohne Verbrecher*...

During the immediate period after the Nazi seizure of power, the measures carried out against the *Berufsverbrecher* remained within the interpretative frame given in Robert Heindl's text, although the police's anti-crime rhetoric provided for a more radical approach. Within a few days after the seizure of power by the Nazis, a flood of propaganda poured out of the *Kriminalpolizei* headquarters in Berlin, announcing the extermination – the *Vernichtung* – of the *Berufsverbrechertum*. As soon as November, 1933, Herman Göring, by that time head of the Prussian government, signed a decree concerning the 'application of preventive police custody against professional criminals,' about the *Anwendung der vorbeugenden Polizeihaft gegen Berufsverbrecher*, to be issued against criminals before trial.[21] Also in November, 1933, the national German criminal code (*Reichsstrafgesetzbuch*) was changed, introducing permanent preventive detention after trial (*Sicherungsverwahrung*) for specific categories of criminals.[22] Basically, the *Sicherungsverwahrung* introduced by this *Gesetz gegen gefährliche Gewohnheitsverbrecher und über Maßnahmen der Sicherung und Besserung* is still a part of the German criminal code and the German criminal justice system today (2004).

The Prussian decree concerning the application of preventive police detention against professional criminals, signed by Hermann Göring, stated that the police could place someone in preventive – and indefinite – police custody provided that this person had committed premeditated crimes or misdemeanours and had been sentenced to at least six months in prison on different occasions. The regulations of this decree also included quotas of criminals, known to the police, who were to be arrested in each police district. During the second half of the 1930s, these regulations turned into a police prerogative the right to put people with no prior conviction at all into preventive permanent detention, provided that the police perceived them as having a 'criminal will' and being a potential future danger to public security. But until the mid-1930s, these preventive custodial practices pursued by the *Kriminalpolizei* were directed against a more or less precisely defined group of professional criminals, most of them recidivists. This core group of criminals was held responsible for most of the criminality that took place in Germany during these years. This perception was accompanied by the idea that after having detained these criminals on the basis of preventive custodial confinement, criminality would disappear.[23]

The categories of criminals which were to fall under this decree loosely followed the concepts Robert Heindl had developed about the *Berufsverbrecher*. During the first years of the Nazi regime, the number of people detained and put into preventive police custody remained relatively low, the annual figures of people put into preventive custody did not exceed the estimations Robert Heindl had made about the

21 Gerhard Werle, *Justiz-Strafrecht und polizeiliche Verbrechensbekämpfung im Dritten Reich*, Berlin, 1989; Wagner, *Volksgemeinschaft ohne Verbrecher*...
22 Werle, *Justiz-Strafrecht und polizeiliche Verbrechensbekämpfung im Dritten Reich*...; Lother Gruchmann, *Justiz im Dritten Reich. Anpassung und Unterwerfung in der Ära Grüttner*, München, 1990 (2nd ed.); Christian Müller, *Das Gewohnneitsverbrechergesetz vom 24. November 1933. Kriminalpolitik als Rassepolitik*, Baden-Baden, 1997; Nikolaus Wachsmann, 'From Indefinite Confinement to Extermination. "Habitual Criminals" in the Third Reich,' in Robert Gellately and Nathan Stoltzfus, (eds.), *Social Outsiders in Nazi Germany*, Princeton, 2001, pp. 165-191.
23 Wagner, *Volksgemeinschaft ohne Verbrecher*...

number of people who were to be locked away permanently as *Berufsverbrecher*.[24] These figures included those convicted criminals who were put into permanent preventive detention after the prison term. To some extent, the courts and the *Kriminalpolizei* remained within the interpretative scope of Robert Heindl's text.

In February, 1934, a 'police-ordered planned supervision' was added to the measures of the decree against the *Berufsverbrecher* which gave the *Kriminalpolizei* the power to keep perpetrators, whom the police perceived as 'dangerous,' under close surveillance. This supervision went far beyond simple parole measures. The *Kriminalpolizei* was allowed to control the entire daily (and nightly) activities of criminals and to impose up to twenty different restrictions on them for an indefinite period. The police were allowed to determine place of residence and leisure activities, forbid alcohol consumption, any social contacts, driving, the possession of pets, and visits or stays in public places.[25]

In the second half of the 1930s, the practice of the *Kriminalpolizei* was radicalized;[26] it went far beyond the framework given by the ideas and proposals of Robert Heindl's text. There are a number of reasons for this extension, including the increasing influence of the Nazi ideology on the police. Let me point to only one of them: In June 1936, Heinrich Himmler, already head of the S.S., was appointed head of the entire German police, thereby creating a double role for him as *Reichsführer SS und Chef der Deutschen Polizei*. During the mid-1930s, Berlin and its surroundings experienced a series of armed robberies which received wide coverage by the press. Himmler, who was an ardent Nazi and racist, but who was a political man as well, perceived this situation as a threat to the law-and-order policies of the Nazi regime and soon reacted by ordering sweeping arrests of criminals. Early in 1937, the *Kriminalpolizei* was ordered to prepare lists of *Berufsverbrecher*. This was just a preparatory step for another action in the spring of 1937 when Himmler ordered the immediate arrest of 2,000 professional or habitual criminals who were to be sent to the concentration camps. Himmler gave just one of the criterion for the selection of these 2,000 people. His decree said that those who 'in the opinion of the Kriminalpolizei' – *nach Auffassung der Kriminalpolizei* were professional criminals, recidivists or – a new category in this context – sexual offenders, had to be arrested and put into protective police custody. No further reference to 'legal' or 'normative' – whatever legal or normative means in this context – was necessary.

In December of 1937 Heinrich Himmler, by then the *Reich*'s Minister of the Interior, issued a 'fundamental decree on preventive crime fighting by the police' – *Grunderlaß über vorbeugende Verbrechensbekämpfung durch die Polizei*.[27] This instruction standardized (from the mid-1930s) a growing practice of the *Kriminalpolizei*, and provided a pseudo-normative basis, used until the end of the Nazi period, for fighting

---

24   *Ibid.*

25   *Ibid.*; Andreas Roth, *Kriminalitätsbekämpfung in deutschen Großstädten. Ein Beitrag zur Geschichte des strafrechtlichen Ermittlungsverfahrens*, Berlin, 1997; Robert Gellately, *Backing Hitler Consent and Coercion in Nazi Germany*, Oxford, 2001.

26   Wagner, *Volksgemeinschaft ohne Verbrecher...*; Roth, *Kriminalitätsbekämpfung in deutschen Großstädten...*

27   Werle, *Justiz-Strafrecht und polizeiliche Verbrechensbekämpfung im Dritten Reich...*; Wagner, *Volksgemeinschaft ohne Verbrecher...*; Roth, *Kriminalitätsbekämpfung in deutschen Großstädten...*

the enemies of the *Volksgemeinschaft*. But this 'crime fighting' instruction meant a significant escalation of the *Kriminalpolizei's* strategy as well: the *Kriminalpolizei* gave police the power to send professional criminals with police records into preventive police detainment, and also extended their powers, putting them into the category of those placed in preventive police detainment, a broadly defined category of so-called 'a-socials.' When dealing with these people, the police could exercise more or less unlimited discretionary powers.[28]

Nazi officials and senior officers of the *Kriminalpolizei* made much publicity about these police strategies by pretending they were successful and by having the press report growing security in the streets and decreasing crime rates. However, the *Kriminalpolizei* did not manage to catch all of the so-called *Berufsverbrecher*, and above all, they did not succeed in making criminality disappear. One of the consequences, which Nazi officials and senior *Kriminalpolizei* officers drew from this failure (which of course was not admitted as a failure to the public), was to expand the criteria for preventive permanent detentions: anti-social individuals were defined even more broadly, including people, such as beggars and prostitutes, who did not fit into the norms and the ideals of the Nazi *Volksgemeinschaft*. As early as September 1933, the authorities in Nazi Germany had ordered a round-up of beggars in the streets of many German towns and cities, but in the final years before the Second World War major actions against these a-socials were carried out by the *Kriminalpolizei*. In an instruction given to the *Kriminalpolizei* in April 1938, a-socials were defined as people 'who demonstrate through their behaviour which is alien to the community, but not necessarily criminal that they will not adapt themselves to the community.'[29] In this instruction the list of these a-socials also included those who had shown 'that they will not comply with the social order that is a fundamental condition of the National Socialist state, *e.g.* beggars, vagrants, prostitutes, drunkards, people with contagious diseases, particularly transmitted diseases, who evade the measures taken by the public health authorities.' Also included were 'persons, regardless of any previous conviction, who evade the obligation to work and are dependent on the public for their maintenance (*e.g.* the work-shy, work evaders, drunkards).'[30] At the beginning of June 1938, the *Kriminalpolizei* was ordered to arrest a minimum of 200 unemployed a-socials in each of the 15 German police districts. This would have meant up to 3,000 arrests of so-called a-socials in Germany, but the police went far beyond this figure, finally arresting 8,000 a-socials in all of Germany and sending them to the concentration camps.[31] Because of this focus on the 'work-shy' (*Arbeitsscheue*) and 'work evaders,' the actions during the first half of 1938 went beyond 'crime-fighting' in the narrow sense. As the Nazi-regime was intensively preparing for war in 1937-1938, a severe labor shortage had developed. This shortage forced the regime to regulate the labor market with

---

28 Werle, *Justiz-Strafrecht und polizeiliche Verbrechensbekämpfung im Dritten Reich...*; Wolfgang Ayass, *'Asoziale' im Nationalsozialismus*, Stuttgart, 1995; Wolfgang Ayass, *'Gemeinschaftsfremde.' Quellen zur Verfolgung von 'Asozialen' 1933-1945, Materialien aus dem Bundesarchiv*, 5, Koblenz, 1998; Gellately, *Backing Hitler...*

29 Translation by Gellately, *Backing Hitler...*; Ayass, *'Asoziale' im Nationalsozialismus...*

30 Translation by Gellately, *Backing Hitler...*

31 Ayass, *'Asoziale' im Nationalsozialismus...*; Ayass, *'Gemeinschaftsfremde'...*; Wagner, *Volksgemeinschaft ohne Verbrecher...*; Roth, *Kriminalitätsbekämpfung in deutschen Großstädten...*

disciplinary measures; the actions against the 'work-shy' and the 'work evaders' were part of these regulative strategies.

Even before the war, the *Kriminalpolizei* had already grown into a role far beyond that of controling criminality. Its role and functions more and more focused on surveying societal developments that could harm or threaten social order as defined by the Nazi state – in other words, the *Kriminalpolizei* gained the function of fighting the enemies of the national-socialist *Volksgemeinschaft*. This proved to be an appropriate preparation for the role the *Kriminalpolizei* performed during the war years. With the increasing threat to the regime from the outside, the *Kriminalpolizei* felt compelled to defend and to strengthen the *Volksgemeinschaft* by fighting an increasing number of enemies from within. This fight was given an 'official label' by a legislative project under the heading *Gesetz über die Behandlung Gemeinschaftsfremder* (law about the treatment of aliens to the community), which would have given the *Kriminalpolizei* a general power to cleanse the *Volksgemeinschaft*. During the early war years, the police estimated that the number of *Gemeinschaftsfremde* among the German population could amount up to one and a half million Germans.[32] With this legislative project, the *Kriminalpolizei* certainly went beyond the framework offered by Heindl's concept about the *Berufsverbrecher*. The law was definitely not decided upon until the end of the regime, partially because the *Kriminalpolizei* already exercised many of the prerogatives proposed by the legislative project. This meant that between 1933 and 1945, as a result of their preventive policies in combination with almost unlimited executive powers, the *Kriminalpolizei* were able to send more than 70,000 people into the concentration camps.[33]

The *Berufsverbrecher* after 1945

What happened to Robert Heindl's *Berufsverbrecher* after 1945? As already mentioned, Robert Heindl himself became reemployed by the American Forces for rebuilding the Bavarian State *Kriminalpolizei*'s identification service. But the *Kriminalpolizei*, which had operated during the Nazi period, was never seriously purged – neither in terms of dismissals of officers, nor in terms of purges of work routines and professional philosophies. The British Forces in their respective zone of occupation in Western Germany used or reemployed *Kriminalpolizei* members who had been in the police service between 1933 and 1945, because – as the British argued – 'to exploit this product of German business is surely good business.'[34] Very soon after the end of the war, the British established a central *Kriminalpolizei* office for their zone of occupation, employing mostly pre-1945 detectives for this office. In the early 1950s this office was

---

32 Wagner, *Hitlers Kriminalisten...*
33 *Ibid.*
34 Stephan Linck, *Der Ordnung verpflichtet: Deutsche Polizei 1933-1945. Der Fall Flensburg*, Paderborn, 2000; Stephan Linck, "To exploit this product of German genius... is surely good business." Zur Personalpolitik der britischen Besatzungsmacht gegenüber der deutschen Kriminalpolizei nach 1945,' in Gerhard Fürmetz, Herbert Reinke and Klaus Weinhauer, (eds.), *Nachkriegspolizei. Sicherheit und Ordnung in Ost- und Westdeutschland 1945-1969*, Hamburg, 2001.

turned into the Federal Office of the *Kriminalpolizei*, the *Bundeskriminalamt*. Most of the men in these offices had practised or experienced preventive police detention during the war and before, and they therefore placed the *Berufsverbrecher* on the police agenda again. The reintroduction of this concept was facilitated by the fact that the legislation on permanent preventive detention after trial, the *Sicherungsverwahrung*, was not abolished because it was basically seen as an outcome of non-Nazi legislative efforts. Even the decrees on the preventive police detention, issued between 1933 and 1945, were not abolished, although they were no longer applied. But large parts of the *Kriminalpolizei* still viewed the preventive strategies they had exercised during the Nazi period as efficient strategies to fight crime. Many of the *Kriminalpolizisten* therefore regretted that the means and possibilities for fighting crime that they had had at their disposal before the end of the war were no longer available. But memories and stories about 'good' policing and efficient fighting against crime during the Nazi period still lingered on among many *Kriminalpolizisten* during the first decade of the Federal Republic.

Their attempts to put the *Berufsverbrecher* back on the police agenda during the 1950s were meant primarily to brief the public about the dangers this criminal category posed and to propose strategies for tackling this danger effectively.[35] But there was a problem with these proposals. These strategies were no longer compatible with the *Rechtsstaat* of the Federal Republic. This led many senior members of the *Kriminalpolizei* to regret the impossibility of cleansing society effectively of 'criminal, a-social elements.'[36] But the newly established rule of law in the (at that time) still young Federal Republic of Germany no longer had any (legal) place for preventive police detention.[37]

---

[35] Wagner, *Hitlers Kriminalisten…*

[36] Herbert Reinke and Robert Seidel, 'Die Entnazifizierung und die Säuberung der Polizei in West- und Ostdeutschland nach 1945,' *Schriftenreihe der Polizeiführungsakademie*, 04/1997-01/1998, pp. 53-67.

[37] Wagner, *Hitlers Kriminalisten…*

PART III
THE RECONSTRUCTION OF EVENTS IN POLICE AND CRIMINAL JUSTICE HISTORY

Chapter 5

Narratives of Crime, Historical Interpretation and the Course of Human Events: The Becker Case and American Progressivism

Allen Steinberg

Early on the morning of 15 July 1912, at New York City's popular midtown nightspot, the Metropole Café, small-time gambler Herman Rosenthal was waiting for a big-time payoff. His complaints about police harassment had finally made headlines, and at any moment he expected to be offered a handsome bribe from fellow gamblers to keep quiet. When a large group of them arrived at the café, Rosenthal excitedly gathered his belongings and scurried out into the street, but before he could even see beyond the glare of the streetlights the shots that would ensure his eternal silence rang out around him.

Three years later, early on the morning of 30 July 1915, at New York State's Sing Sing penitentiary, former New York City Police Lieutenant Charles Becker walked uneasily out of his cell towards the last act of the drama that began that night three years before. With an overflow throng of official guests and reporters watching, Becker was strapped into an electric chair and, for giving the order to kill Herman Rosenthal, became one of the few policemen ever to receive capital punishment in the history of the United States.

'It was one of the great crime stories of all time'[1]

Indeed it was. This kind of hyperbole has become typical of journalists in the twentieth century but this comment is noteworthy because it was expressed by two professors of American history, one of them, Richard B. Morris, a giant of his generation. Their assessment of the Becker/Rosenthal case raises the two main issues that will be explored in this paper. First, to consider why historians believe that a crime story is 'a great crime story,' and how this understanding is related to the 'stories' that become the dominant popular interpretations of American history;

---

[1]   'Herbert Bayard Swope of *The World* Breaks the Becker Case and Tears New York Wide Open,' in Louis L. Snyder and Richard B. Morris, *A Treasury of Great Reporting*, New York, 1962, p. 303.

second, to consider why 'stories,' like the one about Becker and Rosenthal, sometimes take on greater historical significance than the event itself.

When Morris and Snyder wrote these words in the mid-twentieth century, historians' voices still had great political influence. In the United States, for example, the dominant scholarly interpretation of the era of Reconstruction (1865-1877) as a mean-spirited carnival of corruption and incompetence not only shaped popular portrayals of Reconstruction, like those expressed in the enormously popular films *Birth of a Nation* and *Gone with the Wind*, it also helped to legitimate the Jim Crow system of racial apartheid that was still in full force in the American South. Another period of American history in which popular understanding was greatly influenced by historians is the Progressive era (roughly 1896 to World War I). This period, much like Reconstruction, was also interpreted by mid-century historians as one characterized by a battle between mean-spirited predators and their helpless victims, and this version also helped to legitimate a political order and doctrine still in effect today: the liberal state and the ideology of municipal reform.

If films like *Birth of a Nation* and *Gone With the Wind* were the vehicles through which most people received historical understanding of Reconstruction, 'great crime' stories and exposes of urban venality were the vehicles that transmitted historical wisdom about Progressivism. And while this period saw the flowering of urban crime and detective fiction generally, the most influential 'great crime' stories from this period had as their prototypes stories, like the Becker case, that were considered to be 'true.'

Morris and Snyder recognized that the greatness of the Becker case rested on its immersion in the mythology of the Progressive era, an interpretation that they and most historians of their generation supported. But in ways that neither of them (nor anyone else in the mid-century United States) was prepared to properly appreciate, almost the entire episode, from the events that precipitated Rosenthal's murder to its lasting symbolic significance, were the product of the 'stories' and myths told about Progressive-era municipal corruption and crime.

*

Abusive policemen were stock characters in the Progressives' morality play about urban corruption, and in 1912 Charles Becker fit the description. He was a New York City policeman with a past no more checkered than many other members of the force, but with a chesty hubris that brought him to the attention of his superiors, and, much to his long-term detriment, of journalists. In 1897, for example, Becker arrested and roughed up a young prostitute who, unbeknownst to him, was accompanied by the writer Stephen Crane. Crane, earning his living at this time by writing newspaper accounts about urban misery, was outraged and he not only testified in the woman's defense, but convinced Police Commissioner Theodore Roosevelt to convene a departmental trial of Becker. And, although Becker was ultimately acquitted, Crane and other reporters exhaustively told the story and continued to portray Becker as an example of all that was wrong with the police.

Journalism of the sort that Crane practiced was, of course, a major feature of the Progressive era, and it remains one of our chief windows on that period. This literature was a primary force behind the popular Progressive efforts to restructure state and local government and to cope with the massive problems of the new, huge, industrial capitalist city. But if the vast bulk of this 'muckraking' was political, in both the subject of its investigations and the intent of its authors, it was also often a literature of crime. The villains, frequently characterized as criminals, were big industrial capitalists, financial speculators, corrupt public officials, and urban political machines. And especially when its subject was the Tammany Hall political machine that dominated New York City politics, muckraking became explicitly a literature of crime, in which Tammany had to be overthrown because it was, above all, a criminal organization. Proving this assertion became the main objective of the popular literature about Tammany Hall and its leaders. What came to be known as the Becker case became an essential element of these politics.

The Progressive crusade against Tammany began in 1893 when the Rev. Charles Parkhurst delivered a famous sermon denouncing the city's vice economy and the 'polluted harpies' of the Tammany Hall political machine who ran it. Parkhurst was to New York City roughly what Anthony Comstock was to the nation as a whole – a tireless religiously-inspired fighter against vice. Like Comstock, he favored private vigilante enforcement of vice laws by voluntary organizations. In New York the most prominent of these was the Society for the Prevention of Crime (SPC), headed by Parkhurst himself.

The most important result of Parkhurst's sermon was the Lexow Committee hearings of 1894, organized by Republicans in the New York State legislature. These demonstrated, for the first time, the full extent of corruption in the city's police and cast the mold for the police investigating committee, one of the recurring passion plays of the American twentieth century. Parkhurst's crusade also produced one of the first pieces of popular literature for the municipal reform movement, a crime expose called *The Doctor and the Devil, or Midnight Adventures of Dr. Parkhurst*. It was written by the SPC detective, Charles Gardner with whom Parkhurst, elaborately disguised, investigated New York's underworld of dank saloons, brothels and gambling dives and it provided a lurid tale of undercover sleuthing, unbridled sex, race mixing, violence, drugs and debauchery. In his travels, Parkhurst witnessed drunken brawls, live sex acts and, according to his account, he was repeatedly accosted by half-naked women and girls. More than once he narrowly escaped arrest and other threats to his cover, and everywhere he found policemen actively protecting, or involved in, these activities.[2]

Gardner's tract was soon followed by another effort, this one by Parkhurst's associate Frank Moss, who, more than anyone else was responsible for the development of vigilante-like elite private law enforcement in New York. In the 1880s, as director of a property-owner's association, Moss gathered evidence against brothels operating under the protection of the notorious Police Captain Alexander 'Clubber' Williams, and he used policemen from other precincts to conduct raids against them. In 1894 Moss was assistant counsel for the Lexow Committee, and immediately afterwards he became counsel for the SPC. Like many Republican reformers of his generation, Moss was uneasy about unrestricted immigration. This feeling – in part an

---

2   Charles W. Gardner, *The Doctor and the Devil, or the Midnight Adventures of Dr. Parkhurst*, New York, 1894.

inheritance of the nativism intrinsic to the Republican Party during its founding in the 1850s, in part a consequence of the militant Protestantism that was central to the faith in reform – motivated Moss (and others like him) to, ironically, take courageous stands in defense of blacks, but Moss made nativism a local issue in 1898 when he published a three-volume history of New York City called *The American Metropolis*. A cumbersome tome (one reviewer described its style as 'much less than none'), the book was less a history than a compendium of Moss's impressions of various neighborhoods. More often than not these impressions turned on his favorite subject: crime. The chapter on the Lower East Side, or 'New Israel,' as he referred to it, Moss titled 'A Modern School of Crime.' Moss's point was that these 'ignorant and unclean' recently arrived New Yorkers were the inheritors of traditions of crime cultivated in earlier decades in other neighborhoods. Moss, of course, defended himself from charges of bigotry, claiming that it was only the 'ward-heelers' and 'cadets' (procurers of prostitutes) whom he disparaged. He even conceded that he 'may have gone too far' in condemning immigrants in his book, but he never repudiated the link between immigrants, crime and political corruption. These remained the pillars on which his world-view, as well as those of many other late nineteenth century Protestant reformers, was based.[3]

During the 1890s, the leader of Tammany Hall was the brazenly corrupt Richard Croker, who once, famously, admitted to an investigating committee that he was, just like his critics, 'working for my own pocket all the time.' Along with his imperious 300-pound Police Chief William Devery, Croker ruled New York like the lordly English squire he imagined himself to be. In the Police Department, Chief Devery centralized authority and the organization of protection to such an extent that even many policemen came to resent him. This resentment was reinforced because Devery, like Croker, was blatant about his self-interestedness and disregard of rules he disliked. One, of many, famous Devery stories tells how he imposed a fine of only thirty days on a policeman accused of firing his revolver wildly in the street 'for not hittin' nobody.'[4] Croker and Devery were easy targets, and, after another series of investigations around 1900, both of them were dispatched into early retirement in 1903.

Under new leader Charles F. Murphy, Tammany was much less tolerant of official collusion with vice, but characterizing Tammany as 'organized crime' remained its opponents' most effective weapon. Despite Murphy's disapproval, this was still not entirely without some foundation. In New York gambling and other illegal but widely popular pastimes – Sunday drinking, boxing, commercial sex, dancing and sometimes even baseball – were tolerated through a system of protection run by the police, especially the district Captains. By Murphy's time this system had acquired enormous political significance because prominent politicians were the main organizers of much illegal leisure. The most popular politician in New York at this time (and probably in its entire history), for example, was State Senator 'Big' Tim Sullivan, the city's unapologetic kingpin of both gambling and prize fighting.

3　*New York Times*, 24 July 1901; The *Nation*, 11 August 1898; Frank Moss, *The American Metropolis*, 3 vols., New York, 1898.

4　Richard O'Connor, *Courtroom Warrior: The Combative Career of William Travers Jerome*, New York, 1963, p. 74.

Therefore, in the first decade of the new century, the portrayal of Tammany politicians as criminals only intensified. Thanks primarily to Judge William Travers Jerome, Sullivan himself was the primary target when, in 1901, the spirit of the 'crime-fighting lawman' leapt from the pages of dime novels and into the streets of New York. New York City was consolidated in 1897, and the first Tammany administration to encompass this much larger field of opportunity was legendary in the annals of municipal corruption. In response, state Republicans and the anti-vice forces organized, in 1899, another public investigation into city government – the Mazet Committee, which had only a modest effect aside from boss Croker's proud declaration of his own self-interestedness, because it produced relatively little that was new and scandalous.

The attorney for the Mazet Committee, Frank Moss, would not however be deterred. Long associated with private, elite, vigilante law enforcement, Moss now sought to revive this practice on a grander scale. In 1900 the SPC, the City Vigilance League (another Parkhurst vehicle for which Moss was also counsel), several of Parkhurst's allies among the city's clergy and reform community, the Chamber of Commerce, and other businessmen, financed the famous Committee of Fifteen, which was, ostensibly, directed at suppressing prostitution. Moss began to hire undercover investigators and organize raids, but he found policemen much less willing to cross Devery and cooperate than they had been years before. The first raids carried out by the Committee proved futile – the targets were tipped off by the police. The Committee responded by enlisting the support of Judge William Travers Jerome, also a former assistant counsel to the Lexow Committee. Instead of supplying the police with the results of his investigations, Moss turned the information over to Jerome; Jerome issued warrants, put them in his pocket, and joined the raiding party. Then, after breaking in, often with fisticuffs and sometimes with gunfire, Jerome pulled out the warrants and his Bible and held court on the spot.

Jerome and Moss conducted 114 raids like this during the first ten months of 1901. Their primary targets were gambling halls rather than brothels, but their real goal was to promote public relations: to gather favorable publicity for themselves and negative press for their real targets, the policemen and politicians who profited from the vice they protected, especially Croker, Sullivan, and Devery. At every raid Jerome brought with him 'John Doe' warrants, intended to be used against one of these leaders, should someone arrested inside give them up. Reporters were advised of every raid in advance and each time Jerome set out he was trailed by a coterie of writers and photographers. He even had among his supporters literary figures who could be trusted to produce lasting records of tribute to their hero. Thus, according to the novelist A.L. Hodder, who participated in a number of raids, Jerome's raiders were 'a pick-up force of bailiffs, friends, and members of the Committee of Fifteen,' men who were held together by bonds not unlike those 'uniting a group of Western ranchmen.' Though urban, college-educated and 'super-civilized,' they, nonetheless, 'conjured up an image of the plains,' and armed with axes and Bibles they 'rushed' the city's centers of outlawry. Like the vigilantes they resembled, Jerome, Moss, and their comrades relied upon the lawlessness of official law enforcers and the widespread distrust of their authority for legitimacy.[5]

Jerome's intense cultivation of the press during his raiding campaign, and their delight at the image of the axe-wielding jurist he presented, brought a wild-west character to New York and achieved what the Mazet hearings could not. This was not the repression of vice; rather it was a revitalized, riveting, real-life saga about corrupt officials and their heroic foes, stories that were capable of moving people politically. In October, the Citizen's Union, the main good government organization, and the driving force behind the inevitable 'fusion' movement among Tammany's foes, insisted that Jerome be their candidate for District Attorney. Besides appreciating Jerome's dramatic appeal, CU leaders also appreciated the importance of having a public prosecutor who was independent of both political parties in the struggle for 'good government.' Then, in what may still be the most widely covered campaign for New York District Attorney in the city's history, Jerome barnstormed Manhattan for fifty-five days in the fall of 1901. He astonished everyone by campaigning aggressively in all the Tammany-dominated immigrant neighborhoods, and he ran well ahead of the rest of the ticket in leading a fusion sweep of the city elections. Without question, Jerome's image as a fearless crime fighter was responsible for his popularity, achieved in large part because he employed and publicized, as never before, the practice of private vigilante law enforcement, a practice which he himself likened, admiringly, to lynching parties.[6]

Jerome and most of his supporters were not, however, advocates of police repression of what they called vice. Jerome himself came from a famous line of gamblers and roustabouts and he was primarily concerned with corrupt government and what he called 'Anglo-Saxon hypocrisy.' He believed that there was a perverse alliance between 'the puritan and the grafter' that kept them both constantly busy and flush. Jerome's obsession with crime and his encouragement of vigilantism was political; his point was to effect political change by portraying Tammany men as outlaws, and himself as the effective lawman. This saga remained the Progressives' best route to success in New York City, and it was one they continued to propagate after Jerome's election, even though as District Attorney Jerome himself proved to be a disappointment, especially to the Republicans. Two years after Jerome's election, in part because the massive increase of arrests (for minor offenses) that followed in its wake, Tammany recaptured control of the Mayor's office and city government. For the rest of the decade the literature of city government as criminal syndicate flourished.

In 1903, the outspoken State Supreme Court Justice, William Jay Gaynor, wrote several articles severely chastising Jerome, private vigilantes, and the police for the unscrupulousness with which they made arrests. Gaynor, a loyal Democrat, was also a long-time critic of Tammany, advocate of progressive reform, and foe of the police.

---

5   Alfred Hodder, *A Fight For The City*, New York, 1903, pp. vi-vii; O'Connor, *Courtroom Warrior*, pp. 69-74.

6   Gilfoyle, *City of Eros*, p. 303; Hodder, *A Fight For The City*, pp. 28, 38-41 and 46-48; O'Connor, *Courtroom Warrior*, pp. 75-76 and 79; *New York Times*, 21 October 1901, 23 October 1901, 25 October 1901 and 30-31 October 1901.

The key here was the latter: Gaynor's significance lies in his refusal to accept the anti-vice forces dramatization about the problem of the police.

Most historians have seen Gaynor as either a Jeffersonian anachronism or as an apologist for the Tammany machine, criticizing police brutality and violations of civil liberties in order to deflect attention from the machine's real interest, graft.[7] Actually, Gaynor was a spokesman for a widely popular perspective on the role of the criminal law and police power in American life, and a leader in the struggle to shape its future. Gaynor was a single-taxer and strong supporter of the radical economic reformer Henry George. Within the Democratic Party, he was a friend of William Jennings Bryan. As a judge, he was an outspoken opponent of the reigning judicial philosophy of substantive due process that shackled the labor movement wherever it sought to challenge the imperatives of private property. His fellow judges had forgotten, he declared, 'that no ownership of property gives anyone a right to use his property in any way which is inconsistent with the rights, safety or comfort of the community.'[8]

Gaynor was never hesitant to express his opinions on the great national issues of his time, and that brought him considerable criticism from conservatives, but it was also the source of his popularity and the following he amassed was rooted, in part, in the alternatives he offered to the dominant philosophies of both major parties, as well as to reformers and the machine. This was especially true of his opinions on law enforcement during the first decade of the twentieth century. Gaynor was extremely wary of any organized institutional effort to enforce the criminal law. Strict adherence to the requirement that a warrant be obtained for all searches, seizures and felony arrests, and scrupulous following of the specific content of each warrant were, for him, inviolable principles. Policemen, he maintained, had virtually no powers of arrest beyond those of ordinary citizens, and were not permitted to use more than minimum force necessary to make an arrest, and none at all where arrests were not necessary. When confronted with the objection it was often impossible for policemen and public prosecutors to detect crime and apprehend criminals 'by keeping within the law,' Gaynor replied simply, 'then don't.' Throughout his career Gaynor repeatedly objected to the use of proactive police power, whether by the NYPD or organized private citizens. Although he was highly critical of police corruption and the protection of vice, he was much more critical of police brutality and invasions of constitutional rights. Rather than wanting the police to enforce the law more vigorously (and in accord with his private moral beliefs), he wanted their authority to be more subject to democratic and constitutional control.

Gaynor's widely publicized opinions made him not only a well-known antagonist of the police, but also an opponent of the anti-vice forces and their organized law enforcement practices. He was well known for overturning convictions based on arrests that he considered to be violations of due process, regardless of who made

---

[7]   See Mortimer Smith, *William Jay Gaynor: Mayor of New York*, Chicago, 1951, ch. 10; Christopher P. Thale, *Civilizing New York: Police Patrol, 1880-1935*, Ph.D. dissertation, University of Chicago, 1995, pp. 890-891 and 933-934; Samuel P. Walker, *A Critical History of Police Reform: The Emergence of Professionalism*, Lexington (Mass.), 1977, pp. 104-106. Puzzled, Walker found it 'curious' that 'a representative of Tammany Hall' defended civil liberties.

[8]   Smith, *William Jay Gaynor*, pp. 41-42 and 51-53. See also Louis H. Pink, *Gaynor: The Tammany Mayor Who Swallowed the Tiger*, Freeport (NY), 1931.

them. 'Lawlessness pure and simple,' was his dismissive explanation.[9] This was quite a different lawlessness from that which troubled Jerome, and Gaynor maintained this position, even as most reformers and journalists waxed rhapsodic over the new District Attorney. He moved to the forefront of the debate with his two 1903 articles on the conduct of the New York City police that appeared in the widely read *North American Review*. In them he repeated the same points about the limits of police authority he had made many times before. But rather than group these criticisms together with those about police protection of vice to form a blanket condemnation of the police, Gaynor ignored the vice question entirely, including the issue of police abuse of power with that of the private vigilante forces. To Gaynor, the police under the control of reformers was just as dangerous as the police controlled by the machine. 'Societies, and private enthusiasts, for the "suppression of vice"' should remember that a free people 'have more to fear from the growth of the one vice of arbitrary power in government than from all the other vices and crimes combined.' He scorned reformers for behaving as if society could 'be reformed and made better… instead of being debased and demoralized, by the policeman's club and axe.' Continuing, he said, '[t]he idea that the police may trample on the law regulating their conduct in order to make other people observe the law regulating theirs, can arise only out of a total lack of understanding of the principles on which free government rests.'[10]

The response was immediate. In fact, Gaynor's second article was accompanied by a reply written by one of Jerome's senior aides who was unambiguous about what he believed was the source of the 'true lawlessness' in New York. It was not the overzealousness of those making arrests, he maintained, but rather the alliance of the police (and by extension their lords in Tammany Hall) with 'the keepers of brothels and of gambling houses, their partnership with criminals and their acceptance of the proceeds of thefts and burglaries, their stolid and compact organization for perjury' and 'their systematized corruption and blackmail.'[11]

By the end of the decade muckraking had become the rage of American journalism, which would be changed by it forever; and the debate about the criminal government of New York remained one of its most prominent features. *McClure's* Magazine had emerged as the nation's leading muckraking journal, and in 1909, a Mayoral election year in New York, the editors devoted an enormous amount of space to New York City and the 'professional criminals' whom, they claimed, controlled it. The greatest popularizer of this interpretation was George Kibbe Turner, an exposer of municipal corruption second in prominence only to Lincoln Steffens. In his *McClure's* article, 'Tammany's Control of New York by Professional Criminals,' Turner left nothing to the imagination. He began by insisting that the Democrats had stolen every election they had won for the last fifteen years, and went on to describe the process through which this had taken place. Turner's main target was the same person who most of the critics of city government had fingered since the turn of the century: Big Tim Sullivan. Sullivan's great achievement had been to attract into the Tammany fold the vast number of Jewish and Italian immigrants flocking into the city,

---

9   Smith, *William Jay Gaynor*, p. 168.
10   William J. Gaynor, 'Lawlessness of the Police in New York,' *North American Review*, 176, January 1903, pp. 19 and 25-26.
11   Gans, 'Reply,' p. 290.

thereby keeping the machine, which had been closely identified with the older Irish and German ethnic groups, thriving and powerful into the new century. As a result, Sullivan was beloved among the poor people of New York.

For Turner, however, this accomplishment represented the height of villainy. Sullivan, he went to great lengths to describe, did this by first organizing the new immigrants into gangs of pimps and gamblers, and then, with the help of gangsters from other parts of the city, he mobilized them to vote repeatedly in every election, as many times as would be necessary to secure victory. It was therefore, for Turner, a literal reality that professional criminals – pimps, thieves, thugs and gamblers – intimidated and organized immigrants into voting illegally for Tammany candidates. Then, of course, they went on to ply their nefarious trades, especially prostitution, between elections with as little interference from city authorities as possible.[12] Sullivan had been defending himself from charges of this sort for years, of course, and no one was ever successful in connecting him directly to prostitution, a practice he steadfastly maintained he abhorred. Gambling, however, which many immigrants saw as a harmless pastime, was another matter. Nevertheless, the portraits of the city as a place of vice and crime, only intensified. In November, both Turner and S.S. McClure, the magazine's publisher, contributed essays that argued not only that New York was controlled by organized criminals, but by the most easily despised criminal, the 'white slaver,' the immigrant procurer of young girls for prostitution. Not only did these men run New York, but, according to Turner, they were responsible for the spread of prostitution throughout the United States; for McClure, they were responsible for nothing less than the degrading of American 'civilization into barbarism.' Even at the dawn of the twentieth century, the murder rate in the United States was ten to twenty times higher than that of northern and western Europe. For McClure, this was because 'the criminal element among... immigrants is protected by, and strongly allied with, the political criminals who manage our cities.'[13]

It was not entirely coincidental that these articles appeared in the November 1909 issue of *McClure's*. That month saw the Mayoral election in New York, the first one to follow the dismissal of the controversial Police Commissioner Theodore Bingham, a military man who offended many by publicly blaming Jewish immigrants for increasing crime, but who, for the likes of McClure, was 'deposed... because he would not fall in with the corrupt political schemes of some party boss.'[14] The criminality of Tammany Hall and its police was the dominant issue that year, as it often was in the early twentieth century, and the articles in *McClure's* were a major part of the campaign by Tammany's 'fusion' opponents to unseat them.

But the reformers were facing some severe difficulties in the 1909 election, which was perhaps why they tried so hard to portray Tammany as organized crime. When coalitions of Progressive reformers had previously succeeded in ousting Tammany from power, in 1895 and 1901, they did so in the wake of a police corruption scandal.

---

[12] George Kibbe Turner, 'Tammany's control of New York by professional criminals,' *McClure's Magazine*, 33, 2, June 1909, pp. 117-134.

[13] George Kibbe Turner, 'The daughters of the poor,' *McClure's Magazine*, 34, 1, November 1909, pp. 45-61; S.S. McClure, 'The Tammanyizing of a Civilization,' *McClure's Magazine*, 34, 1, November 1909, pp. 117-128, quotes at pp. 124-125.

[14] McClure, 'The Tammanyizing of a Civilization,' p. 127.

Articles like Turner's and those published in *McClure's* were designed to stir up another. Though it was not hard to persuade New Yorkers that Tammany leaders were corrupt or even morally suspect, it was another thing altogether to pry voters away from them. In order to do that 'fusion' leaders had to either convince enough people of Tammany's utter repulsiveness, find a candidate charismatic enough to overcome the bonds Tammany politicians had worked so hard to forge with their constituents, or both. Unfortunately for them, District Attorney William Travers Jerome, who turned that trick in 1901, had fallen from reform grace during his two terms in office and was unavailable. Instead, 'fusion' settled upon the latest exploiter of the symbolic significance of anti-vice raiding, the until recently little-known Magistrate, Charles Whitman, who had escaped his obscurity by drinking at saloons after closing hours and then, Jerome-like, holding court on the spot using his own consumption of alcohol as evidence. Whitman, however, proved to be too bland to carry an uninspiring candidate for Mayor on his shoulders, as Jerome had done eight years before. This was infinitely more difficult for Whitman than it had been for Jerome because Tammany leader Charles Murphy made the master stroke of persuading the person who, besides Jerome, had established the greatest legitimacy with the city's people on law enforcement matters, to be the Tammany candidate for Mayor, the long-time thorn in Tammany's side, Justice William Jay Gaynor. So 'fusion' won the battle but lost the war. Every successful candidate that fall was an outspoken critic of the police and their criminality, but the big prize, the mayoralty, went to Gaynor, and thus remained, if only titularly, in Tammany's hands. Nevertheless, it definitely was not in 'fusion's.'

After assuming office in January 1910, it took no time for Gaynor to earn the enmity of both Tammany and the reformers by demonstrating that a popular police reform program could be established around *his* priorities. He initiated an unprecedented campaign against police violence and invasion of constitutional rights. Dozens of investigations into police brutality were commenced, and the police became noticeably less brutal. Arrests fell by 30 per cent during his first six months in office. He abolished the special police squads, which had been let out to private citizens (usually businesses) to be used for their private purposes (often to police strikes). Criticism was widespread and came from both reformers and machine politicians, but Gaynor held fast and his popularity soared.[15]

Gaynor succeeded by concentrating on the real grievances of ordinary New Yorkers about abusive policemen, grievances that had more to do with brutality and arbitrary arrest than with the toleration of vice. This made the reformers' dramatizations of police criminality all the more necessary from their point of view, but Gaynor was prepared with dramatizations of his own. His political standing was based in large part on his judicial outspokenness and the wide attention his opinions attracted. In his *North American Review* articles Gaynor had cut right to the bone. He blasted Jerome's celebrated raiding campaign as 'cheap reform' that takes 'for granted that there is only one vice in the world, and that great city reforms are to follow the knowledge of how many women of ill repute there are on Houston or Hester Streets.' When the raids resumed after Jerome was elected District Attorney, Gaynor insisted

---

[15]   Smith, *William Jay Gaynor*, pp. 111-112 and 169-171; Thale, 'Civilizing New York,' pp. 553 and 890-891; *New York Times*, January 8 1910, pp. 12-15.

that it was 'often of little consequence' whether an individual suspected of a crime 'be arrested or convicted,' but it was 'of transcendent importance' that he be arrested and convicted 'in accordance with those restrictions and safeguards' prescribed by the constitutions and laws. 'To say that a "suspicious" or "bad" place should be entered and searched without a warrant would be to beg the whole question.'[16]

The power of communication remained key for Gaynor now that he was Mayor. Ordinary New Yorkers quickly learned that they could write Gaynor and that he would reply personally, sometimes at considerable length, to as many of his correspondents as possible. When he was particularly enamored of one of his responses, Gaynor made sure to send it to the newspapers for publication. Often he just wrote letters to the newspapers on his own initiative. The New York press was widely read throughout the nation and many local papers picked up much of their national editorial content from the New York papers. Before long Gaynor was exchanging letters with people from across the country. So when a book-length collection of his letters and speeches was published during Gaynor's last year in office, the editors could begin by confidently asserting that 'Mayor Gaynor's letters need no introduction to the American public.' The letters covered the gamut of Gaynor's concerns: his outrage at policemen working for private employers or preventing boys from playing ball; his support for the 'single tax' platform of the reformer Henry George; the complexities of police enforcement of vice laws; great literature and ancient philosophy; and the health benefits of walking, to name just a few. Before the end of his first year in office, Gaynor was without question the most widely known and well respected Mayor in New York's history.[17]

Gaynor had taken control of the discourse, severely limiting the appeal and effectiveness of the reformers' story. They needed to strike back, and Gaynor, even more than Tammany, now became their target. Gambling indeed was thriving around the city, as it had been for decades. Gaynor's hamstringing of the police didn't help discourage it, but in truth gambling was very popular. With Gaynor's success in combating police brutality and arbitrary arrest, the really unpopular forms of police misconduct, reformers feared that it would now be much more difficult for them to exploit those sensitivities in their war against another, much less unpopular, form of police misconduct. So the tendency to portray the police and their political patrons as organized crime intensified. Only days after Gaynor assumed office, a reform-minded judge empanelled a special grand jury, with John D. Rockefeller, Jr. as foreman, to investigate the charges about organized 'white slavery' in New York made by George Kibbe Turner in his *McClure's* articles. Therefore, more or less immediately, the new District Attorney Whitman was in a position to keep the heat on Tammany by stirring up a scandal about organized crime. Rockefeller, for his part, was a reluctant participant, interested as much to demonstrate that Turner's articles were 'sensational slanders against the city' as to prove their veracity. However, thanks to Whitman, the inquest gave a platform to those wanting to portray the city as a vicious hotbed of violence and sin during Gaynor's first months in office.[18]

---

[16]   Gaynor, 'Lawlessness', pp. 10-26.

[17]   *Mayor Gaynor's Letters and Speeches*, New York, 1913, p. 5.

[18]   *New York Times*, 6 January 1910; *New York World*, 6 January 1910.

Rockefeller ultimately concluded that there was no 'organization trafficking in women,' nor even any 'organized traffic.' Even the zealous reformer, now Whitman's chief Assistant District Attorney, Frank Moss, not only agreed, but asserted, that this was one crime with which not even Tammany Hall could be stained, even if the public had a different impression. The grand jury heard from Turner and also from Cornell University professor and immigration expert Jeremiah Jencks. Jencks repeated lurid tales of immigrants, pimps and their young female victims, but could not provide any specific evidence of organized procuring. However, Whitman and his assistants continued to feed the press stories about suspected organizations and dance halls, saloons, and movie theaters where women were deceived into lives of prostitution. And before the end of January at least eight people had been indicted under a 'white slave' law that had been rushed through the state legislature.[19] Because it was easy to find unorganized prostitution runners, Whitman was able to keep the specter of organized crime alive enough to secure funds in early February from the city's reform-dominated Board of Estimate to continue the grand jury's investigations. This dismayed both Rockefeller and Mayor Gaynor, who warned Whitman against using the investigation simply to 'make noise.'[20]

Though there were some indictments and convictions, most of what the investigation produced was indeed 'noise,' and the absence of the organization the jurors had set out to find mattered little. By spring every time a case arose involving a man who lived off the earnings of a prostitute, newspapers blared stories about 'white slavers.' When two college women working as detectives for the grand jury 'purchased' several girls, sensational stories followed about 'slavers' who promised to tell all, about their child victims gone missing, and about the numerous indictments promised by District Attorney Whitman. William Randolph Hearst's *American* made sure to juxtapose stories about the grand jury sting operation with one about a speech by Gaynor that criticized the investigations and, just so no one would forget whose political ox was to be gored by the hysteria, proclaimed New York the most 'moral' city in the nation.[21]

Only a few minor convictions resulted from this particular ruckus, but the impression of a city overrun by white slavery was inescapable from the press reports of the Rockefeller investigation. Throughout the year the reform press continued to portray a sense of peril. While the warring sensationalist newspapers of William Randolph Hearst and Joseph Pulitzer competed with one another with saturation coverage of crimes both spectacular and bizarre, the more temperate *New York Times* ran a series of thoughtful articles to more or less the same effect in its Sunday magazine section. Professors and jurists solemnly discussed organized crime and police corruption in lengthy articles. Prominent among them was state Supreme Court Justice John Goff, most famous for having been the chief counsel for the Lexow Commission, the great investigation of police conditions in New York in 1895. Goff

19   John D. Rockefeller Jr., to John P. Mitchel, 6 January 1911, *John Purroy Mitchel Papers*, Box 4, Library of Congress, Washington DC; *New York Times*, January 9 1910, pp. 18-20; *New York World*, January 7 1910, pp. 9-10, 12 and 18; *New York Herald*, 6-7 January 1910.
20   *New York Times*, 5 February 1910.
21   *New York Herald*, 30 April 1910; *New York American*, 3 May 1910, p. 1; *New York World*, 3-5 May 1910, p. 1; *New York Times*, 2 May 1910.

blamed the problem of excessive power wielded by ordinary policemen, referring not on their billy clubs, but their union. The efficiency experts of the Bureau of Municipal Research argued for a re-organization of the force and greater oversight of day-to-day activities by the Commissioner and Mayor. Other experts declared that organized crime had New York in its grip, but when pressed they only talked about gangs of pickpockets and shoplifters.[22]

Nevertheless, the publicity was enough to counter Gaynor's advances, and the battle reached a head in the Spring of 1911, when city Magistrate and former Jerome assistant Joseph Corrigan attacked Gaynor directly for the city's 'great and alarming increase of crime and of the still more alarming decrease in its detection and punishment,' turning Gaynor's proudest achievement, the reduction in arrests, back against him. The Mayor had made the police afraid to enforce the law, Corrigan charged, and as a result 'crime of almost every kind is being flagrantly and openly committed' and 'criminals from all over the country have come to New York in droves.' William Randolph Hearst, who was feuding bitterly with Gaynor (and competing with him for the same political constituency), made it sound like Corrigan was confirming *his* charges about Gaynor in the giant headlines in the Hearst newspapers. Gaynor called Corrigan's remarks 'seditious' and threatened to have him ousted from office, a charge that briefly caused more of a stir than the Magistrate's charges. Within days Whitman had another grand jury investigating the 'crime wave' and reform community leaders were scrambling after one another to help finance the inquiry and supply detectives. Chief Assistant District Attorney Frank Moss promised to find the secret police 'squeal books' that recorded all the crimes the police didn't pursue. He failed, of course, but not in making the impression that such documents, and such crimes, indeed existed. Though this grand jury, like Rockefeller's, would fail to sustain the charges that led to its empanelling, the months of publicity about gangs, vice and police corruption had the desired effect. Gaynor suffered abuse, his Police Commissioner was forced to resign, and he allowed the new one, Rhinelander Waldo, to organize three special squads operating out of headquarters to combat gangs, gamblers, and other forms of organized crime.[23]

The squads, therefore, were the direct consequence of a battle between opposing political agendas regarding criminal justice, and their conflicting representations of the same conditions and policies. Given the depth of public dissatisfaction with the police in all quarters, it was easy for both sides to stir passions and to raise public fear of both crime and law enforcement. Gaynor himself approached the new squads in the context in which they arose – as concessions to his enemies – and he ignored them. That left it up to Waldo to assemble the squads, and the men he picked to head them could not have been worse for Gaynor. In order to please the reformers, Waldo chose their favorite, Lt. Daniel Costigan, to head one squad. To balance the scales, he picked Lt. Charles Becker, an officer with no reform credentials at all but with a record of violence and a willingness to do dirty jobs for headquarters, to head another. Neither of them were the kind of men Gaynor would want anything to do with, and his

---

[22] *New York Times*, 25 September 1910, 27 November 1910, 11 December 1910 and 9 April 1911.

[23] *New York Times*, 23-28 March 1911; *New York World*, 23-28 March 1911; *New York American*, 23-24 March 1911.

neglect of what was going on with these squads, especially Becker's, would cost him dearly.

The absence of a policy commitment at the top left Becker with considerable freedom to conduct himself as he chose, and, like most of the cops he had known in his career, he chose to feather his own nest. Becker, who was especially close to Commissioner Waldo, was given the anti-gang squad in the tenderloin district, and he quickly sought to make the most of his situation. His squad carried out many raids, but Becker also used his position to collect the graft that he had been excluded from earlier in his career. Now he could rack up arrests, earn a promotion to Captain, and collect handsomely from gamblers to ensure that their arrests would not turn into convictions and that their business could resume promptly. Becker hired a press agent to report on his exploits, and went to work ablaze with ambition. He raided gambling houses at twice the rate of the other two squads, raiding some houses that had not been touched by the police for decades. He made the largest bank deposits of his life and restored his fearsome reputation.

Becker also made enemies among jealous fellow policemen and especially among vengeful gamblers. He arranged for the notable gambler 'Bald' Jack Rose to be his bagman, or collector, from the many, mostly Jewish, establishments that had opened recently in the tenderloin with the approval of Big Tim Sullivan. Becker's demands, and the publicity surrounding the vice squads, reinforced the opportunistic behavior of this ordinarily petty and thin-skinned lot. After less than a month Becker was warned of a plot against him. Then he began to receive threats. Pseudonymous complaints about him turned up at police headquarters. Becker was clearly making trouble as well as money. More than once in early 1912 he asked the Commissioner for a transfer out of the vice squad, but by then Becker had already made his biggest mistake. In March he raided the 46th Street faro house of Arnold Rothstein. Among the regulars at Rothstein's resplendent resort, indeed perhaps Rothstein's best friend, was the brilliant, arrogant young star of the *New York World*'s city desk, Herbert Bayard Swope. Shortly after the raid, Commissioner Waldo began receiving more anonymous letters suggesting that he investigate Becker, who once again asked to be reassigned.

The gambler Herman Rosenthal, unlike Rothstein, was not thriving. He lost his main source of income when off-track betting was outlawed by the Republican Legislature in 1909, and since then he had survived by running a series of small gambling rooms. He made some enemies by refusing to pay off on several debts, and the police began to raid his operations. He began to complain loudly, to the press, to police officials, to politicians. He went to the Mayor, wrote to the police commissioner, and knocked on District Attorney Whitman's door. He moved his operations to new neighborhoods – Queens, Harlem, and finally the Tenderloin. Everywhere he feuded with other gamblers, clashed with police, and complained loudly, accusing them all of being grafters and of harassing him. In April 1912, Becker's squad closed down Rosenthal's second Tenderloin gambling house, and humiliated Rosenthal further by stationing a vice squad member permanently in his apartment.

In July, still steaming from the officer on duty in his home, Herman Rosenthal complained for what would be the last time, because this time his whining fell on the interested ears of Herbert Bayard Swope, whose friend Arnold Rothstein had been raided by Becker just before Rosenthal. In addition to his relationship with Rothstein, Swope made sure to give himself access to all sides of a story by establishing a mutually beneficial relationship with District Attorney Whitman. Whitman gave Swope advance tips on his plans; Swope portrayed Whitman as a crusading knight.

On 13 July 1912 Swope set in motion the events that would lead directly to the Becker-Rosenthal case with yet another story, a long article in the *World* in which Rosenthal named Becker as his partner, who had betrayed and raided his establishment. Rosenthal was, Swope insisted, a victim of the 'system.' Becker, understandably outraged at what was obviously an unbelievable claim by a desperate man, prepared to sue Rosenthal for libel. Swope, his integrity in question, was worried because Whitman, until then, had steadfastly refused to investigate Rosenthal's charges. Now he convinced Whitman of the benefits of proving that a policeman was actually Rosenthal's partner, regardless of the truth, and so persuaded him to take such a claim seriously. It was a claim that would be easily accepted within the reform community. The skeptical but still headline-seeking District Attorney perked up. He met with Rosenthal and agreed to have him testify before his latest anti-vice grand jury. Becker publicly scoffed at Rosenthal's charges, and spent his days preparing affidavits to refute them. The night before Rosenthal's expected testimony, Becker was confidently enjoying the fights with journalist friends at Madison Square Garden.

The day before, right after Swope's *World* article appeared, a group of Rosenthal's fellow gamblers, including 'Bald' Jack Rose (a man who also knew that Rosenthal's charges were baseless), resolved to kidnap him and put an end to his shenanigans. They let it be known that they were willing to pay Rosenthal off in return for his silence, and late that Monday evening Rosenthal went to the popular Metropole Café in Times Square to await their arrival, expecting his pay day. Instead, the group of five or six men hired to seize Rosenthal bungled the job and shot him to death on the sidewalk in front of the cafe.

The sensation that ensued continued through Charles Becker's trial, conviction and death sentence in October 1912, was largely the product of the conflicts that led initially to the murder of Rosenthal. Indeed, it was the culminating battle of that conflict, in which Charles Becker became a symbol and an image; the actual man's fate was an afterthought. Herbert Bayard Swope 'hit the top in journalism' with this story, according to Snyder and Morris, whose judgment about such matters was authoritative. It was not an accident. During the next several months Swope and the city's reform community guided Whitman every step of the way. According to Snyder and Morris, Swope even wrote Whitman's press releases. From the beginning, Whitman had insisted that the murder was the result of vice squad corruption, Gaynor's policies, and Tammany's venality; that is, he took the truth of Rosenthal's heretofore dubious contentions for granted and jumped head first into the political struggle over law enforcement. Quickly Whitman's agents set out to capture the four shooters – four immigrants, three Jews and one Italian. Their ominous nicknames, like 'Gyp the Blood' and 'Dago' Frank, would help Swope and the rest of the press terrify the city. 'Bald' Jack Rose and the other gamblers who hired them, turned themselves in.[24]

---

[24]   Snyder and Morris, 'Herbert Bayard Swope,' pp. 303 and 310.

The anti-vice police reform community sprung into furious activity. They held mass meetings, formed grand juries and citizens' committees to investigate vice, arranged city council hearings on the police, and, most importantly, financed Whitman's investigation. Jews, horrified at the revelation of gamblers and gangsters in their midst, began their own investigation. Whitman charged all the gamblers and gangsters involved with capital murder. He put his chief deputy, the anti-vice zealot Frank Moss, in charge of the prosecution. In 1912 it was still possible to empanel an elite 'blue ribbon' jury comprised entirely of well-to-do men who would be sympathetic to the reformers' point of view, and Whitman did just that. He also arranged for Justice John W. Goff, chief counsel to the Lexow Committee, fierce opponent of Tammany and the police, and Moss's long-time associate, to be the judge. Among his other attributes, Goff was an enthusiastic supporter of capital punishment, and was the city's most feared 'hanging' judge.

Though the shooters and gamblers who arranged what turned out to be Rosenthal's murder were quickly identified, the newspapers, and Whitman, continuously speculated on the involvement of Becker and high police officials. Becker eagerly accepted Whitman's invitation to testify before the Grand Jury about his relationship with Rosenthal and his activities on the night of Rosenthal's death. But before that testimony was given, Rose and the other gamblers secretly met with Whitman, and, in exchange for immunity from prosecution, named Becker as the instigator of the murder plot. On 29 July, instead of summoning Becker, the *Grand Jury* indicted him for ordering and planning the assassination of Herman Rosenthal.

The Rosenthal murder case was thoroughly immersed in the dueling discourses about law enforcement. Over the next several months, Whitman, Moss and Swope orchestrated a campaign to convict Becker in the press and to persuade him to save himself by implicating even more prominent policemen and politicians. Believing their own constructions in the heat of hysteria, Swope and Whitman thought that they could destroy Tammany. They concocted the testimony of the chief witnesses and then Swope leaked it in articles in the *World*, proclaiming, for example that 'Rose's Charges Against Becker Are Found True by Mr. Whitman.' When Rose privately confessed to the District Attorney, his confession somehow turned up as an exclusive in the *World*. Justice Goff, presiding over the Becker case, also held a wide-ranging grand jury inquiry that was intended to uncover the full dimensions of the dreaded 'system.' He subpoenaed witnesses such as Tammany figures 'Big' Tim Sullivan and his notorious Jewish associates Max Hochstim and Martin Engel; the press carried on about impending indictments of 'higher ups' and prominent politicians. The *World* published (with banner headlines) Swope's stories containing Rose's assertion that Becker and three others divided over $2,000,000 a year in police graft. According to the stories spread by the *World* as well as other newspapers, and still argued by popularizers of American crime history, after Becker became a 'strong-arm' squad leader, 'every pimp and gambler on Broadway and in Manhattan knew that failure to pay Becker the cut he demanded meant swift and sure retaliation.' His enforcers, they continued, were 'the cream of New York's thugs.' This picture of Becker was undoubtedly enhanced when both the reputed leader of the gunmen's gang, as well as the man who gave one of them up to the authorities, were murdered, gangland style, in the weeks before the trial.[25]

For most of September, just before Becker's trial, the city was treated to hearings that were held by a committee of city Aldermen, inspired by the Rosenthal murder. In reality, they were directed squarely at Gaynor – who was the first, hostile, witness – and his police policies. William Randolph Hearst published explicitly drawn contrasts between Whitman's courage and Gaynor's degradation of the Mayoralty. He claimed that it had reached as 'low an ebb' as it ever had. Perhaps Hearst's most effective blow at Gaynor was a cartoon that ridiculed him with a caption that had him saying 'Everything is all right. Becker is all right. You're all right. I'm all right. There is no gambling. Rosenthal isn't even dead. Everything is all right except the blackleg newspapers.'[26] In retaliation, Gaynor lashed out at journalists as 'corrupt scamps,' but he lost the argument.

By the time of Becker's early October trial, after the Aldermanic hearings, grand jury investigations, and the daily barrage of revelations in the press, the city seemed convinced not only of the existence of the insidious police 'system,' but also that the ruthless and devious Becker was its kingpin. Editors throughout the world offered opinions about whether the New York police had executed Herman Rosenthal. That had become the story, the question that made the murder a sensation. Becker refused to budge from his claim of innocence and would not co-operate with Whitman by giving up any of the higher police officials or politicians the District Attorney wanted to implicate in the crime. So, confident of Goff's co-operation, Whitman and Moss prepared for a blatantly prejudicial trial. Becker insisted that he was the victim of a political frame-up, but because the venality of the police was one of the few things that virtually all New Yorkers agreed upon, most people were already convinced that Becker was guilty. Becker found few supporters, despite the fact that no credible evidence would ever be offered against him by anyone not already under indictment for a capital crime.

When Becker's trial began on 7 October, the murder of Herman Rosenthal was, indeed, the biggest story in New York; it would continue to be front-page news in the city as well as much of the nation for nearly a year. The trial itself lasted two dramatic weeks, and ran like a serial in papers everywhere. Whitman and Moss plotted most of the action. They chose 'Bald' Jack Rose to be their chief witness, not only because his 'confession' was the key evidence against Becker, but because, utterly hairless since birth, he was also sure to be memorable. Rose put in a star turn.

But hubris, perhaps understandable in these circumstances, got the best of Whitman and Swope in the courts, where they had to fulfill technical legal requirements and could not just stampede a credulous public with a compelling story. They ran into two problems. One was the requirement that in order to convict someone of a capital crime, the prosecution had to have at least one corroborating

---

25   Stephen G. Christianson, 'Charles Becker Trials: 1912-1914,' in Edward W. Knappman, (ed.), *Great American Trials*, Detroit, 1994, p. 263; *New York World*, 27 July 1912 and 31 July 1912.

26   *New York World*, 27 July 1912, 31 July 1912, 6-7 August 1912 and 8 August 1912; *New York American*, 7 August 1912; Andy Logan, *Against the Evidence: the Becker-Rosenthal Affair*, New York, 1970, pp. 95-96.

witness who was not an accomplice in the crime; of course, all the witnesses whose testimony had been arranged were themselves the perpetrators. The other was simply the issue of due process, which, to an extraordinary extent, they denied to Becker. In order to meet the first requirement, Rose testified that there were two planning meetings, one in Harlem and one at a Turkish bath, and tried to make it look like one of the conspirators was actually uninvolved. But, in order to make these unlikely stories stick, it would be necessary to obstruct Becker from making his best defense, and with this Goff complied.

His co-operation with the prosecution was reflected by little things, such as forbidding Helen Becker from sitting within view of the jury, and by big things, such as repeatedly preventing Becker's attorney from cross-examining Rose. The defense, naturally enough, concentrated on impugning the testimony of the prosecution's witnesses and the conduct of the District Attorney. They had witnesses who would testify that they were offered bribes by Whitman to help frame Becker, and that before the immunity arrangement had been made, Rose and the others had sworn that Becker had nothing to do with the murder. Goff never admitted the testimony. He summarily halted cross-examinations when they were about to elicit testimony favorable to Becker, including that which would reveal the complicity of the conspirator Whitman was trying to pass off as a non-accomplice. Goff refused to let former District Attorney Jerome testify for Becker. His obstruction of Becker's case was so extreme that on the last day of the trial Whitman persuaded Goff to put one of Becker's strongest supporters back on the stand, and the trial ended with the bizarre sight of the judge forcing a witness to answer questions that he had disallowed just a few days before. Finally, Goff delivered a charge to the jury that was, as Becker put it, 'virtually a direction to the jury to find me guilty.'[27]

It is a testament to the depth of the public hostility to the police that, even with the obvious flaws in Whitman's case, and the extremely biased conduct of the judge, it took only eight hours of deliberation for the jury to return a verdict of guilty. They could, after all, only consider the very biased evidence put before them. Six days later Judge Goff sentenced Becker to death in the electric chair.

Swope wrote the story a few days later that became the defining version of the Becker case, and was lionized by Snyder and Morris for having 'tilted lances with the "System."' In Swope's telling, Rosenthal had affronted that "System," in whose labyrinthine maze men are killed, others are robbed, and women are made slaves.' Becker not only 'had his being through the grace he found in its eyes,' but 'like Caesar, all things were rendered unto Becker in the underworld.' He gave the order to Jack Rose: 'I want Herman Rosenthal croaked!' Even Swope himself understood that his story 'would seem to be a work of art – an unreal thing,' but he had no doubt that this would only make the world all the more aghast at the awful truth he had helped uncover.[28]

But if Whitman and Goff could stampede a jury as effectively as they could the public, they had gone too far for the Court of Appeals. In 1914, with a scathing rebuke of Goff's 'forceful... prejudgment' of the case, they ordered a new trial. Goff, the court concluded, left the jury with no choice but to believe 'an improbable tale

---

27   Logan, *Against the Evidence*, p. 209.
28   *New York World*, 27 October 1912; Snyder and Morris, 'Herbert Bayard Swope,' p. 303.

told by four vile criminals to shift the death penalty from themselves to another.' There had been no credible testimony from a non-accomplice, and the key Harlem planning conference was 'a pure fabrication.'[29]

But then fabrication was what had fueled the entire chain of events, and it was not about to end. The political environment in 1914 was in many ways even worse for Becker. Mayor Gaynor had been made to look foolish by the Becker case, and he had literally been driven to his grave. He was replaced by John Purroy Mitchel, an anti-vice true believer. With Mitchel's election in 1913 as its ultimate validation, the story of the 'system' was firmly implanted in the public mind, the Court of Appeals' criticism of Goff notwithstanding. Whitman and Swope had convinced most people that the stories woven by reformers for two decades were true. Becker's association with Rosenthal and the immigrant gamblers, and the gamblers' ties to Big Tim Sullivan, were concrete proof that the 'system' through which Tammany politicians and policemen controlled organized vice and crime really existed. Most of the press was outraged at the appellate court. Swope was determined that the conviction in what he called 'my murder' should stand. He made sure that the *World* would strongly urge Whitman to prosecute Becker again.[30]

Whitman needed little persuading, but he was chastened. The theatrics, no longer necessary for a convinced city, could be dispensed with. He made sure to keep the case away from anti-vice zealots like Frank Moss and John Goff, and found less impeachable ways to cover the holes in his first case. The much calmer and more scrupulously conducted second trial also resulted in a conviction, which was upheld, despite continued uneasiness because all the crucial evidence against Becker remained rooted in the testimony of men who were desperate to save themselves. As the Court of Appeals explained this time, they could only ensure that the process was proper. Judging the evidence was up to the jury.

With this victory, Whitman rode his reputation in the Gubernatorial election in 1914, portraying himself as a kind of successor to New York's previous Progressive Republican Governors (and, not incidentally, Presidential candidates) Theodore Roosevelt and Charles Evans Hughes. Therefore, when Becker had to make his final appeal for executive clemency on the eve of his scheduled July, 1915 execution, it was to Whitman. The Governor, of course, did not recuse himself and, to no one's surprise, Becker kept his final appointment with the electric chair at the famous Sing Sing Penitentiary.

Whitman turned out not to be a Progressive at all, but a reactionary and opportunist (he was a prohibitionist who drank too much). His tenure is generally considered a failure by historians and was, without question, a disaster for the advocates of labor, social welfare and regulatory legislation. To Tammany's delight, he was defeated in the 1918 gubernatorial election by their vice-besotted 'happy warrior,' Al Smith.

Nevertheless, as long as the heroic version of American Progressivism remained dominant, which meant basically that as long as American social history was dominated by the champions of the liberal state the Progressives created (despite the obstructionism of Whitman and other conservatives), the version of the Becker case

---

[29] Logan, *Against the Evidence*, pp. 244-245.

[30] *Ibid.*, p. 248.

that his prosecutors created remained unchallenged. According to this version, the 'squeaky clean' Whitman courageously listened to Rosenthal, attacked 'the powerful Becker head-on,' and the case remained 'great' because of 'the attention it focused on urban corruption and the efforts of people like Whitman to combat it.'[31]

Maverick New York journalist and attorney Henry H. Klein continued into the 1950s to insist on an alternative story: he maintained that Becker was innocent, that he had been framed by Whitman and the gamblers, with the passive connivance of politicians who hoped the case would put the police graft issue to bed for good. This version was probably a lot closer to the truth, and was more or less validated in 1971 by the *New Yorker* magazine City Hall reporter, Andy Logan. In the context of the considerable anti-police sentiment prevalent at that time, she was asked by a Hollywood producer to write a screenplay about the case. Logan did her research, almost exclusively in the city's daily newspapers, and, using evidence fully available to everyone at the time of the case itself, came to the conclusion that Becker was framed. He was also probably innocent, but either way the *story* was not Becker's corruption but rather Whitman's shameless opportunism and disregard of due process, and Herbert Bayard Swopes's excessive ambition and hubris. Needless to say, her producer didn't want a movie about *that*, and so this expose rests in Logan's now out of print and scarcely read book, *Against the Evidence*.[32]

For nearly a century, despite the continuous existence of a much more plausible counter-narrative, Swope's version of the Becker case has remained the prevalent one. Partly this is because the case has become obscure with the passage of time (and not much is written about it any more), but it is also because the version of the history of American urban Progressivism that it supposedly illustrates still reigns as the dominant interpretation in the popular imagination. But if there is a more plausible story of the Becker case, there is also an alternative to the popular version of urban Progressivism. Much of this scholarship emphasizes that the battle between reformers and corrupt officials was largely a rhetorical device that obscured more complex conflicts among shifting coalitions of reformers and regular politicians. Drawn from both political parties they understood that laissez-faire, nineteenth-century tribalism was a thing of the past and they fought to shape a new version of statecraft, which they had difficulty conceptualizing, let alone implementing. In many places, the political reforms of this time served, as Amy Bridges puts it, to 'constrict the political community.' At the same time, the state and local governments run by this shrunken political community accrued ever more authority as well as the capacity to act. And one of the fronts on which they typically acted, unsurprisingly given the salience of the issue, was criminal law enforcement, which became markedly more efficient and extensive.[33]

[31]   Christianson, 'Charles Becker Trials: 1912-1914,' pp. 263-264 and 267. See also Jay Robert Nash, *Bloodletters and Badmen: A Narrative Encyclopedia of American Criminals From the Pilgrims to the Present*, New York, 1995, pp. 65-67; Sir Harold Scott, *Concise Encyclopedia of Crime and Criminals*, New York, 1961, pp. 22-23.

[32]   Henry H. Klein, *Sacrificed: The Story of Police Lt. Charles Becker*, New York, 1927; Henry H. Klein, *My Forty Year Fight For Justice*, New York, 1953.

[33]   Amy Bridges, *Morning Glories: Municipal Reform in the Southwest*, Princeton, 1997. See also, among many other things, Samuel P. Hays, 'The politics of municipal reform in the progressive era', *Pacific Northwest Quarterly*, 1961; Jon Teaford, *The Unheralded Triumph: City*

Since the traditional interpretation of Progressivism, the one set forth by historians like Louis Snyder and Richard Morris, rests on the conventional understanding of the Becker case, how should we now understand the significance of this famous case and what does it tell us about our understanding of the period? In the final analysis, the central historical drama was not the battle between corruption and reform, but rather between the alternative visions of the policy-making state and criminal justice, versions represented by, for example, William Travers Jerome and William Jay Gaynor. While Charles Whitman was surely not a heroic fighter of corruption, neither was he a failure as a reformer. Rather, he was something else: a new, pro-penal state conservative who exploited the vice reformers narrative to his advantage. He was instrumental in incorporating their methods into public policy, and also demonstrated the efficacy of fashioning a politics not around social reform, but around criminal law enforcement. Governor Whitman started the New York State Police and fought a ferocious battle to destroy the period's one prison reformer who took democratic and rehabilitory principles seriously, Sing Sing warden (and Becker supporter) Thomas Mott Osborne. Becker's fall, the product of Swopes's story and Whitman's case, is emblematic not because it represented the destruction of an evil 'system,' but because it is a cautionary tale about the extent to which people will exploit circumstances in the cynical pursuit of power. And, for serious students of history, it serves as a reminder that we must always approach enduring historical interpretations and received wisdom with a healthy dose of skepticism.

Government in American, 1870-1900, Baltimore, 1984; Daniel Rodgers, 'In search of progressivism,' *Reviews in American History*, 1982; Michael H. Ebner and Eugene M. Tobin, (eds.), *The Age of Urban Reform: New Perspectives on the Progressive Era*, Port Washington (NY), 1977; Bruce M. Stave and Sondra Astor Stave, *Urban Bosses, Machines, and Progressive Reformers*, Malabar (Flo.), 1984.

Chapter 6

Sergeant Goddard:
The Story of a Rotten Apple,
or a Diseased Orchard?[1]

Clive Emsley

On 29 January 1929 George Goddard, a former Station Sergeant of the Metropolitan Police with twenty-eight years' police service, was sentenced at the Old Bailey to eighteen months' hard labour, with a £2,000 fine and the requirement that he pay the costs of the prosecution. His co-defendants were Kate Meyrick, a well-known nightclub proprietor who received a fifteen months' prison sentence, and Luigi Ribuffini, a restaurateur and nightclub proprietor, who also received fifteen months. Goddard had been found guilty of corruptly accepting and obtaining money from Meyrick, Ribuffini and Anna Gadda – the latter had fled abroad. Meyrick and Ribuffini had been found guilty of paying money to Goddard. And all three had been found guilty of conspiracy to pervert the course of justice. A few weeks after Goddard's sentence Horace Josling, a former sergeant who had informed on Goddard six and a half years before and been forced to resign for his pains, was exonerated. Justice appeared to have been done.[2]

Sir John Moylan, the Receiver of the Police, subsequently commented in his book on Scotland Yard that 'it was justly remarked, as a reassuring feature, that it was the police themselves who brought the facts so fully to light.' For Moylan, Goddard was an isolated offender, and it was the nature of his tasks in being required to supervise the underworld of London's principal vice district, Soho, which led to him being tempted, and succumbing to that temptation.[3] H.M. Howgrave-Graham, Secretary to the Metropolitan Police, did not address the Goddard case as such in the book on Scotland Yard that he published in the aftermath of the Second World War but,

---

[1]   My thanks to Mark Roodhouse, Heather Shore, Graham Smith and Chris Williams for comments on an earlier draft of this paper. My particular thanks also to Ray Seal of the Metropolitan Police Archive for his assistance in collecting information on some of the individual police officers mentioned.

[2]   The trial was fully reported in the national press. The account that follows draws on the extensive trial reports in *The Times*, 22 Jan. (p. 7), 23 Jan. (p. 11), 24 Jan. (p. 17), 25 Jan. (p. 10), 26 Jan. (p. 8), 29 Jan. (p. 9) and 30 Jan. (p. 9.) Court transcripts can be found in PRO DPP 4/55 and DPP 4/56. Unless otherwise stated, the information on Goddard and his trial is drawn from these sources.

[3]   Sir John Moylan, *Scotland Yard and the Metropolitan Police*, London, 1934, 2nd ed., pp. 126 and 328.

writing of the late 1920s, he was critical of the fickleness of public opinion and of the press. One minute these could be praising the police, and the next minute 'the pendulum' swung back.

> In the news world, as in any other business, demand creates supply; Press reporters realized that any story about misconduct amongst the Metropolitan Police was good copy and they nosed about for any little tit-bit to form the basis of a new sensation. ANOTHER SCOTLAND YARD SCANDAL was on the placards twice a week and, as often as not, the only foundation was some perfectly ordinary discipline case such as must necessarily crop up at fairly frequent intervals in a body of 20,000 men.[4]

A decade later Douglas G. Browne published a history of Scotland Yard which combined both Moylan's and Howgrave-Graham's assessments of the Goddard case. Newspapers of the 1920s had embarked on a 'campaign of abuse based on a series of incidents of which the worst that can be said of most of the officers concerned was that their actions were sometimes injudicious.' The problem was aggravated by the fact that a majority of the instances reported in the press involved 'women who either are of doubtful reputation, or act in a highly indiscreet manner.' On Goddard's case specifically, Browne quoted Moylan's 'reassuring feature' and continued with a paragraph that comes close to exonerating Goddard as an unfortunate victim who had been tempted by foreigners 'of the lowest type' at a time of economic uncertainty and mass unemployment.[5] T.A. Critchley, who wrote what is probably the most astute of the Whig histories of the English police, ignored the Goddard case but noted that within two years of the General Strike of 1926 'the Press and public opinion had once again decided, as they were apt to do from time to time, that the police were corrupt and oppressive.'[6] David Ascoli published the semi-official history of the Metropolitan Police for its 150th Anniversary in 1979. His book is detailed and thorough on the attempt to clean up police corruption during the 1970s, but he chose to discuss the Goddard case in terms similar to his predecessors. He stressed the 'degenerate society' and 'the pursuit of pleasure' in the London of the 1920s, the growth of disreputable clubs where drinking laws were flouted and where prostitution was rife, and where 'most of the proprietors were foreigners of very doubtful repute.'[7]

These authors were all close to the police, indeed it was not until the mid-1970s that police history began to be explored on a more critical academic level, though most of the resulting research has tended to concentrate on the English police during

---

4   H.M. Howgrave-Graham, *Light and Shade at Scotland Yard*, London, 1947, p. 18, and see also p. 1.
5   Douglas G. Browne, *The Rise of Scotland Yard: A History of the Metropolitan Police*, London, 1956, pp. 326 and 335.
6   T.A. Critchley, *A History of Police in England and Wales*, revised ed., London, 1978, p. 200.
7   David Ascoli, *The Queen's Peace: The Origins and Development of the Metropolitan Police 1829-1979*, London, 1979, pp. 214-215. Browne and Ascoli's criticism of 'degeneracy' and 'foreigners' picks up on some of the contemporary anxieties expressed about nightclubs, vulnerable and predatory women, jazz, drugs, and the fact that two of the most notorious 'dope' kings of the period were the Chinese 'Brilliant' Chang and the Jamaican jazz drummer Edgar Manning. See Marek Kohn, *Dope Girls: The Birth of the British Drug Underground*, London, 1992.

the nineteenth century. The official and semi-official line on the Goddard case, and on similar occurrences, has always tended to be that such offenders were isolated individuals – 'rotten apples' or 'black sheep', the latter being a particularly favored term[8] – who were brought to justice by honest policemen. At the same time, by seeking to shift blame from the police institution to society for its 'degeneracy,' to the press and the public for their fickleness, and to unsavory foreigners and 'women of doubtful reputation,' the police are further absolved. Police officers, the occasional black sheep excepted, thus appear as honest, courageous individuals, doing their difficult job with professionalism, and standing above the capriciousness of the public that they serve. In general, police officers probably are no different from the public that they serve and from whom they are drawn. The question that has to be explored, however, is the extent to which this official and semi-official discourse served, and perhaps serves, to sideline problems within the Metropolitan Police, which were possibly institutional, both during the inter-war period and afterwards. In short, was Goddard an isolated rotten apple? Were the other instances reported in the press at worst 'injudicious' and really only 'ordinary' disciplinary cases? Or were there more serious problems within the institution.

I

George Goddard had been born in 1879 in Guildford, Surrey, some thirty miles from central London. He began his working life as a bricklayer, but joined the Metropolitan Police in 1900. He served in a cross-section of London districts: in Marylebone, 'D' Division, a busy central district, in Wandsworth, 'V' Division, a mixed suburb to the west of the center, and in Hampstead, 'S' Division, the suburb with many elegant districts to the north of the center. In 1910 he was fined, severely reprimanded and cautioned for heavy drinking. Three years later, however, he was posted as a sergeant to 'C' Division, St. James's. By this time he had conquered his drink problem and was regarded as 'practically a total abstainer.'[9] In Goddard's time St. James's was the smallest of the twenty-three divisional areas of the Metropolitan Police; it covered just under a square mile. There were three police stations in the division, Vine Street, Great Marlborough Street and Tottenham Court Road. At the time of Goddard's trial there were 528 men in the division: a superintendent, 21 inspectors, 61 sergeants and 445 constables. The police presence was heavy since this was a central division, but equally important, 'C' division covered the vice district in and around Soho.[10] In 1918 Goddard had been given responsibility for supervising the nightclubs and 'disorderly houses' – the euphemism for brothels – of the district. Nightclubs were legal, but they

---

8 See, inter alia, *Police Review*, 1 Mar. 1929, p. 158; *Report of the Royal Commission on Police Powers and Procedure*, 1929, Cmd. 3297, London, paragraph 262; and Andrew Boyle, *Trenchard*, London, 1962, p. 585.

9 PRO HO 45.25425.440186/37, Correspondence with Capt. T.J. O'Connor, r.e. Goddard.

10 Arthur Tietjen, *Soho: London's Vicious Circle*, London, 1956, provides a racy, journalistic account of the district between the wars and up to the early 1950s that touches on the drugs trade, prostitution, racetrack gangs, nightclubs and, of course, the Goddard case. See also Kohn, *Dope Girls*.

were commonly believed to sell alcohol after licensing hours. Brothels were illegal but, of course, did not advertise themselves as such. It was Goddard's task to follow up information, often anonymous, about illegal behavior. For this purpose he could direct young constables to enter nightclubs in plain clothes and he could also furnish them with sufficient funds to make them appear genuine club clientele. The constables reported to Goddard, and he, in turn, reported to the superior officers in the division. Evidence of illegal behavior on the strength of these reports meant that an application could be made for a magistrate's warrant authorizing a police raid on suspect premises. If the subsequent raid found evidence of illegal behavior, then the proprietor might be prosecuted. The opportunities for corruption are obvious. Goddard was able to construct reports to the effect that the anonymous information on a particular club, restaurant or any other premises, appeared, on investigation, to be incorrect. Alternatively, he could tip-off club proprietors about a raid so that there was no evidence of any alcohol being sold, or having been sold, at the moment when the police entered the building. Goddard's wage was £6 -15s (£6.75) a week. Evidence presented at his trial, however, showed that he was able to draw over £100 in a month in Treasury notes to finance the 20 or so young constables who entered nightclubs on his behalf. Some of these Treasury notes were laundered through an Italian restaurant proprietor who entertained Goddard to a free lunch or dinner five or six times a week.[11] At the time of his arrest Goddard lived in a house in the south London suburb of Streatham which he had purchased for £1850; he owned a Chrysler car which he had purchased for around £400; and he had various safe deposits and bank accounts. One of the safe deposits, registered in the fictional name of Joseph Eagles resident at the address of Goddard's brother-in-law, contained £12,000 in bank notes, some of which could be traced back to Meyrick and Ribuffini. In all it was estimated that the £6-a-week police sergeant had assets amounting to almost £18,000.

Goddard's ultimate exposure began with an anonymous letter received by Sir William Horwood, the Commissioner of the Metropolitan Police, on 20 September 1928. This accused Goddard of taking bribes to protect the proprietors of the suspect clubs, and of having a personal financial interest in them. It drew attention to his house and car, and noted further that he had established his brother-in-law in a pawnbroker's business. Enquiries were begun within two weeks. Indeed, a request to

---

[11] Travelling in Italy as one of the Bill Hall Trio in the late 1940s, Spike Milligan met a Poppa Rocca who lived in a villa on the shore of Lake Maggiore. Rocca claimed to have been a restaurateur in Soho who let out rooms above his restaurant to prostitutes. He also claimed that he was picked on for not paying protection money to members of the Metropolitan Police, and that he was deported following the Goddard affair. His grand-daughter explained to Milligan that Poppa Rocca had paid money to Goddard, and that 'big names' were involved in the affair and had given Goddard 'a golden handshake' to take the blame. Spike Milligan, *Peace Work*, London, 1992, pp. 104-105 and 119-121. There was no one called Rocca named at Goddard's trial, but several other Italians were: Vittorio Pianciola and Luigi Varesio were involved with rooms in Kingly St, and Giulio Pelotto and Alfonso Mariani were joint proprietors of the Star and Garter Restaurant in Bloomsbury. As to the question of deportations, *The News-Sheet of the Bribery and Secrecy Commission Prevention League*, no. 57, March 1929, p. 27, noted: 'The Home Secretary is said to have ordered the deportation of a number of aliens supposed to have been mixed up in the Goddard case. Many would feel more comfortable if such cases came into court in the first place.'

the car firm from whom Goddard had purchased his Chrysler gave him warning that investigations were afoot. The manager of the firm telephoned Goddard to ask permission to pass information about the purchase to the police; Goddard responded by setting up the safe deposit box in the name of Joseph Eagles and transferring money held in his own name. When shown the anonymous letter Goddard protested that his wealth had been accumulated over a long period: his wife had money; he had been thrifty and had saved; he had been given some very good racing tips, and he had speculated successfully in foreign currency. On 29 October, however, he appeared before a disciplinary board at Scotland Yard, and admitted guilt on two charges: neglect of duty in failing to give a satisfactory account of large sums of money that he had received from unknown sources; and discreditable conduct, namely betting and associating with bookmakers and other undesirable persons. This admission led to dismissal. He was arrested on the criminal charges involving Meyrick and Ribuffini a few days later. But the anonymous letter of September 1928 was not the first accusation levelled against Goddard, and involvement with bookmakers never figured in the criminal charges.

Charles Morton was Goddard's divisional superintendent from 1926 to 1928.[12] In the witness box he produced a number of anonymous letters which he had received during those years about restaurants and hotels functioning as brothels and about nightclubs selling drink after hours and trafficking in cocaine. These letters had been passed on to Goddard for investigation, and Goddard had reported that there was no truth in them. Some of the letters produced for 1927 accused Goddard of tipping off proprietors about raids and of receiving free meals at a hotel suspected of being a brothel. In March 1928 the Home Secretary, Sir William Joynson-Hicks, wrote to the Commissioner with information that he had received concerning a club in 'C' Division's district, 'a place of the most intense mischief and immorality' and a haven for 'doped women and drunken men.' He requested that the Commissioner 'put this matter in the hands of your most experienced men and whatever the cost may be, find out the truth about this Club and if it is as bad as I am informed prosecute with the utmost vigour of the law.' In reply Horwood declared that he had 'every confidence' in Morton and that he was unwilling to bring in men from elsewhere to investigate 'C' Division. He requested that the Home Secretary's informants make their allegations directly to him.[13] Possibly as a follow up to this Morton organized a raid on Mrs. Meyrick's '43 Club' in May without informing Goddard or any of the constables who worked under him. The raid took place at 1.30 a.m.; some 250 to 300 people were found in the club, and alcoholic drinks were being consumed. But there were no repercussions within 'C' Division. At the trial Sir Henry Maddocks, acting for Mrs. Meyrick, asked Morton: 'Did you have Goddard and the other "officers" on the

---

[12] *The Times* gives Morton's rank as divisional inspector. However Morton's Record of Service, held in the Metropolitan Police Museum, Charlton, shows him promoted to superintendent on 1 May 1926. Morton, born in Norfolk in 1875, began his working life as a railway porter. He joined the Metropolitan Police in October 1897, received eight commendations, and retired in December 1933.

[13] PRO HO 144/17667, Home Secretary to Commissioner, 3 Mar. 1928, and Commissioner to Home Secretary, 5 Mar. 1928.

carpet to ask them what was meant by their previous reports?' and 'Did you take any steps to ask them?' On each occasion the reply was 'No.'

In Morton's defence it might be argued with reference to the letters produced in court that an effective vice-squad officer might be the victim of anonymous accusations by offenders seeking to have him removed from his position. On at least one occasion, in September 1927, Goddard had responded to an anonymous letter protesting about the 'insidious lying and unfounded allegations against the police who are powerless to defend themselves against writers who write in anonymity.' Furthermore, it might be argued that even the most effective vice-squad officers might not always know the scale and whereabouts of major offending. However, if Morton's failure to press Goddard on the contrast between the reports and the results of the raid remains puzzling for historians, it does not seem to have puzzled the police authorities. At the time of Goddard's trial Morton was no longer an inspector with 'C' Division but had been transferred to be the Superintendent of 'Y' Division, Highgate, North London. Three day's after Goddard's appearance before the Police Discipline Board, the Commissioner informed the Home Office that he was

> calling on the Chief Constable of the District and certain senior officers of 'C' Division for an explanation as to how it is that this Station Police Sergeant's consistently corrupt practices extending over so long a period have remained undetected by them if they have been exercising proper supervision and care in discharging their duties.[14]

Whether anything came of this meeting is unclear and, aside from the transfer of Morton, no one responsible for supervising Goddard appears to have been reprimanded or disciplined. Shortly after the Discipline Board Chief Constable Frederick Wensley, one of Scotland Yard's top detectives, questioned a contable who was later to give evidence against Goddard. 'Goddard said he was going to stand alone rather than bring other people into it,' declared Wensley. 'I don't know who the other people are, do you?' Constable Wilkin replied that he did not, and Wensley did not pursue the matter.[15] In the following February Johnson-Hicks was asked in the Commons whether he was satisfied that Goddard's behavior could have continued without the connivance of any superior officers, and how many were still serving. Joynson-Hicks reported that the new Metropolitan Police Commissioner, Lord Byng of Vimy, had gone into the matter and taken 'certain steps.' Subsequently, in a written reply, he explained that 19 senior officers had supervision of Goddard during his time in 'C' Division; 11 of these were serving at the time Goddard was suspended, and all 11 were still serving.[16]

Horace Josling was less fortunate. The son of an engine driver for the Great Eastern Railway, he had attended Brentwood Grammar School. He began his working

---

14   PRO HO 45.25425.440186/21, Commissioner to Home Office, 1 Nov. 1928.
15   PRO DPP 1/87, interview of PC Wilkin, 31 Oct. 1928.
16   *Times*, 15 Feb. 1929, p. 11, and 1 Mar. 1929, p. 13. In June 1929 however, Chief Inspector Mears, one of Goddard's former superiors, was suspended from command of the Metropolitan Police Dock contingent at Devonport. *Police Review*, 21 June 1929, p. 484.

life as a schoolteacher but, to better himself, he joined the Metropolitan Police in July 1912.

[B]ad as the pay and pension prospects were in the Police in 1912, they were then (...) infinitely better than those obtaining in the teaching profession, especially so as the teaching world at that time was flooded with young men and women.[17]

Josling's academic abilities led to his appointment to the administrative staff of a central division then, at the end of the First World War when the Metropolitan Police recruits' school reopened, he was posted to it as a sergeant instructor. The financial cuts of the 'Geddes axe' forced a reduction in the school's staff and Josling was transferred to the bustle of Great Marlborough Street Police Station where Goddard was already serving. But Josling was incorruptible and perhaps, as the Scotland Yard Disciplinary Board of July 1922, which investigated his case, concluded, he was also a little 'self-righteous.' According to Josling there was a weekly shareout of bribes from local bookmakers at Great Marlborough Street and Goddard was the key police figure in the distribution. Enforcement of the 1906 Street Betting Act had fostered police corruption. It appeared impossible to prevent the working class from passing bets to bookies' runners and a significant number of police officers of all ranks connived with bookmakers to produce arrests and convictions sufficient to suggest police efficiency, together with little interruption to the practice of betting and a satisfactory distribution of profits to both bookmakers and policemen.[18] Josling claimed that, even after he had several times refused to participate in the shareout, plain envelopes filled with money were placed in his locker. He addressed his charges directly to the Commissioner on the grounds that, since he and Goddard had the same immediate superiors, it would be difficult to bring his allegations before them. The Commissioner responded by passing the information to the Home Office which, in turn, set up a two-man enquiry. The results of the enquiry were never published, but shortly afterwards Josling found himself on the disciplinary charge of bringing false allegations against brother officers.

According to Josling, speaking at a press conference held in the House of Commons after Goddard's trial, the Disciplinary Board that met in July 1922 appeared to see him as the offender rather than Goddard. The latter was allowed two witnesses, but Josling was not allowed to cross-examine them. No bookmakers were summoned.

I was cross-examined for two days to the point of almost physical and mental exhaustion. On the first day I was examined for eight hours with a break for luncheon. On the second day I was kept before the Board from 1 o'clock until 20 minutes to 8 at night. The members of the Board had tea, but I was not offered any.[19]

Josling was found guilty of making false allegations against Goddard and was called upon to resign. He lost his pension rights, and spent the next two years

---

17   *Police Review*, 15 Mar. 1929, p. 192.
18   David Dixon, *From Prohibition to Regulation: Bookmaking, Anti-Gambling, and the Law*, Oxford, 1991, chap. 7.
19   *Times*, 21 Feb. 1929, p. 5. .

supported financially by his wife while he trained at Goldsmith's College to return to his original career. At the time of Goddard's trial he was the master of a village school in Shropshire and on Goddard's conviction he presented a claim for compensation backed by the Labour M.P. for Edge Hill, Jack Hayes, himself a former Metropolitan Police sergeant. In March 1929 the Home Office declared that Josling's resignation would be amended to having been 'voluntary' and awarded him £1,500 from the Metropolitan Police Fund.[20] With hindsight it is easy to be critical of the Disciplinary Board that compelled Josling to resign. He probably did come over as something of a prig. But it would also be surprising if the board were not aware of the stories of police corruption and links with bookmakers. The Royal Commission on the Duties of the Metropolitan Police which sat between 1906 and 1908 produced considerable evidence to this effect as did the Select Committee of the House of Commons on Betting Duty which met the year after Josling's resignation. The suspicion has to be that the Disciplinary Board preferred to sacrifice Josling rather than to open up the opportunity for a scandal that might extend well beyond Goddard.

None of the semi-official police histories by Ascoli, Browne, Howgrave-Graham and Moylan contain any reference to Josling. However, in the aftermath of the Goddard case Josling's story was given considerable prominence as the heroic, moral counterpart. 'Out of evil cometh good!' declared the *Police Review*, and it reprinted a lengthy article written by Jack Hayes for the *Liverpool Post* that spoke of

> a man whose conscience was his master, and whose sense of rectitude and honour demanded of him the blighting of his career and the sacrifice of some of his fondest hopes.' Josling's strong Christian faith was stressed, as was that of 'his brave wife…. [who] with her Spartan spirit, bade him be of good cheer, and (…) buckled to and turned breadwinner.' Moreover, Hayes was moved that Josling could even find generous words for Goddard: 'I cannot help but feel sorry for [him]. Better men perhaps than he have succumbed to lesser temptations. I have no spleen or feeling against him or anyone else.'[21] There was also significance that could be drawn from Josling's return to teaching. Again to quote Hayes, following Josling's death early in 1941 at the comparatively young age of 51, 'he buried his sorrow in his struggle to teach village youngsters a way of life which would make them good citizens. [22]

The Goddard story is unpleasant and it offers a picture of London's Metropolitan Police that is very different from the usual. Of course the semi-official historians were right when they noted that it was a police investigation that brought Goddard to book. Yet this does not excuse the fact that an earlier investigation led to an innocent man being compelled to resign and to lose his pension rights. Jack Hayes had raised the issue of Josling indirectly with a question to the Home Secretary in November 1928 after Goddard's dismissal from the police and before his arrest on the corruption charges. Hayes also posed a series of questions regarding the action taken against Goddard that were never answered; in particular, at what point was the decision taken

---

20 *Times*, 5 Mar. 1929, p. 8.
21 *Police Review*, 22 Feb. 1929, pp. 135 and 138-140; see also, 23 Nov. 1928, p. 916, and 30 Nov. 1928, p. 939.
22 *Police Review*, 24 Jan. 1941, p. 52. Josling had been promoted to headmaster of a school at Oswestry in 1930. *Police Review*, 19 Sep. 1930, p. 764.

to prosecute Goddard? And if this was before the disciplinary board that resulted in his dismissal, why was he not simply suspended before the trial and only dismissed once the guilty verdict was passed, as was normal practice? 'However bad he may have been, his trial should not have been pre-judged by dismissal from the Force.'[23] Questions might also be posed as to why there were not casualties among Goddard's superiors who were guilty, at the very least, of complacency. Some newspapers raised this issue at the time of the trial,[24] as did H.L. Adam in his journalistic survey of the C.I.D. in 1931.

> [T]he thing that mystifies one most of all is how an officer in Goddard's humble position – that of a mere sergeant – was able to carry on such an extensive system of 'graft' without being unmasked or in any serious degree interfered with.

But neither the newspapers nor Adam pressed the matter. Indeed, in terms which appear patronizing to the contemporary eye but which would have produced little criticism during the inter-war years, Adam went on to suggest that the ordinary individual did not need to press the matter, after all the important people were aware.

> [T]here are certain thin portions of the veil of obscurity through which one may get unpleasant glimpses of the truth. Further than that one must not go. But there are those who know, among them the late Home Secretary, whose knowledge, however, is secured by an official seal.[25]

A rather similar line was taken by the semi-official journal *Justice of the Peace*. The general public was 'in no position to judge' corruption in the police from resignations or brief allegations in the press. Rather it would be 'far more reasonable, as well as more optimistic, to take the recent events as evidence of increasing vigilance on the part of responsible authorities and of a determination not to gloss over any unpleasant discoveries.'[26] Such a statement is redolent of the culture of secrecy that David Vincent has described as pervading British administration in the nineteenth and twentieth centuries. 'Withholding information became at once a claim to probity and a demand for deference. It implied a sense of responsibility which arose from and defined a position of moral authority.'[27] At the same time, putting all the focus and blame upon an individual convicted of a criminal offence is a means of reassuring the public and of insisting that the authorities are vigilant, but it also avoids any root and branch investigation of an institution and thereby avoids the risks of more serious revelations. Emphasizing the positive side of developments is, perhaps understandably, a common trait among official and semi-official historians of institutions. It has been common among a variety of official British institutions during the nineteenth and twentieth centuries.[28] In the case of the Metropolitan Police early in 1929, moreover,

---

23   *Police Review*, 1 Mar. 1929, p. 158.
24   *The News-Sheet of the Bribery and Secret Commissions Prevention League*, No. 156, Feb. 1929, pp. 15-16, and No. 157, March 1929, p. 27.
25   H.L. Adam, *C.I.D. Behind the Scenes at Scotland Yard*, London, 1931, p. 32.
26   *Justice of the Peace*, 22 June 1929, p. 391.
27   David Vincent, *The Culture of Secrecy: Britain, 1832-1998*, Oxford, 1998, p. 15.
28   Alan Doig, *Corruption and Misconduct in Contemporary British Politics*, Harmondsworth, 1984.

there was a particular reason for not wanting to bring dirty washing before the public. 1929 was the force's centenary. On 25 May, the hundredth anniversary of the passage of the bill creating the force, there was an inspection by the Prince of Wales in Hyde Park, followed by a March Past of Buckingham Palace. However, a closer investigation of the Metropolitan Police during the 1920s and early 1930s, suggests that Goddard was not a solitary 'black sheep' or 'rotten apple,' but that corruption and feelings of inviolability went much deeper than a single, or even one or two isolated individuals. Moreover, the idea that the press were seizing upon and magnifying a few minor disciplinary cases becomes difficult to accept when the details of these cases are examined.

II

At the beginning of 1922, the year in which Josling was forced to resign, the *Daily Graphic* published an article on 'Modern Gambling Dens' in which it alleged that gaming houses in London 'having a rich and extensive clientele, can afford to bribe the Police to a certain extent.' The furious Commissioner of the Metropolitan Police forced an apology from the *Graphic*, which was published at the top of Police Orders.[29] Towards the end of the year several newspapers and journals carried articles about police involvement with prostitutes, either blackmailing them or accepting bribes from them to permit them to solicit unhindered. The home secretary responded to MPs' questions with a written answer to the effect that no specific evidence could be acquired from those who made the allegations.[30] However, over the next few years there were a series of incidents involving Metropolitan Police officers that are suggestive, not of corruption, but of a degree of high-handedness and a sense of immunity for their actions. In July 1925 a Tribunal of Enquiry was held into the arrest of Major R.O. Sheppard of the Royal Army Ordnance Corps. Sheppard had been accused of theft by Miss Deltah Dennistown. It appeared that Miss Dennistown was mistaken in identifying the major, while the tribunal found the police at fault for delay in admitting him to bail, wrongful questioning, laxity in an identification parade, wrongful fingerprinting, failure to allow the accused to communicate with friends, and a general inability to expedite and facilitate matters when such might put them to some inconvenience.[31] *The Times* found the report 'disquieting' and sensed 'a bureaucratic undertone in some of [the police] answers (…) which has an 'autoritaire' flavour of an unpleasant kind.'[32] The Home Secretary, however, could respond that 'the case was a quite exceptional one,' that he had rectified the defects which it had highlighted, and that he was 'satisfied that there [was] no justification for any serious mistrust of the attitude or practice of the police in the discharge of their very difficult duties.'[33] In October 1927, however, the Home Secretary thought it necessary to appoint the

29   *Metropolitan Police Orders 1922*, 10 Jan., p. 23.
30   PRO HO.45.25425.440186/1-2; *Times*, 15 Dec. 1922, p. 9.
31   *Arrest of Major R.O. Sheppard, D.S.O., R.A.O.C. Report by The Right Hon. J.F.P. Rawlinson, K.C., M.P. of Enquiry held under Tribunals of Enquiry (Evidence) Act, 1921*, Cmd. 2497, London, 1925.
32   *Times*, 17 Aug. 1925, p. 11.
33   *Times*, 28 Aug. 1925, p. 9.

Street Offences Committee under Hugh MacMillan, K.C. to enquire into prostitution and offences against 'decency and good order.'[34] Amongst the issues discussed by the committee were reports of the bribery of police by prostitutes. 'I believe it is inevitable that there should be corruption in police forces,' explained an experienced London magistrate who continued with the traditional cliché, 'in the same way that there are black sheep in every flock.'[35] The Committee itself concluded 'that such instances must inevitably happen' given the possibilities for temptation, and believed that 'street betting and motor offences (...) afforded similar opportunities for temptation' as prostitution.[36] According to Harry Daley, who was transferred to 'C' Division seven years after Goddard's exposure, this was another racket in which Goddard had been involved.

> Each whore paid a regular lump sum to Goddard, which entitled her to be arrested in proper rotation with the other girls, never unexpectedly, and enabled her to give full attention to passing men without the nervous wear and tear of keeping constant look-out for coppers. The arrangement was so convenient to the girls that on the appointed day, in places like Lisle Street, they formed small queues waiting to pay their dues to Goddard. It must have been wonderful.

By the time that Daley moved into the district, however, prostitutes could not be arrested by any policeman, but only by a policeman in uniform. This reduced the opportunities for the bribery of plain-clothes men. Since any uniformed officer could make an arrest, it meant that a protection system was more difficult to guarantee. Finally, it cut the opportunities for men seeking to extort money or favors from prostitutes on the grounds that they were plain-clothes policemen.[37]

A sub-group of the MacMillan Committee was asked to investigate the case of Major Graham Bell Murray, acquitted in the preceding August on a charge of being

---

34 *Times*, 15 Oct. 1927, p. 12.

35 *Times*, 3 Dec. 1927, p. 12. This report appeared in the column adjacent to a report of a bookmaker appearing in court alongside nine members of the Liverpool Borough Police all charged with corruption and conspiracy.

36 *Report of the Street Offences Committee*, Cmd. 3231, London, 1928, paragraph 26.

37 Harry Daley, *This Small Cloud. A Personal Memoir*, London, 1986, p. 149. The Street Offences Committee recommended the deployment of larger numbers of uniformed officers in areas where prostitution was rife to facilitate 'prevention.' It thought that there was a particular problem in deploying plain-clothes officers to detect and prevent offences involving male homosexuals because of the risk that the officers become *agents provocateurs*. *Report of the Street Offences Committee*, paragraph 57. The problem of corrupt police behavior towards prostitutes was not immediately resolved however. *Metropolitan Police Orders* for 29 November 1929 report the dismissal of a constable in T Division who, while off duty and in plain clothes, had approached two 'well known prostitutes', declared he was a police officer, and demanded money from them. When the women refused he assaulted one of them, at which point a uniformed officer interfered. The offender compounded his misdemeanor by denying to his uniformed colleague that he was, in fact, a policeman.

drunk and disorderly, notably by molesting young women in Piccadilly. The findings of the sub-committee forwarded to Murray in May 1928 stated:

> that due care and judgement were not exhibited by the police officer in arresting you; that proper steps as required by the Metropolitan Police General Orders were not taken in the police station to inform you of your right to communicate with your friends and call in a private doctor, and that proper regard was not paid to your requests in the matter; and that the evidence of the police officer at Quarter Sessions on the subject of your condition was recklessly inadequate.

In recompense Murray was offered an *ex-gratia* grant of £500 from the Metropolitan Police Fund.[38]

But the real *causes célèbres* in the cases of public decency and suspect police behavior during this period involved women stigmatized by Browne, and others, as 'of doubtful reputation.' In April 1928 two plain-clothes officers arrested Sir Leo Chiozza Money and Irene Savidge in Hyde Park and charged them with an offence against public decency. Sir Leo, a well-known economist with friends in high places, brought his not inconsiderable influence into play. The case was dismissed at the Great Marlborough Street Magistrates' Court, costs were awarded against the police and questions were asked in Parliament. In an attempt to exonerate the police institution Miss Savidge was invited to Scotland Yard to give a statement on the affair. But the interview was badly mismanaged. A woman police officer in attendance at the outset was dismissed from the proceedings, which then continued for several hours. While the evidence is contradictory, the interview and the surrounding events appear to have been patronizing, clumsy and possibly suggestive. A parliamentary committee of enquiry was set up which could not agree; one member was very critical of the police, the other two largely exonerated them.[39] The Helene Adele affair followed hard on the heels of the Money-Savidge case. Miss Adele was sleeping in the back of a parked taxi when, she claimed, a uniformed patrol officer of 'Y' division, in the presence of another uniformed officer, climbed in and attempted sexual intercourse with her. When she vociferously protested she was arrested and charged with insulting words and behavior. Miss Adele was acquitted at the Clerkenwell Magistrates' Court. The two officers were then charged, found guilty of perjury and sentenced to 18 months' hard labor. The judge, in words reminiscent of those used with reference to the discovery of Goddard's offences, expressed his satisfaction 'that the Force to which you belong have been the means of bringing you to justice and showing that you were unworthy of the uniform which you wore.' Nevertheless, a police sergeant

---

38   *Times*, 31 May, 1928, p. 11.
39   *Inquiry in Regard to the Interrogation by the Police of Miss Savidge*, Cmd. 3147, London, 1928. It is interesting to note that Ascoli, *Queen's Peace*, pp. 213-214, Browne, *Rise of Scotland Yard*, pp. 327-328, and Critchley, *A History of Police*, p. 201, stress that the Labour member of the committee was the critic of the police. For Browne he was 'a poor judge of character.' For Ascoli he acted 'for transparently political reasons'; these may have been transparent to Ascoli, but are not apparent from his text.

who gave false evidence on the defendants' behalf was dismissed.[40] In August 1928, the month following Adele's initial arrest and preceding the trial of the two officers for perjury, the government determined on a Royal Commission into Police Powers and Procedures.

The proceedings of the Royal Commission were reported in newspaper columns that abutted those reporting the Goddard affair. Its report was dated 16 March 1929, just over six weeks after Goddard's conviction. The Commission did not shirk the problem of police corruption. It concluded that such corruption,

> where it exists, seems to be mainly associated with the enforcement of laws which are out of harmony with public opinion, or in enforcing which the Police are compelled by lack of adequate powers to have recourse to unsatisfactory methods of detection.

Nevertheless, the testimony received 'from responsible and judicial authorities' led the Commission 'to form a very favourable opinion of the conduct, tone, and efficiency of the Police Service as a whole.' The recent offenders brought to book had been tempted because of the problems of enforcing the law relating to betting, to nightclubs and to public decency. '[T]he culprits in these conspicuous cases were in no sense typical of the Service which they have disgraced and (...) their detection and punishment are welcomed and approved by the Police Force as a whole.'[41] Yet within a year of the Commission's Report and Goddard's conviction there was evidence that matters in 'C' Division remained far from perfect.

In the early summer of 1929 Lord Byng of Vimy, the new Commissioner of the Metropolitan Police, called for volunteers to transfer into 'C' Division. Such volunteers appeared hard to come by. '[T]here is a general feeling in the Force' wrote the *Police Review*, 'that 'C' Division is not now looked upon as being so desirable a ground as previously.'[42] It is unclear whether this 'general feeling' stemmed from the stigma left by Goddard or from concerns that men in the division would find themselves constantly under strict surveillance. As the call for volunteers went out two sergeants and two constables at the Great Marlborough Street Police Station were dismissed on the grounds of:

> Corrupt practice – did improperly use their position as members of the Force to their private advantage, namely did accept meals from restaurant keepers without paying for them. Further discreditable conduct – did act in a manner likely to bring discredit on the reputation of the Service by associating with persons whom they might reasonably be expected to suspect of keeping brothels.[43]

---

40 *Times*, 15 Sept. 1928, p. 7 for the final verdict, and see also 6 Aug., p. 7; 10 Aug., p. 7; 13 Aug., p. 9; 23 Aug., p. 7; 27 Aug., p. 7; 30 Aug., p. 9; 12 Sept., p. 9; 13 Sept., p. 14; and 14 Sept., p. 14.

41 *Report of the Royal Commission on Police Powers and Procedure*, 1929, paragraphs 280 and 297-298.

42 *Metropolitan Police Orders 1929*, 29 May (p. 486) and 11 June (p. 537); *Police Review*, 21 June 1929, p. 483.

43 *Metropolitan Police Orders 1929*, 22 May (p. 456) and 5 June (p. 519); *Police Review*, 19 July 1929, p. 564.

Goddard, it will be remembered, had been accused of similar practices. An un-named source informed the press, and the press jumped on the story, much to the annoyance of Lord Byng who drafted an angry letter to Lord Riddell, chairman of the Newspaper Publishers' Association. 'We did not wish to give this information to the Press because we still prefer to deal with our own domestic troubles in our own domestic way.' He expressed concern that the story might tarnish the centenary parade scheduled for the Saturday following the press revelations, and concluded that, if newspapers did not show a little more 'goodwill' then it might be hard to justify the expenditure on the police's relatively new Press Bureau. The draft was shortened and toned down, with references to closing the Press Bureau removed. Riddell was sympathetic, but also raised the important point about sources: 'who gives out this information? What is an "illicit source"? I am not defending the press. At the same time there are two ends to this troublesome question.'[44] The following August two inspectors, four sergeants and six constables of 'C' Division were separated and transferred to other divisions. The reasons for the transfers are unclear, but it seems probable that this was a further attempt to cleanse the division by removing men who had fallen under suspicion but against whom there was little evidence.[45] On this occasion the press were silent, but not so two years later when dealings with bookmakers brought other members of 'C' Division down.

In the summer of 1931 one inspector and 26 police constables from Great Marlborough Street Police Station were dismissed for accepting money from bookmakers and other tradesmen in the district.[46] At the same time another inspector and at least 23 PCs were separated and transferred from 'C' Division.[47] The press reported the dismissals and commented unfavorably on the reluctance of the Metropolitan Police to make any official statement. 'We have had occasion before' protested the *News Chronicle*, 'to plead that Scotland Yard should be less secretive about matters of this kind, if only because nothing so undermines public confidence as over-elaborate secrecy.'[48] The newspapers rapidly picked up on the fact that a sergeant had been reduced to the rank of constable and that three other constables had been disciplined and fined. Once again Lord Byng expressed his anger to the Newspaper Publishers' Association. 'The Commissioner had hoped that, after the correspondence which took place in 1929, it was realised that the public interest was not served by treating disciplinary enquiries of this nature as matters of more than domestic concern.' The *Sunday Express* wrote to Byng concerned that 'the reputation of the fine body of men under your control suffers from the action of a few black sheep' and suggested that he might like to put the record straight by giving the paper

---

44 PRO MEPO 3.739, Leakage of Information to the Press, 1929-1931.

45 *Metropolitan Police Orders 1929*, 9 Aug., p. 750.

46 *Metropolitan Police Orders 1931*, 16 July, p. 781, 6 Aug., p. 847, 13 Aug., pp. 877-878, 27 Aug., p. 923, and 1 Sep., p. 951.

47 *Metropolitan Police Orders 1931*, 26 Aug., p. 910, and 2 Sep., p. 956. HO 45.25425.440186/63 has a slightly shorter list of men investigated and transferred, but this list also includes two other constables, McBean and Offord.

48 *News Chronicle*, 3 July 1931; cutting in PRO HO.25425.440186/55.

an interview. Byng's secretary curtly replied that the commissioner never gave interviews.[49]

The *Daily Mail* noted that the accused officers came from 'C' Division, which had been Goddard's division, though it also told its readers that some of the alleged offences were trivial. 'One is charged with accepting a pound of strawberries, and another with taking a small sum of money ten years ago.'[50] Nevertheless the removal of fifty men was a considerable reorganization of one police station and it meant that almost one third of the station's total complement, and nearly one man in ten in the whole division, had been either dismissed or disciplined. 'For quite a considerable time,' a senior officer at Scotland Yard explained to the Home Office,

> we have had reliable information that some systemic corruption is going on in this district. As usual, we have had intense difficulty in getting anyone to come forward and give us specific details upon which we could act. We have now, however, got a certain amount of evidence which should enable us to deal with at any rate some of the worst offenders.[51]

Among the men dismissed were an inspector and a constable who had volunteered for transfer to the division in June 1929; the sergeant reduced in rank and transferred, and four of the constables transferred to new divisions had also joined the division that summer.[52] The time that the defaulters had served in the police and, in particular, in 'C' Division shows that it was not simply old sweats who were involved but a cross section, some of whom had spent their entire police career in 'C' Division, and some who had scarcely been members of the police when Goddard was dismissed. There is rather more information available on the men who were transferred than on those who were dismissed. Their records suggest that the men transferred were a fairly typical cross-section of police officers; some had commendations for making arrests, some had been reprimanded for petty offences such as drunkenness, gambling, failure to detect an unlocked door while on their beat. Moreover a few successfully put the mistakes and/or suspicions of 1931 behind them and rose in rank. The demoted sergeant, for example, had reached the rank of inspector when he died in service in 1942; and one of the three men disciplined and fined alongside him was promoted to sergeant within three years and was an inspector within ten.

---

49 PRO MEPO 3.739, Leakage of Information to the Press, 1929-1931.
50 *Daily Mail*, 29 June and 7 July 1931; all cuttings in PRO HO 45.25425.440186/55 and MEPO 3.739. See also, *Times*, 16 July, p. 12, 17 July, p. 11, 1 Aug., p. 7, 14 Aug., p. 12, 21 Aug., p. 12, 28 Aug., p. 10, 9 Sept., p. 9, and 7 Oct., p. 6. PS Cornell was severely reprimanded and cautioned for not reporting that a constable was 'improperly associating' with a bookmaker who was under observation, and for 'improperly drinking' with a bookmaker and constables in a pub. PCs Atkin, Zurcher and Macaskill were all fined four days pay, severely reprimanded and cautioned for associating with bookmakers. *Metropolitan Police Orders 1931*, 18 Aug., p. 890.
51 PRO HO 45.25425.440186/55, Bingham to Anderson, 3 July 1931.
52 *Metropolitan Police Orders 1929*, 10 May, p. 419, 12 June, p. 539, and 21 June, p. 579.

Table 6.1 The 27 men dismissed from 'C' Division, Summer 1931

Rank and name	Date of joining Metropolitan Police	Date of joining 'C' Division
Inspector George Dyer	17 April 1911	12 June 1929
PC Arthur Underdown	5 August 1907	30 November 1908
PC Thomas Tozer	9 March 1908	30 November 1908
PC Edmund Burchell	1 February 1909	17 January 1916
PC Philip Bence	2 May 1910	24 April 1912
PC Nelson Grimwood	8 May 1911	10 February 1919
PC John Crafer	15 July 1912	15 July 1912
PC Frederick Warren	26 August 1912	26 August 1912
PC Walter Bradbeer	7 October 1912	7 October 1912
PC Percy Robinson	2 December 1912	19 June 1914
PC Robert Marler*	10 February 1913	10 February 1913
PC William Carswell*	14 April 1913	14 April 1913
PC Fitzgerald Foreman*	24 November 1913	24 November 1913
PC Arthur Callahan	28 July 1919	28 July 1919
PC Arthur Wakeman	3 November 1919	3 November 1919
PC Richard Thorpe	3 November 1919	3 November 1919
PC Herring	1 May 1920	1 May 1920
PC Meering	16 August 1920	16 August 1920
PC William Tompkins	19 September 1921	1 October 1923
PC Henry Lees	19 November 1923	19 November 1923
PC Frederick Holt	25 February 1924	25 February 1924
PC John Robbins	16 June 1924	16 June 1924
PC Jack Jackson	21 July 1924	21 July 1924
PC James Sutton	14 April 1925	14 April 1925
PC Charles German	7 December 1925	7 December 1925
PC George Davis	11 April 1927	21 June 1929
PC John Howe	4 July 1927	12 August 1929

* Marler, Carswell and Foreman were all transferred into the army for war service in 1918. Marler and Carswell both served from 29 October 1918 to 14 January 1919, and Foreman from 19 May 1918 to 21 January 1919.

Table 6.2 The 24 men transferred from 'C' Division, Summer 1931

Name and rank	Date of joining Metropolitan Police	Date of joining 'C' Division	Final rank and date of leaving police
Inspector William Cameron	5 September 1910	30 August 1929	Chief Inspector, 21 November 1937
PS John Hall	12 June 1911	15 December 1922	Sergeant, 14 June 1936
PS Charles Cornell (reduced in rank, 1931)	20 October 1919	?	Inspector, Died in service 10 May 1942
PC William Macaskill	10 August 1908	24 September 1926	Constable, 29 September 1933
PC Walter Mills	5 December 1910	14 December 1918	Constable, 19 January 1936
PC John Lewis	2 October 1911	2 October 1911	Constable, 4 October 1936
PC Albert Williams	27 December 1911	29 November 1919	Constable, 27 December 1936
PC Thomas Dymock	9 May 1913	6 May 1927	Sergeant, ?
PC John Kemp*	4 October 1915	14 December 1918	Constable, 31 December 1945
PC Charles Wyatt	3 November 1919	3 November 1919	Constable, 31 December 1945
PC Frank Lewry	12 April 1920	12 April 1920	?
PC Leslie Tidey	16 August 1920	16 August 1920	Constable, 31 December 1945
PC Arthur Burrow	11 July 1921	11 July 1921	Constable, 22 August 1945
PC John Atkin	19 September 1921	1 October 1923	?
PC Stanley Garner	10 October 1921	24 August 1926	Constable, 14 October 1951
PC James Butler	16 March 1925	16 March 1925	?
PC Herbert Zurcher	29 June 1925	29 June 1925	Inspector, 20 November 1946
PC Lewis Law	4 January 1926	4 January 1926	?
PC David Hughes	18 January 1926	18 January 1926	?
PC George Peddie	26 April 1926	12 June 1929	Constable, 29 May 1946
PC Donald Millar	4 October 1926	12 June 1929	Constable, 13 November 1949
PC Herbert Pepper	22 November 1926	12 June 1929	?
PC Charles Willmington	10 January 1927	10 January 1927	?
PC William Cartwright	30 May 1927	30 May 1927	?

* Kemp joined the police exceptionally in wartime after 13 years' service in the Royal Horse Guards.

While 'C' Division may have been the center of the most extreme and the most publicized instances of corruption, the problems were not confined to this division, nor, indeed, to the Metropolitan Police.[53] At the end of 1931 a court case involving a police officer in 'F' Division revealed the existence of an agreement between police and bookmakers similar to that which Josling had sought to expose nine years earlier. In September 1931 Sergeant James Hogg and P.C. Robert Reid had been transferred from the largely suburban 'S' Division to the more bustling 'F', Paddington, Division. Hogg's and Reid's role in Paddington was the pursuit of street bookmakers. Not long after their arrival Hogg was approached by Sergeant Malcolm Watts Jones, a man of good character who was due shortly to retire on a full pension. Jones offered to introduce Hogg to the local bookies. According to evidence offered in court, he told Hogg:

> Now, you are a man of the world, and if you care to fall in line and do as I tell you, you will not only be able to show a return on your charges, but also a nice return for yourself at the end of the week, which I am sure you can do with...[54]

Unfortunately Jones had picked the wrong man. After consultation with Reid, Hogg reported the incident to his inspector. Hogg then agreed to go along with Jones's proposal and was introduced to a Paddington bookmaker, William O'Connor. O'Connor complained that four of his runners had been arrested in five days. He suggested that some arrangement could be negotiated whereby his runners might take bets on certain pitches while another individual could be established elsewhere specifically as a target for the police to apprehend. O'Connor concluded by giving Hogg £2 -10s. (£2.50) on account. The case was eventually heard at the Old Bailey in February 1932. O'Connor was found guilty of corruptly giving money to Hogg, and Jones was found guilty of aiding and abetting. O'Connor was sentenced to nine months imprisonment, and Jones to 18 months. What appears to have infuriated the Recorder, Sir Ernest Wild, K.C., was that the defence had sought to blacken Hogg's name in order to discredit his evidence. He was also disquieted by the evidence of bookies setting up 'dummies' for arrest so that their runners might proceed with their business unhindered.[55]

---

53 At the beginning of 1928 there was a court case in Liverpool that resulted in the conviction of a bookmaker for offering bribes, and of nine former members of the city's police for accepting them. *Prevention of Bribery*, No. 145, Feb. 1928, p. 11, No. 146, March 1928, pp. 18-19, No. 147, April 1928, p. 26 and No. 148, May 1928, p. 34.

54 *Times*, 23 Oct. 1931, p. 9; *Police Review*, 30 Oct. 1931, p. 889.

55 *Times*, 4 Feb. 1932, p. 7; see also, 5 Nov. 1931, p. 9, 12 Nov. p. 4, 26 Nov. p. 4, and 3 Dec. p. 4. The use of 'dummies' shocked the judge trying the case in Liverpool. 'Police-constable Harris, giving evidence, said four constables all made up their note books for the purpose of giving evidence in the same way. That was a matter of form. He wrote in his notebook, copying another officer's, that he had seen one of the dummies taking bets, but he had not seen him doing so.

Mr. Justice Swift: I have often heard it suggested that policemen do these things, but I have never heard a policeman on oath say that he did them.

[Ex-P.C.] Harold [one of the accused]: Well, they do. That is the system,' *Prevention of Bribery*, No. 146, March 1928, p.18.

III

As the scandal of 'C' Division unfolded in July 1931 the *Morning Post* published a leading article, 'Pointing the Moral.'

> No police force in the world has a higher reputation for probity and chivalrous devotion to duty than has ours. One can hardly expect every man in so large a force to be a paragon of virtue. In every public service there are backsliders who bring discredit on their comrades. Human nature is sometimes weak even in a uniform, yielding to temptation rather through thoughtlessness than with any intent to act disloyally. If the present inquiry focuses attention on the weaknesses it also throws up in high relief the essential strength and soundness of our police personnel and organisation. So long as we have men like Lord BYNG in control, we need have no fear of the fate which has overtaken some Transatlantic cities overtaking us.[56]

The traditional histories of the Metropolitan Police describe Byng, and his successor as Commissioner, Lord Trenchard, as men brought in to sort out disciplinary problems that the press had played upon. The unfortunate Horwood was not up to the task; his successors were. The Goddard affair and the 'ordinary disciplinary cases' of which the press had made so much were minor blemishes, soon removed by a firm hand, on the reputation of 'the best police in the world.' The image of the incorruptible, non-political, even avuncular British bobby remains a powerful and a potent one within the police itself and also among the general public. But there is also an alternative image which, except for occasional instances like the Goddard affair, was rarely much publicized in Britain before the Second World War. A succession of scandals beginning in the 1950s, running through the corruption revelations of the 1970s and beyond, together with a critical sociological approach building on research into police forces in the United States, all contributed to the new approach. The Goddard affair highlights two important issues for the police that are not easily solved. It reveals also that these are not as new as some of the recent research might imply, but rather that they have been permanent elements of English policing and have, in spite of the traditional historians' claims to the contrary, survived the strong disciplinary hand of men like Byng and Trenchard.

First, there is the very real problem of temptation. Police officers in Goddard and Josling's day may have received better pay than schoolteachers, but they were not well paid, and in an area like Soho particularly, they were surrounded by considerable wealth, much of which was linked with illegal activities. Once a few individuals had opted to compromise with those involved in such activities, the second problem arose. As Josling himself put it:

> To be seen speaking to me was a fearsome thing. Comrades' wives who had hitherto been more than on the visiting list, shunned the company of my wife – not because they had less regard for her, but because they had been in the Service atmosphere sufficiently long to know that the unpopularity of such friends was not calculated to enhance their husbands' Service interests.[57]

---

[56] *Morning Post*, 10 July 1931.
[57] *Police Review*, 15 Mar. 1929, p. 191.

Esprit de corps can be an essential quality for any institution, but it can also prompt a closing of ranks and a refusal to acknowledge institutional problems as anything other than, at worst, minor peccadilloes. In such instances the informant, however noted for honesty and integrity – and few can have appeared more honest and upright than Josling – can become the outsider. The way in which Josling has been written out of most of the traditional histories of the police can be seen as a further reflection of this trend.[58]

There is a final problem that the historiography of the Goddard affair poses. For the traditional police historians, with the possible exception of Ascoli's account of the corruption scandals of the 1970s, police history is about individuals – commissioners and chief constables at the top, constables at the bottom. Focusing more on the institution, and looking beyond individuals who seize the attention with a colorful narrative, can present a much drier story. But it can also present one that challenges some of the complacent assertions about the British Bobby. Goddard the individual was not an isolated offender. His whole division appears to have been infected; old sweats had the infection, and new men caught it. And the symptoms can be found beyond Goddard's division. This is not to suggest that, at the close of the 1920s and in the early 1930s the entire Metropolitan Police was corrupt, but rather the problems were more significant and more deep-rooted than has been allowed. Given the problems that arose after the Second World War and which led to another Royal Commission, questions might be posed about the extent to which Byng and Trenchard did succeed in sorting out certain problems and the extent to which such problems might be systemic.

---

[58] The exception here is Martin Fido and Keith Skinner, (eds.), *The Official Encyclopedia of Scotland Yard*, London, 1999, which contains articles on both Goddard and Josling.

Chapter 7

Competing Memories:
Resistance, Collaboration
and the Purge of the French Police
after World War II[1]

Jean-Marc Berlière

Of all the countries conquered by Hitler, France alone signed an armistice with Germany and kept a government of its own. The provisions of the armistice,[2] the existence of a legal government and the policy of 'collaboration' set in place by the 'French State' – as much to curry favor with the victor and to gain a place in a German-dominated Europe as to implement its own ideological program – account for the uncomfortable and ambiguous situation of the French police, which was at once a symbol of the legitimacy and prerogatives of a would-be state and at the same time the instrument of an anti-democratic policy rooted in repression. Trapped by the legitimacy of the Vichy government, but also by its own corporate interests and a professional culture that shared some of the aversions of the new masters, the police came to play a role that explains the profound discredit attached to it at the time of the Liberation.

As with all of the issues connected with the reconstruction of the State and the construction of post-war France, the problem of the police preoccupied General De Gaulle in 1944. Faced with two contradictory imperatives – the need to preserve a strong, effective police to restore State authority and keep order in the face of possible revolutionary uprisings, while at the same time accommodating public opinion and a desire for revenge rampant in freshly liberated France – the head of the provisional government needed to actively encourage an unflinching purge.[3] However this had to be done without dismantling an essential instrument of power.

The purge was no less delicate a task for being indispensable and inevitable: *who* was to be purged and on *what grounds*?[4] In spite of threats proffered by the Resistance,

---

1 Translated by Nora Scott.
2 Among which article 3 obliged the French adminisrations to enforce the German *ordonnances* (orders with legal status, issued by the MBF = *Militär Befehlshaber in Frankreich*.)
3 'To pass over so many crimes and excesses would be to allow a monstrous abscess forever to infect the country. Justice had to prevail.'
4 Not only was it necessary to punish the police responsible for arrests that had often led to the death or deportation of French citizens, but it seemed difficult to entrust civil servants compromised by their espousal of Vichy ideals with the tasks of hunting down those guilty

it was not the intent of General De Gaulle to 'raze to the ground the great majority of functionaries, most of whom, during the terrible years of the Occupation and usurpation, had sought primarily to serve the public interest to the best of their ability';[5] and above all, not the police, whose only sin had been to serve the de facto State as they had been led to do by a culture of obedience. This obedience was their essential quality and the very essence of their function.

The provisional government was well aware that discipline, following orders and obeying the law, were fundamental principles of the civil service and must not be shaken;[6] it needed to define what constituted 'collaboration' for functionaries placed in the position of enforcing the occupier's *ordonnances* and obeying the orders of a government whose legality was not questioned at the time. Their very mandate - keep order, fight crime and those offenses defined by laws it was not their job to question - involved the police directly in putting down a Resistance whose actions necessarily took the form of illegal acts, and in the enforcement of laws that, by incriminating the membership of political, religious or philosophical movements – trampled the 'basic freedoms of the Republic.' But these police – closely watched by the occupier, denounced by the collaborating 'ultras' or proponents of the new order, under constant threat of reprisals or sanctions - were simply obeying the Law and following the orders of government officials and magistrates who were often the same people who were in those positions before the war.

Obedience alone could not be regarded as a crime. That is why the post-Liberation power recognized – in article 3 of the *ordonnance* of 28 November 1944 – an 'absolving excuse' (*excuse absolutoire*) for functionaries who *acted exclusively on orders*: 'neither crime nor misdemeanor can be charged to the authors and accomplices when the deeds entailed no more than the strict execution (...) of orders or instructions received, without exceeding these in any way, or the simple fulfillment of professional obligations, with no voluntary participation in an act of anti-national nature. However, the text goes on, 'the laws, decrees, regulations or authorizations of the de facto authority in no way justify acts of collaboration when the accused had the option (*faculté*) to avoid their execution through personal initiative and when his responsibility or moral authority were such that his refusal would have served the Nation.' The difficulty, of course, lay in assessing the extent of this 'option to avoid' execution of an order when it involved a simple policeman on the beat or an inspector.[7]

---

of collaboration: 'The police must be strong and respected, its authority must come from public trust' (typed note from the services of the Interior Ministry, AN 72, AJ/4).

5   Charles De Gaulle, '25 July 1944,' *Discours et messages*, Paris, 1970, 1, p. 458.

6   These principles were swept away – with grave consequences for the Fourth Republic – by those carrying out the purges, for whom a 'disciplined' agent was a 'servile' agent, good evaluations, rewards, initiative, a bonus, an 'act of courage,' were grounds for punishment; whereas, punishments, mediocre evaluations, a wait-and-see attitude, passivity, refusal to obey orders and instructions, lack of discipline, were proof of 'resistance' and grounds for promotion.

7   In order to facilitate the task of those carrying out the purge, who were often hampered by the difficulty of interpreting this text, the Interior Ministry took care to define seven grounds that would provide more specific reasons for purging and make it possible to suit the punishment to the gravity of the acts: 'Having openly manifested collaborationist sentiments; having actively propagated the ideas and doctrines of the countries under

And, too, how and on the basis of what sources can the attitudes of the police be assessed? Those carrying out the purge received and sought denunciations from colleagues and testimonies and complaints from victims or their families; they collated the police lists of accused or suspected of anti-national acts or attitudes drawn up by the 'committees of Resistance' that had, often spontaneously, sprung up in the different departments. To find the names of those who had arrested 'patriots,' Jews, and young men who refused forced labor in Germany, they combed the arresting officers' reports, and the archives and files of cases handled by the anti-terrorist services. They pursued every sign of overly zealous compliance, scrutinizing the departmental evaluations, the applications for bonuses the rewards and promotions handed out during the occupation. All of this material needs to be used with infinite caution.

The very nature of the purge archives, the context and climate in which they were produced, the testimonies sought and 'arranged,' even when not actually dictated, and above all, the stakes involved, are enough to explain why everything can be found in these archives, but rarely the direct truth. Many of these documents, reports, investigations, accusations, defense statements, testimonies (usually for the prosecution, less often for the defense), as well as interviews of witnesses, statements of the accused, obviously, and of necessity, fall short of the truth! But whether they serve the interests of the defense or the prosecution, witnesses 'reconstruct,' they adapt the facts, lie, embroider, elude, forget, interpret, exaggerate, accuse, arrange or minimize. Taken one by one, most of the documents in the purge archives therefore express and contain no more than the accused's efforts to convince so as to avoid punishment or, on the contrary, the accuser's efforts to 'do down' a colleague or a policeman and obtain the harshest sentence possible.

Just as the historian must handle these archives with the utmost care,[8] so too the same care should have been exercised with the police archives used by those in charge of the purge, men who cannot have been unaware of their very particular nature. Individual records, applications for rewards, bonuses, decorations and promotions, recommendations, arrest reports, records of incarceration, searches, archives and case files all obey certain laws and belong to categories which the historian must be familiar with and which he must understand in order to avoid serious blunders of interpretation.

---

totalitarian government; having adopted an unmistakably anti-national attitude; having served with zeal and admiration the de facto government; having been a member of any anti-national group disbanded by the *ordonnance* of 9 August 1944; having, without holding membership, been active in or sympathetic to one of these anti-national groups; having shown marked hostility to the Resistance; having knowingly derived direct material advantages from the enforcement of the regulations of the de facto authority in contradiction with the laws in force on 16 June 1940.'

8   Not only are the testimonies and files bent on vengeance and accusation, but also those meant to lend a helping hand, are full of inaccuracies, errors and mix-ups owing to the material conditions in which the purge was carried out, to the frequent absence of the victims or witnesses, whose viewpoint is sadly lacking, to the difficulties of the investigation, and finally, to the partisan nature of those in charge of the purge. For further information, see Jean-Marc Berlière, *Les policiers français sous l'Occupation à partir des archives inédites de l'épuration*, Paris, 2001.

Frequently, for instance, the signature on an arrest record is not the same as that of the arresting officer: a policeman brought in his 'catch' and another colleague wrote and signed the report. This is even more apparent in the cases of the Jewish inhabitants arrested in the street by the henchmen of the *Police aux questions juives* or the *Section d'enquête et de contrôle*, both para-police departments of the *Commissariat général à la question juive*, staffed by anti-Semitic fanatics who, without being members of the police force and having no official right to make arrests, turned in Jews for 'violation of the German *ordonnances*' (not wearing the yellow star, being in places where they were not allowed, etc.), thereby leaving it to the police at the station, who were powerless to do otherwise, to transfer them to the detention camp at Drancy.[9] Likewise, the presence of the names of police officers on a report tracing the history of a case and the resulting arrests is not proof that these men actually played a role in the case. In the department of the *Renseignements Généraux*, it was a widespread practice – in order to inflate expense accounts – to put the maximum number of officers' names on the case. An application for a reward of any kind, therefore, is always hyperbolic, extolling the qualities and role of each participant in order to justify the request.

But the details – which in 1942 were meant solely to underscore a sometimes imaginary zeal, and wholly invented initiatives – appear in an altogether different light when understood in the climate of the purge. The following three examples show the problems raised by the interpretation of these sources in a different context and chronology.

The Investigation of the Brigade Spéciale Criminelle of the Police Judiciaire into the Nantes Case

On 20 October 1941, a three-man commando sent to Nantes by the *Comité Militaire National* of the clandestine Communist party gunned down *Feldkommandant* Holtz. This was the first time such a high-ranking German officer had been assassinated. While the occupation authorities carried out their threat of reprisals by shooting dozens of hostages in Nantes, Paris and Châteaubriant, the French police feverishly looked for the culprits, for whom the Germans had announced a considerable reward as well as a suspension of the executions. While the investigation marked time in Nantes, a brigade from the *Police Judiciaire* in Paris identified the shooter and, in late October, arrested his 'gang': young members of the 'youth battalion,' the fighting arm of the *Jeunesses Communistes*.[10] In early November, as usual after a successful 'wrap,'

---

[9] These arrest records must be signed by a policeman. Every evening the (anti-Semetic) 'IV J' department of the SIPO-SD would check the list of new detainees against the lists provided by the SEC, which severely reduced any initiative the police captains might have. But since theirs was the only signature on the transfer orders, it was they who were pursued by the victims or their families after the war; Alternatively, most of the 'amateur policemen' in the SEC – using pseudonyms or numbers – escaped prosecution.

[10] See Jean-Marc Berlière and Franck Liaigre, *Le sang des communistes. Les bataillons de la jeunesse et les débuts de la lutte armée (automne 1941)*, Paris, 2004.

Captain (*Commissaire*) Veber wrote up a report designed to display his department's excellent work and the zeal, merit, and professional qualities of his men.

An apparently useless piece of information rapidly exploited and a keen professional sense enabled these investigators, on 30 October last, to arrest:

Hanlet Robert, born 4 December 1922, bicycle deliveryman, living at 4 rue Henri Ranvier

Milan Pierre, born 29 August 1924, postman, living at 3 rue Henri Ranvier

A search of whose residence led to the discovery of numerous weapons and Communist propaganda material.

Subjected to thorough questioning, they said they were part of a group of three militants whose activity entailed acts of sabotage. Their revelations permitted the rapid identification of their leader, Zalkinov Fernand, a Jew of Russian origin...

It was quickly established that he lived at 126 avenue Philippe Auguste and he was arrested there that very evening after having injured Inspector Debernardi, who overpowered him before he could use his weapon.

Subjected to hard and close questioning under my direction by Messieurs Loupias and Badin, assisted by Inspector Henon, which lasted that night and the following days, Hanlet, Milan and Zalkinov admitted their participation in, among others:

1. an attempt to destroy a German post at Goussainville
2. sabotage of the railroad by explosives at Lagny
3. the burning of trucks at the SOGA garage, boulevard Pershing
4. a similar operation at the TODT garage, rue de Lagny in Montreuil
5. the burning of a German truck at the Cours de Vincennes
6. the burning of silage barns at Jouy-le-Châtel
7. theft of large socket wrenches [for unscrewing rail bolts] at Orry-la-Ville
8. a similar theft at the Cambronne métro station.

Examination and comparison of their statements further permitted the identification and arrest of their accomplice, Peltier Robert, born 9 October 1921, living at 3 rue Danton, in Goussainville, and the identification of their leader Brustlein Gilbert, born 20 March 1919, an upholsterer living at 1 rue de Montreuil in Paris. Independently of the acts of sabotage carried out under his direction, which I have just enumerated, he is believed to be the author of the assassinations of officer cadet Alfons Moser, killed at the Barbès metro station, and of Lieutenant-Colonel Hotz, Feldkommandant of Nantes. He is also believed to have destroyed military trucks with the help of dynamite sticks.

In addition, during the search, examination of the walls of the top-story room occupied by Brustlein and Zalkinov at 126 avenue Philippe Auguste led to discovery of the group's arsenal, namely: five pistols or revolvers, numerous rounds of ammunition, charges of dynamite and tolamite equipped with detonators, three socket wrenches, shears, bottles containing incendiary liquids, ordnance survey maps, floor plans and travel routes, compasses, a supply of stencils, plans concerning acts of sabotage with detailed instructions, a large quantity of military and Communist documents, etc.

It is owing to the brilliant professional qualities and to the sustained zeal of the inspectors whom it is my honor to call to your attention and who labored unstintingly day and night, that it was possible, in such a short time, to put an end to the nefarious activities of this terrorist organization that represents a constant danger to the French community.

I would also like to mention Inspectors Batut, Nicolas, Prince, Henry and Bouygues, who performed a particularly thankless task, that of keeping 24-hour surveillance in all weather, thus playing a role in the successful completion of this case.

A bonus would be a fitting reward for their efforts.

Following this report, on 13 November, the director of the *Police Judiciaire*, after consulting the Prefect, announced the following bonuses: 1000 f for the captain of the brigade, 500 f for his secretary, 300 f for the principal inspectors, between 200 and 100 f for the others.[11] Far from the amounts they had dreamed about, given the rewards promised by the Germans, but bonuses and praise that would ultimately compromise them three years later and justify their appearance before the purge courts to explain this zeal extolled with such lyricism and emphasis in Captain Veber's report.

While these policemen did indeed arrest a group of young Communist resisters, all of whom were shot, it would be naive to attribute more 'objective' value to this text than it actually has.

A preliminary remark for those new to this kind of literature. This report belongs to a special genre, one which has its own rules: 'The recommendation for an award is always written in elegiac terms, to the detriment of the pure truth, the terms increasing in extravagance with the importance of the role of the candidate for the award, or when a large amount of work is to be recompensed. A visit to the administration offices of the *Police Judiciaire* in order to consult the recommendations for awards on the occasion of any case will rapidly establish the truth of what I have said, in particular about stretching the truth...'[12] And indeed, the 'sustained zeal of the inspectors (...) who labored unstintingly day and night,' the 'keen professional sense,' the 'brilliant professional qualities' are all conventional formulas, that are emptied of their meaning by their systematic and mandatory use in all similar reports. A few details give an idea of the hyperbole and systematic exaggeration. Inspector Debernardi's injury, for instance, had no clinical reality – no medical report was filed, no sick leave prescribed – it was meant solely to show the risks and dangers incurred by those policemen when tracking down 'dangerous terrorists.' The examination of the room on the Avenue Philippe Auguste in search of the weapons cache was pure fiction, since the panel hiding the 'cache' was lying on the floor, leaving the cache 'gaping,' as the original search report put it. The same was true of the 'hard and close questioning.' In reality, one of the young men arrested seems to have proven astonishingly talkative upon arrest. His comrades, on the other hand, despite a night of interrogation, did not talk.[13]

'As is the custom, hierarchical order was respected.'[14] In effect, the distribution of the awards strictly followed the hierarchy. It is clear, then, that style of these documents as well as their reading and interpretation must always be put into context.

---

[11] At the time, an inspector earned between 2,000 and 3,000 francs a month, and a captain in the Paris force between 5,000 and 8,000 francs.

[12] Report by Loupias on his summons before the purge court, to the *Département des Renseignements Généraux*, 4 May 1945.

[13] The transcript of Zalkinov's first interrogation, dated 30 October 1941, reports him saying: 'I don't want to give any information that might enable the arrest of those who directed me on this case' (APP, GB 49.) Captain Vilchien's report to Captain Delgay, of 11 November 1941, confirms: 'Questioning of Zalkinov adds first of all only a very few elements to the investigation underway, since he is most reluctant to furnish explanations about his activity and that of his accomplices (...) he has so far refused to divulge the identities of any possible accomplices [in the attack of 15 October 1941]' (AN.Z6 29), p. 3.

[14] Loupias, Report, 1945.

Variations on the Circumstances of the Arrest of a 'Terrorist' (1942-1949)

Tony Bloncourt, a young student with the group led by Brustlein – the Nantes shooter – escaped the police raid in late October 1941. With the help of a few friends, he held out all that fall and early winter with difficulty and without help or assistance from the Communist party, which, at the same time as its leaders-in-hiding were smugly recounting their exploits in their telegrams to Moscow,[15] laid no claim to any of their actions,[16] which were presented in the clandestine press as German 'provocations.'[17] These actions were condemned by Marcel Cachin, a historic figure of the Communist party and editor of the Communist daily *Humanité*, in a document written in October in exchange for his release.[18]

But the net was drawing in day by day. At the beginning of November 1941, a wanted poster distributed by the *'Direction de la Police Judiciaire de la Préfecture de Police, Brigade Spéciale Criminelle, 36 Quai des Orfèvres,'* alerted the Paris police: 'Wanted, Bloncourt, Tony Louis, born 25/02/1921, chemistry student, living at the home of his aunt, 4 Rue Félix Voisin, fugitive, photograph attached. Bloncourt is wanted for participation in numerous armed attacks on businesses, factories, garages, etc., working for or occupied by the German Army, as well as on members of the occupation army. Description: looks about 20 years of age, 1m76… usually carries a leather briefcase. If found, he is to be arrested together with anyone in his company or with whom he may be staying and immediately inform the *Direction de la Police Judiciaire*, Turbigo 92-00.'[19]

---

[15] 3 October, from Jacques Duclos (head of the clandestine French Communist party) to Dimitrov (general secretary of the Komintern): 'Steps taken by Germans attest to their fury as the attacks on their men begin to look like a mass movement. Every day numerous victims, and that is the result of many individual initiatives. Attacked by enemy, Party holding up well and proves worthy of Stalin's great cause.' 13 October, Duclos to Dimitrov: 'Sabotage become so widespread that Germans giving secret instructions.' 2 December (Duclos to Dimitrov): 'German bookshop Paris blown up by 2 bombs. Garage in Paris with trucks burned. 20 truck tires slashed in Paris. German's telephone wires cut at Courneuve, Le Bourget, Passy.' Quoted in Bernhard Bayerlein, Brigitte Studer, Mikhaïl Narinski and Serge Wolikow, (eds.), *Moscou-Paris-Berlin, Télégrammes chiffrés du Komintern 1939-1941*, Paris, 2003, pp. 501, 505 and 519.

[16] Whereas the September (n° 127) issue of *Humanité* saluted the assassination attempt by Paul Collette – a young Gaullist patriot – on Déat and Laval, it was not until February or March 1942 that the use of force and guerilla warfare was admitted.

[17] *Humanité* (n° 140), 5 December 1941.

[18] Arrested on 5 September 1941 by the SIPO-SD and incarcerated in the Santé prison, Marcel Cachin wrote a document – of 21 handwritten pages – on 17 October, of which the passages condemning terrorism were reproduced on placards in the spring of 1942: 'They asked me if I approved of the individual assassination attempts on German soldiers. I replied that individual attacks worked against the goal their authors claim to be aiming at. I have never recommended nor encouraged them. I have always discouraged my comrades from taking such action' (see Denis Peschanski, 'Marcel Cachin face à la Gestapo,' *Communisme*, 1983, 3, pp. 85-102).

[19] Box 7 of BS2, folder 'Bloncourt, Weis, Frémont, Daix, Lédé.'

Everything about this manhunt, with its constant anxiety, in this month of December in a cold, hostile Paris that was profoundly affected by the series of hostage shootings at Mont-Valérien, was difficult: the lack of money, means, ration cards and experience. 'Tony broke down on 6 January. While changing his hiding place from Giuzsi's [Weisberger] apartment, Rue Saint-Jacques, to George Frémont's, Rue Monge, he ran into a police barricade and, instead of showing his ID, he ran. This is how he was caught.'[20]

5 January 1941
Special report
Arrest of terrorist
Police Municipale, Traffic Department
Police officers Guillaume Raymond and Grapin Gilbert of the Special Plainclothes Brigade to Monsieur le Commissaire Principal des Renseignements Généraux, M. Hénocque [*sic*].
We report that at 8 o'clock, at the corner of the rue de l'Épée and the rue Saint-Jacques, we stopped two individuals who were walking along the rue Saint-Jacques towards n° 225 of the aforementioned street. As we approached, one ran up the rue Abbé de l'Épée towards Luxembourg gardens, the other continued down rue St Jacques as fast as his legs would take him, we caught him at the corner of rue Gay-Lussac and rue Saint-Jacques with the help of our colleagues Capra and Cavalier alerted by the repeated blowing of our whistles.
Taken to the central station of the 5th [*arrondissement*], this individual was found to be carrying;
1/ an ID card in the name of Marchand, Georges, Louis, French nationality, accountant, born 7/9/1920 at St Flour, living at 6 rue Denis Roy, which he himself admitted to be false;
2/ a J3 ration card in the name of Blancourtin Antoinette, student, age 28 [*sic*], born 25/02/1921 in Port-au-Prince, also admitted to be false by this individual who also admitted being a certain Bloncourt Tony, Louis, Marie, born 25/02/1920 in Port au Prince (Haiti) of parents Yves and Noémie Collerie, chemistry student, living at the home of his aunt, Melle Bloncourt Yoland, 4, rue Félix Voisin in Paris, 11e, wanted for armed attacks on members of the occupation army;
3/ a J3 bread coupon, n° 5640, a coupon for various items, same number, a d° meat coupon, one for soap products, a semester sheet of d° coupons, a new J3 food card without number or other writing;
4/ all of these coupons and sheets are enclosed in an envelop with a heading of the Prefecture of the Department Seine with a note in ink containing these few words: '4, avenue Corbera, 3e section n° for the sheets? valid until'…;
5/ a white-metal wristwatch,
6/ a billfold containing the sum of 438.40 francs;
7/ a hat, a muffler, a comb, a handkerchief.
This individual was turned over to 2 inspectors from the *Renseignements Généraux* of the Special Brigade headed by M. Hénocque notified by M. Gros, Police captain'
Signed Guillaume, Grapin, Cavalier, Capra.[21]

In the margin, Guillaume, who wrote the report, adds: 'As for the 2nd individual who fled up the rue de l'Épée [*sic*] towards Luxembourg [gardens], [he] seems to have been the same height rather shorter [*sic*], wearing a dark raincoat, bare-headed and appearing to be around 20 years of age.'

---

20   Pierre Daix, *J'ai cru au matin*, Paris, 1976, p. 64.
21   APP, GB 99 bis.

The purge obviously took an interest in this arrest and their records reveal some interesting details about the circumstances of this case, but especially they show not only the divergences between the accounts of the policemen who signed the report, but also the real difficulty of establishing the reality of the facts and of attributing the responsibilities of each of the protagonists. Blamed by the Germans for their inability to ensure their safety and prevent the aggressions and attacks of which they were the target, the Paris 'municipal police' – the police on the beat, in uniform – created, in December 1941, a new special brigade within the companies assigned to (…) traffic control! Entrusted to Captain Gros, the '*Brigade d'Intervention Antiterroriste*,' as it was called, was given the task of ensuring the protection of the hotels requisitioned by the German Army, which had in the past few months become a favorite 'terrorist' target. The policemen in this brigade, in plainclothes so as to be more discrete, were supposed to stop and question pedestrians and cyclists circulating in the vicinity of the hotels. Bonuses and promotions were promised to those who discovered anyone carrying weapons or tracts. On the morning of 5 January, surrounding the Hotel Dagmar, situated on the corner of the rue Saint-Jacques and the rue Abbé de l'Épée, across from the church of Saint-Jacques-du-Haut-le-Pas, was a whole contingent of police from the 5th *arrondissement* and the *Brigade d'Interpellation*. While a policeman and a 'passive defense' agent ostensibly guarded the dimly lit door to the hotel, some twenty meters away, in the shadows, plainclothesmen Grapin and Guillaume were assigned to stop and question the passersby. And so it was that, shortly before eight o'clock, Bloncourt and Weisberger, who were walking down the rue Saint-Jacques towards the rue Gay-Lussac on that dark and rainy January morning, fell into the trap. Leaping out from the shadows, Guillaume shouted – 'Police!' – the two young men broke into a run and split up. Bloncourt, whose false papers were at risk in this sort of control, sped towards the intersection of the rue Saint-Jacques and the rue Gay-Lussac, pursued by Grapin and Guillaume. Unfortunately, Tony ran into two other policemen, Capra and Cavalier, from the team stationed at the intersection... It was Capra who collared the fugitive and handcuffed him.

The four policemen took Bloncourt to the station, and all four signed the report quoted above. After the Liberation, the policemen's testimonies differed on the precise circumstances of the arrest. Cavalier claimed to have heard Bloncourt, who took them for 'civilians,' blurt out that he was wanted by the 'German police.' Capra always denied this. He finally admitted – in 1949 – that Bloncourt said he was 'wanted by the police,' and that information convinced him that he was dealing with a criminal. Grapin and Guillaume, who joined them, affirmed they had attempted, together with Cavalier, to persuade Capra to let his prisoner go, something Capra obstinately refused to do. Both the outcome and certain details cast a reasonable doubt on this dialogue. In effect, the four men seemed at that moment to have been essentially concerned with the advantages – bonuses, promotion – they could derive from a case whose true nature clearly did not escape them. The only problem that occupied them on their way to the station was: who will 'take the responsibility' and write up the report? Because they could not come to an agreement on this thorny subject, the four policemen *together*, and contrary to custom, conducted Bloncourt to the 5th *arrondissement* police station on the corner of rue Soufflot and place du Panthéon. This was also the reason why *all four of them* signed the arrest report for Captain Hénoque.

At the station, while the head of the *Brigade d'Interpellation*, Captain Gros, questioned 'Marchand-Bloncourtin,' the latter, in spite of his beard, was identified by a bicycle patrolman from the same station, Lamartine: 'He looks like the one on the poster over there!' Unmasked, Bloncourt confessed – at once, it seems – that it was indeed him. Captain Gros called the RG, who sent two inspectors to collect him.

Who was responsible for the arrest of Tony Bloncourt, shot by the Germans on the following 9th of March?

'Not me!,' said Grapin, who claimed – in 1945 – to have waited before raising the alarm and not to have pursued the fugitive on the rue 'de l'Épée': something which his sergeant, (*brigadier*) Breulé (who waited in ambush on the boulevard Saint-Michel that morning and who had missed Weisberger), would always bitterly reproach him for.

'Not me!,' said Guillaume, who claimed to have dropped his revolver on purpose so as not to shoot, contrary to formal orders from his sergeant. Furthermore, Guillaume was a resistant, a real one, a member of the 'Front National-Police,' organized by the Communist branch of the Resistance. He produced certificates full of praise from Pierre, the head of FN-Police and... member of the purge commission. It was written, signed and stamped: he had handed out tracts, slashed tires, moved road signs, distributed clandestine newspapers, and even shot a German soldier on 21 August 1944, during the Paris uprising. So he was a hero. And a hero with a heart: his chief in the Front National would attest to the remorse Grapin allegedly expressed over this case.

'Not me!' said Cavalier, who explained that he had tried – in vain – to persuade Capra to let his prey get away that morning.

Capra was therefore the ugly duckling.

Everyone affirmed as much with admirable unanimity. First of all, his political opinions were well known: a member of the Parti Social Français[22] before he was engaged by the police prefecture in February 1937, he was 'a fascist.' 'Moreover, I don't know that he isn't of Italian descent,' Guillaume subtly pointed out. The colleague who arrested him on 19 August 1944, in the midst of the insurrection – some priorities can't wait! – rewarded him with an unequivocal report, the very one found in the purge files concerning about one thousand police from the prefecture, those who were to come 'before a special court with the maximum sentence': 'Fervent admirer of totalitarian regimes (...) servile executor of Vichy's orders (...) thus served the cause of the occupier.' With these kind of accusations, Capra – who seemed above all 'a bit unbalanced' and 'not very bright' – could not escape the firing squad. But with order gradually being reestablished, the Republic had principles. To condemn someone to death, proof was needed, facts, in particular those with evidence of 'intelligence with the enemy.' However Capra's file was a bit 'thin' in this area, and his colleagues were not very clear. Kept in administrative detention [thus without due process] from 19 August 1944, Capra, who had been removed from his job by the purge commission, was therefore set free on 15 February 1946.[23]

---

22   The PSF was a right-wing, and even extreme right-wing, party that replaced the Croix de Feu after the leagues were disbanded by the Popular Front government. Led by Reserve Lieutenant-Colonel La Roque, it was – wrongly – regarded by the Left as a fascist organization.

23   He was released without charge on 6 March 1946.

Lamartine, the cyclist from the 5th *arrondissement*, would have made a presentable enough culprit. It was he – everyone stressed this point – who had identified Bloncourt from the wanted poster on the station wall. Captain Gros – who claimed credit for this identification in his January 1942 report – was just about to free Bloncourt – at least that is what he maintained in 1945! – when that idiot Lamartine recognized him! Unfortunately, Lamartine died shortly after the Liberation: he could not therefore don the suit so carefully cut to fit him, nor give his version of the incident, which did not stop his colleagues from putting most of the blame on him, and having him testify posthumously.

Finally there is Captain Gros. He was in for it: he had commanded an 'anti-national and anti-terrorist brigade' in the Traffic Department! How could he have accepted this disgraceful and compromising post! Because in December 1941, when this political-cyclist brigade was created, he was the last to be appointed and, he claimed in 1945, he had no choice. Nonsense! Those carrying out the purge did not believe a word of it. Furthermore he was regarded with suspicion at the national level. Had he not replied to a policeman who said of the events of August 44: 'It's a revolution,' that 'it wouldn't last as long as taxes [*contributions*]!' As the secretary of the purge section noted with great psychological insight: 'This remark clearly shows the anti-republican mentality of Captain Gros,' who furthermore tried to dissuade his men from striking on 15 August 1944... the same Gros, whom the prefect of police Bussière came to implore – in pajamas on the morning of 17 August 1944 – to bring his men under control. Gros, who was wounded along with 28 policemen on the Champs-Élysées in 1943 during the Doriotiste demonstration[24] – 'in 1943 you had to have guts to resist the Doriotistes!' – would therefore be forced into early retirement.

Everything is clear and reassuring in an episode that features staunch patriots, a certified resistant, a fascist, an anti-republican and a conveniently deceased informer. Only the petty-minded might point out:

– that Guillaume, the FN-police resistant, at the time of the events, reported this arrest to obtain his promotion to the rank of sergeant;

– that the four men – the 'resistant,' the 'patriots' and the 'fascist' – each received a bonus of 100 francs: not only was this not a lot for the arrest of a dangerous terrorist on the run for two months and soon shot, but they were also made to wait for this measly handout. Hennequin, head of the *Police Municipale* was not pleased, he was even furious that his men had reported their deed not to the head of the municipal police but to the captain of *Brigade Spéciale 2*. The result was that Rottée, head of the *Renseignements Généraux* and his arch-rival, had been able to announce the news of the arrest to the prefect before him. 'Since that's the way it is, they won't get a bonus!' Hennequin had said, and he had nearly kept his word.

---

[24] Followers of Jacques Doriot, former Communist leader, founder of the *Parti Populaire Français*, one of the fascist-leaning political organizations that would enthusiastically collaborate with the Germans.

What's that Decoration You're Wearing on Your Lapel?

At 8:15, in rue des Trois Bornes, at the corner of rue Saint-Maur, having heard shots coming from Rue Saint-Maur, I ran over. At that moment, I saw a man wearing a raincoat and carrying a revolver, when he saw me he introduced himself immediately. The man's name was M. Capron (…) who had been attacked by a group of terrorists. Seeing a cyclist armed with a revolver shooting in my direction, I ran after him, exchanging shots and blowing my whistle repeatedly. At that moment, a second cyclist who was stopped along the curb on the odd-numbered side shot at me as I came up to him. Finding myself caught in the crossfire and seeing that the first cyclist was going to get away, I ran after the second while a third on my right also opened fire on me. As the second cyclist was fleeing in the direction of rue Oberkampf, I ran after him, despite being out of bullets. I grabbed a bicycle that was lying in the street and had certainly been abandoned by one of the terrorists but, not having noticed that the chain was broken, I fell to the ground, scraping my right thumb and spraining my right wrist. Keeping my head, I borrowed the bicycle of a passing cyclist and again set off in pursuit of the individual.

The man entered the Passage de la Fonderie. At that moment, police officer Marzin Jean from the *école pratique* was on his way from his home in the passage de la Fonderie to the school, and since he was in civilian dress, and had heard my whistle, he blocked his path, threatening him with his revolver, and we arrested him.[25]

To sum up: that morning, in the 11th *arrondissement*, a four-man commando tried to assassinate the mayor of Alfortville, a former Communist deputy, member of the *Parti Ouvrier et Paysan Français* (POPF).[26] Capron and his bodyguard shot back in self-defense. With seven bullets in his body,[27] Inspector Rougeot, responsible since 6 September 1941 for the secretary general of the POPF, lay in the entrance to a building. He would die from his wounds. Marcel Martin, a policeman alerted by the gunshots, 'listening only to his duty' and blowing away on his whistle, ran after one of the aggressors. A few minutes away, leaving his home to go to work, trainee policeman Marzin, 25 years old, wholly unaware of the nature of the aggression, alerted by the sound of the whistle, blocked the fugitive's path and immobilized him. Believing he was dealing with a petty delinquent, he did not even search him.[28] As they were joined by Martin, the man broke away and tried to escape by firing on the policemen, who managed to immobilize him. It was then that they discovered he was carrying two revolvers, an appointment card and a list of names that would permit some twenty other arrests among the predominantly Communist *Francs-tireurs* and *partisans* in the Resistance. The man's name was Charles Rouxel. Handed over to the Germans, he was executed a few months later. Martin, promoted to the rank of sergeant for his 'zeal and his initiative in the pursuit and arrest of a terrorist,' received

---

[25] Report by police officers Martin and Marzin to the captain of the Folie-Méricourt *quartier*, 10 April 1943 (APP, GB 125.)

[26] Composed of Communists having rejected the Germano-Communist pact, this party would paradoxically collaborate and its leaders would become the privileged targets of the killers from the Communist party 'special squads.'

[27] Three in the back, two in one arm, one in the armpit, one in the chest. He died on 11 April 1943 at 4 am. The aggressors pursued him into a building entrance.

[28] Of course he did not threaten him with his revolver: this detail added by Martin is meant to increase his merit.

the silver medal for *belles actions* ['galant acts'], while young Marzin, officially engaged the day after Rouxel's arrest, received a bronze medal.

This action, the awards, the zeal and initiative expended to arrest a patriot who was subsequently shot, earned the two men an appearance before the police prefecture purge commission. Their attitudes at that time were quite different.

Marzin, the young trainee, who was unaware of what had happened in Rue des Trois Bornes, truly thought he was arresting a criminal, and had always, according to the testimony of his colleagues, expressed regret at having been party to this unfortunate affair and was ashamed of the medal that he had never worn. Sergeant Martin, on the other hand, never took it off. Furthermore, he displayed it with pride before the purge sub-commission[29] that questioned him on 15 February 1945.

Presenting himself as the 'champion' of the purge in Les Lilas,[30] secretary of the 'Front Uni de la Résistance Française aux Lilas' (United Front of the French Resistance in Les Lilas), boasting of the 465 [*sic*] arrests he had ordered of 'collaborators' or those accused of collaboration, Martin thoroughly sickened the members of the sub-committee, who were scandalized by his attitude and especially by the medal won 'with the blood of a patriot,' as one member of the sub-commission reminded him. The sub-commission therefore recommended his dismissal from the police and the transfer of his case to the justice system. The general inspectorate considered that the sub-commission did not have the competence to take such decisions, and so Martin was heard again, but this time by the purge commission. And this time he took the precaution of removing his silver medal for *belles actions*. The commission questioned him at length on his attitude the day of the arrest and on the report he had written.

The problem was simple.

If he really did not know what had happened, it is possible that Martin did not know Capron, as he now claimed. Professional logic and caution would have dictated that he subdue Capron, disarm him, and ask for his papers.[31] Instead, at the risk of his own life, Martin threw himself headlong and determinedly into the pursuit of those whom Capron had designated as his attackers and whom he claimed, in 1945, to have taken for common criminals.

The other possibility is that Capron, as Martin had written in his report, had told him who he was and what had happened. If this is the case, Martin was fully aware that he was no longer pursuing a 'common criminal,' but a 'terrorist' and now a 'patriot.' Moreover, it is doubtful that an experienced resistant, who claimed to have entered the Resistance as a postman in 1940, would not have understood that he was dealing with a political matter, especially after a shootout in the streets of Paris in February, 1943.

As the purge commission considered Martin responsible for the execution of several patriots, it revised the conclusions of the sub-commission and recommended his dismissal from the force and the transfer of his file to the public prosecutor's office.

---

[29] Buried under the number of cases to be examined, the purge commission set up at the police prefecture entrusted, for the space of a few weeks, with the examination of a certain number of cases concerning Municipal policemen on the beat to sub-commissions.

[30] Located in the outskirts of Paris.

[31] He could not have seen Inspector Rougeot, gravely wounded, as he lay in the building entrance.

Yet Martin would be released by the government *commissaire*,[32] who had a rather surprising interpretation of the events: Martin was a genuine patriot, a resistant; risking his life, he gave chase to someone he had taken for a criminal. If Martin, who was unaware of Capron's identity, wrote the contrary in his report, it was on the advice of his captain and his sergeant so as to obtain the promotion and award of which he was so proud!

The prefect, who was waiting for the final decision, disregarded the acquittal and pronounced Martin's dismissal from the police, since it seemed highly unlikely that a seasoned resistant had not understood he was intervening in a case of patriotism. The review commission dealing with promotions given out under the occupation shared this view and had annulled Martin's promotion, 'obtained for the arrest on *his own initiative* of a patriot executed by firing squad.'

Authorized to do so by his acquittal, Martin appealed these decisions. Numerous interventions and petitions from inhabitants, the mayor, and his colleagues at Les Lilas police station (whose Resistance unit Martin had commanded at the time of the street-fighting to liberate Paris and its surrounds), supported his appeal so effectively that the consultative commission that examined his case on 15 October 1948 recommended that his dismissal be annulled, but confirmed his downgrading to simple policeman on the beat [*gardien de la paix*]; the recommendation was approved by the prefect of police.

If everything turned out well for Martin, the post-war period was less kind to inspector Rougeot, the policeman responsible for protecting Capron. Killed in the attack, he was awarded the title 'victim of duty,' promoted, posthumously, to the rank of *brigadier chef*, and decorated with the gold medal for *belles actions*. His case, like that of all police officers having received the title of 'victim of duty' during the Occupation, was examined in the fall of 1945 by the purge commission. In the course of this inquiry, it was discovered that Rougeot had been decorated on the initiative of the prefect 'in view of the circumstances.' The prefect, who believed he should 'pin the gold medal for *belles actions* on the chest of this brave servant,' applied, on 14 April 1943, to the head of the then government to 'kindly regularize this attribution as quickly as possible.' As the morale and the zeal of the policemen of the police prefecture had a tendency to flag in the beginning of 1943, the decision was endorsed.

The problem came up again at the Liberation: 'death in commanded service' of a policeman responsible for the security of a 'collaborator' did not seem to come under the heading of *belles actions* deserving of a gold medal. In the report dated 8 October 1945 by an inspector from the 1st Group of the Purge Department, stating that the inquiry into Rougeot's morality had shown that he was known in his entourage as a 'died-in-the wool Gaullist [who] displayed no political opinions' [sic], the purge commission decided to annul the medal for *belles actions* but to leave Rougeot his title of 'victim of duty.'

In July 1951, in answer to a letter from the Minister for Veterans, who had been asked about the advisability of awarding Rougeot the mention 'died for his country,' the personnel director wrote back that the circumstances of the attack of which he

---

[32]   A judge sitting in the courts set up at the Liberation to judge cases of collaboration who acts as prosecuting attorney.

had been the victim did allow him to say that Inspector Rougeot[:] 'in the event, he was doing his normal duty as a police inspector.'

These examples shed some light on the difficulty of the task of the historian who must read and interpret these archives, and who is well aware that his conclusions never fully meet the expectations of a collective memory that is in constant evolution, undergoing incessant reconstruction, subject to repression and conflicted to boot. This is especially true for the history of the purges, which followed four years of occupation and near civil war, and which continues to be a subject fraught with fantasies and preconceived ideas. It is not easy to recount one's future in the past tense, to recall that vital period of history dubbed by the philosopher Paul Ricoeur 'the future past' *(futur du passé)*, to restore the *uncertainty of the future* to actors incapable of imagining what came next in a history that now seems frozen. Between the speeches for the defense and those for the prosecution, the present obsession with memory and all manner of 'commemorative liturgies,' history has become a mantra, it is even increasingly called to take the stand and tell the truth. But *which truth?* What really happened? What people thought, believed, experienced to be true at different moments? Confronted with such expectations, required to speak to social demand, the historian finds himself in an uncomfortable position, his necessarily shaded replies, his reservations, his desire to understand and explain, regularly lead him to be suspected or accused of indulgence or even negation.

But recounting the past in the present is more than a scientific requisite. The police of a democratic state, for instance, has everything to gain from a rational and objective knowledge of its past[33] for, as Paul Ricœur reminds us:[34] 'In a different telling of a story, the events are no longer the same (...) these narrative variations have a remarkable function when it comes to those forms most frozen by repetition, most ritualized by commemoration (...) to be told differently, to be told by the other side, is already the beginning of the path to reconciliation with the lost objects of love and hatred.'

---

[33] On this subject, see Jean-Marc Berlière, 'Entre pages blanches et légendes: un corps sans mémoire?,' *Pouvoirs*, Paris, 102, 2002, pp. 5-15.

[34] Paul Ricœur, *La mémoire, l'histoire, l'oubli*, Paris, 2000.

Chapter 8

Facts and Fiction in Police Illegalisms: The Case of Controlled Deliveries of Drugs in France in the Early 1990s[1]

René Lévy

On 6 June 1990, at dawn, customs officers on a routine patrol operation in Lyons ordered the driver of a camper to pull over to the side of the road. He tried to escape, collided with the customs vehicle, and came to a halt. The customs officers ran up, searched the car and discovered 1,058 kilos of hashish! They immediately proceeded to arrest five Britishers, described as well-known international traffickers.

On the 5 December of the same year, during another 'routine check' in Pouilly-en-Auxois, in the Burgundy region, customs officers from the same department intercepted two cars, seizing 540 kg of cannabis resin this time. Less than three weeks later, near Vienne, a city south of Lyons, another 519 kilos of cannabis were discovered under similar circumstances. All in all, over a period of one year, 'routine check' after 'routine check, ' the Lyons customs department seized close to three tons of cannabis.[2]

This, at any rate, is how the affair was officially presented. In fact, as subsequent investigations were to reveal, all of these cases and some other ones as well were the outcome of infiltration operations conducted by a group within the Lyons branch of the DNRED (*Direction nationale du renseignement et des enquêtes douanières*, or Intelligence and Investigations Department), an elite agency in charge of the most complex, delicate investigations within the customs administration.

In every instance, these customs officers had played an active role in actually organizing the trafficking, contacting Moroccan go-betweens under forged identities or infiltrating the group, recruiting people to bring the drugs in from Morocco, providing storage places in France, helping to package the substance and organizing

---

1   Translated by Helen Arnold.
2   These cases have been described in detail by Philippe Bordes, *Enquêtes aux frontières de la loi. Les douaniers et le trafic de la drogue*, Paris, 1992; see also the proceedings of the trial: Érich Inciyan, 'Les méthodes des douaniers dans la lutte contre les trafiquants de drogue sont mises en accusation,' *Le Monde*, 16 March 1991; Maurice Peyrot, 'Au tribunal de Dijon, la douane en correctionnelle,' *Le Monde*, 14 October 1994; Robert Belleret, 'Au tribunal correctionnel de Lyon, le dérapage douanier de l'Opération Gisèle', *Le Monde*, 7 October 1992; Robert Belleret, 'Au tribunal correctionnel de Lyon, le procès de cinq trafiquants britanniques relance le débat sur les méthodes des douaniers,' *Le Monde*, 30 January 1993.

122   *Crime and Culture: An Historical Perspective*

its delivery to purchasers – or even doing it themselves – and handling money from the traffic, all of which was theoretically illegal under French law.

In at least one instance, the Pouilly-en-Auxois case, they even agreed to give a go-between 60 kg of cannabis, the resale of which went to finance the transportation of the entire batch. Discovery of this latter maneuver led the examining judge in charge of the case to indict, and place in pretrial detention, not only the customs officer who had mounted the operation but also his immediate superior and the heads of the two customs districts involved, under the charge of drug trafficking. The same individuals were also indicted in five other cases of the same type between February and April 1991.[3]

The decisions of the examining judges touched off a crisis. What had started as a series of irregularities committed by a group of local government workers, an undercover operation that went wrong, suddenly became an affair of State, demanding interventions by the Prime Minister, causing a conflict between ministries, triggering a reform of the code of criminal proceedings and revealing both the national stakes involved in European unification and the latent conflicts between the various police forces and the judiciary institution. A bill was drafted authorizing police and customs officers alike to set up controlled deliveries under certain conditions and under supervision by the Public Prosecutor. The law, passed unanimously by both Chambers in December 1991, included an amnesty for the officers who had been prosecuted. Thus, it took less than a year to draft and pass this piece of legislation, plus an additional 6 months to work out detailed instructions for the security forces involved: about 18 months after the customs officers were jailed they had been cleared and were now allowed to do more or less what they had been prosecuted for. A remarkably fast instance of laundering of police illegalisms, indeed.

*

The present study is based primarily on the archives of the Direction of Criminal Affairs and Pardons (the DACG), which conserves all of the documents written by the Ministry of Justice or received by it during the preparatory phases: drafting of bills and of official instructions for enforcement, and groundwork for parliamentary debate. These include official correspondence between the different ministries involved, in-service notes, consecutive versions of texts, hand-written notes taken during in-house meetings or those involving several administrations, various annotations referring to the internal circulation of documents between the various hierarchical levels within the DACG, documents used by the drafters (case law, accounts of informational

---

[3]   In French criminal procedure, the more serious offenses or the most complicated cases are usually investigated (with assistance of the police) by a specialized magistrate called *juge d'instruction* (translated here as 'examining judge'). This magistrate has extended investigative powers and especially at that time had the right to remand suspects in custody for extended periods of time (see Jacqueline Hodgson, 'The police, the prosecutor and the juge d'instruction. Judicial supervision in France, theory and practice,' *British Journal of Criminology*, 2001, 41, 2, pp. 342-361 and René Lévy, 'Police and the judiciary in France since the XIXth century: the decline of the examining magistrate,' *British Journal of Criminology*, 1993, 33, 2, pp. 167-186.

missions abroad, correspondence with diplomats to obtain information on the legislation and methods employed elsewhere, and so on). It also contains evidence of exchanges between the ministry and the Council of State (which must examine the legality of bills before they are sent to Parliament) as well as the two parliamentary chambers (the National Assembly and the Senate). Given the wealth of documents we found here, plus the fact that this was the very department primarily involved in drafting the bill, we felt it unnecessary to consult the archives of other ministries. We did of course look at parliamentary documents (projects, reports, proceedings of debates, etc.), chronicles of the press and books on the issue.

After the bill had been passed, these documents were forwarded to the Direction's archivist who ordered them into files and subfiles. When one looks at the numerous scribbled – and sometimes almost illegible – notes found in those files, it appears clearly that the archivist did not sort them out, except to put them in some kind of chronological and logical order, without removing anything.

The analysis of these documents started with an inventory aimed at reconstructing the precise chronology of the successive phases of the drafting process . As the documents were not always dated, an internal critique was necessary to order them precisely. This was especially the case with the numerous successive versions of specific provisions, which circulated among various drafters several times a day. This called for a precise comparison of the documents and of the handwriting of the drafters. Once the phases of the process have been reconstructed, each set of documents has been analyzed in order to reconstruct the explicit or hidden agenda of the various individual or institutional actors and the dynamic of the negotiations which led to the final version. The present chapter attempts at giving a synthetic view of these events.

Explanations are required on two points, here – one terminological, and another legal – before we go on to a more detailed analysis of the events.

'Monitored Delivery' or 'Controlled Delivery'?

Whereas in English there are only 'controlled deliveries,' the French make a distinction between *livraison surveillée*, or monitored delivery, and *livraison contrôlée*, or controlled delivery, which correspond to two levels of involvement of the relevant law enforcement agencies. A controlled delivery is an undercover operation in which police or customs officers pose as drug traffickers and infiltrate or otherwise assist a drug trafficking network, in order, supposedly, to identify and arrest the people involved, their providers and customers. A monitored delivery is a less intensive undercover method entailing only more or less extended surveillance of traffickers.

Until 1991 and the reform to be discussed here, 'monitored deliveries' were viewed as legal in France, whereas 'controlled deliveries' were not.

Legality or Illegality of Undercover Practices

This distinction raises the question of whether undercover action is legal. At that time French law allowed undercover or entrapment techniques only insofar as they did not induce the offenses which they were supposed to uncover. In practice, this meant that when an accused person's counsel uses entrapment defense as an excuse, the judge must determine whether the offense would have been committed had the police not intervened. Such intervention is considered legal if it simply provided an opportunity to commit an offense for someone who, it may be reasonably assumed, would have perpetrated it anyway. At the time we are talking about, then, police officers were allowed, for instance, to monitor drug traffickers without interfering with their dealings or to pose as a drug customer, but not as a drug dealer. Conversely, it was illegal to take direct part in the accomplishment of offenses or to act as an accessory and specifically, at the time these events took place, to facilitate drug trafficking by providing money, cars, storage facilities etc. to a drug ring, or to help it in any other way, which is precisely what those customs' officers had done.[4] Consequently, they were indicted as drug traffickers and were liable to receive a stiff sentence.

The Legalization of Police Illegalisms

As Dominique Monjardet and I attempted to show several years ago,[5] undercover policing is a real laboratory for studying the legalization of policing methods. It is in practice that police forces develop methods, techniques or tricks, sometimes importing or adapting them, according to the needs of investigations and to the dynamic process of attack and defense, with the innovations of the hunters and the hunted mutually enriching each other. Consequently, law is constantly out of step with practice, and these innovations are often introduced on the fringes, and sometimes completely outside of the accepted rules. This situation may last, at least as long as no conflict arises, or as long as the competent authorities – including the judiciary authorities – look the other way, for efficiency's sake. As a rule it is a public scandal that prompts them to take action, and in this case, the usual reflex, in France and elsewhere, is to modify the legal status of the particular practices incriminated rather than to attempt to eliminate them.[6] In France, we have the additional peculiarity, most probably due to the combination of a solid administrative tradition and of a lasting, pervasive tendency to cloak action in the reason of State, of having the intermediate solution of administratively codified illegalism, located somewhere between patent illegality and legalization. As will be seen, the case we are examining here comes under that heading.

What interests us here is not so much the issue of monitored or controlled deliveries themselves, or even the expanding struggle to control drug trafficking – one episode of which is described herein – as the process by which a country came to legislate on a particular interventionist policing technique.[7] Consequently, the question

---

4   Patrick Maistre du Chambon, 'La régularité des 'provocations policières': l'évolution de la jurisprudence,' *Semaine Juridique*, 1989, 3422, pp. 51-52.
5   Dominique Monjardet and René Lévy, 'Undercover policing in France: elements for description and analysis,' in Cyrille Fijnaut and Gary T. Marx, (eds.), *Undercover. Police surveillance in comparative perspective*, The Hague, 1995, pp. 29-53.
6   This mechanism was described by Jean-Paul Brodeur, 'La police: mythes et réalités,' *Criminologie*, 1984, 17, 1, pp. 9-42.
7   The question of whether the use of such policing techniques is necessary, opportune or legitimate, from the viewpoint of criminal law, human rights or democracy is beyond our purview here, except when it is relevant for understanding the controversy around the

of whether, under what circumstances and in what way, monitored or controlled deliveries were practiced by the various agencies involved is marginal in regard to this central concern, or in any event, it only interests us inasmuch as it sheds light on the events that led the government, followed by Parliament, and lastly, the *Cour de Cassation*, to look into this issue.[8] There is no doubt, in this respect, that this particular policing technique was widely used for many years, even before any reference to it could be found in national or international juridical instruments. However, I think I can prove that the *decision to legislate* itself was the consequence of some peculiar events, that it was made in an improvised manner and that the resulting legislation is the outcome of a power struggle between the various administrations involved.

There are several ways to describe the context of these events, depending on how closely one looks at them: in the vocabulary of cinema, we may talk of a panoramic view, of a medium close shot or of a close-up. Of course, depending on which focus one uses, one will get different images, which must then be reconciled somehow.

A Panoramic View

If we take a wide-angle lens to look at the French events I have recalled, the whole matter seems rather unproblematic: the French legalization of controlled delivery is but another instance of the spreading of an American investigative technique promoted by the DEA through international agreements and police cooperation, as Ethan Nadelmann has shown in his book, 'Cops Across Borders.'[9]

In the course of the 'War on drugs' launched by President Nixon at the turn of the 70's, and the integration within a single specialized agency – the DEA – of various smaller ones, the American authorities persistently and successfully tried to promote undercover techniques against drug traffic, and this effort went on in the following decades, until today.

And indeed, the late 80s and early 90s – *i.e.* when controlled deliveries were finally allowed in France – were a period of intense international concern about organized crime, drugs and money-laundering. For instance, controlled delivery was promoted by the UN Vienna Convention of 1988, which as a matter of fact was put into effect in France a few months before the legalization. Then there was the Schengen Implementation Convention of 1990, which also mentions the necessity of controlled deliveries (but was not enforced until 1995). One could also mention the influence of the International Group for Financial Action (IGFA), emanating from the G7 summit of 1989, which resulted in the creation, within the French police and customs agencies, of specific branches dealing with money-laundering (as a matter of fact, this is another

---

legislation studied. For a methodical discussion of these issues, see Chantal Joubert and Hans Bevers, *Schengen Investigated. A Comparative Interpretation of the Schengen Provisions on International Police Cooperation in the Light of the European Convention on Human Rights*, The Hague, 1996, pp. 239-242. See also Steward Field, 'The legal framework of covert and proactive policing in France,' in Steward Field and Caroline Pelser, (eds.), *Invading the Private: State Accountability and New Investigative Methods in Europe*, Aldershot, 1998, pp. 67-81.

[8] The *Cour de Cassation* is the highest court in the French justice system; it only judges the legality of Appeals court decisions and not the facts themselves.

[9] Ethan A. Nadelmann, *Cops Across Borders*, University Park (Pa.), 1993.

instance of the rivalry between those agencies, which was also at work in the present case, as I will show).

Thus the French move may appear as a logical consequence of these international developments.

However, when one looks more closely at what happened in France in 1991, things appear to be more complex, or at least, the legalization of controlled deliveries seems not to have been a direct consequence of this international drive. This does not mean that there is no international dimension to these events, but to find it one must look elsewhere and narrow the focus to the consequences of European unification.

A Medium-Close View

The fact that the implicated officials were customs officers rather than police officers reflects a distinct change of policy of the customs department in the wake of the suppression of the European Union's 'internal borders' (*i.e.* borders between EU members) and the correlative emphasis placed on the surveillance of 'external borders' (*i.e.* between member and non-member states, including ports of entry from the latter).

To put it bluntly: this agency was at risk of losing its traditional battleground (the border area) and was forced to redefine its strategy to survive. It did so in two ways:

– by moving its forces from 'internal' towards 'external' European borders; as France is entirely surrounded by EU States, this meant focusing on airports and coastal areas, and

– by adopting much more proactive, mobile and selective tactics based on improved intelligence-gathering, which resulted in an intensification of stings, entrapments and controlled deliveries.

Part of this strategy was the attempt by the Ministry of the Budget, which is responsible for customs, to turn this agency into a third national police force and to have customs officers granted the same investigative and judicial powers as those of police and *gendarmerie* officers.[10] Until then, although the customs officers' powers were in some respects broader than those of the police, they did not have criminal investigation competences, thus being obliged to turn cases over to regular police officers once their customs inquiry was finished, if they intended the case to be prosecuted. Obtaining powers similar to those of police officers would have given them complete autonomy, a claim which was of course resented and fiercely resisted by the ministries of Interior and Defense as an infringement on their territory.

Such a change was also strongly resisted by the Ministry of Justice which was wary of what it considered an excessive independence of customs officers who, contrary to the police, were not subjected to judicial supervision (and still are not, for the most part).

---

10   In France, there are two national police agencies, the National Police, a civilian force operating in urban settings, and the National Gendarmerie, a military force operating mainly in rural and suburban settings (Christine Horton, *Policing Policy in France*, London, 1995; René Lévy, 'Neighbourhood versus Europe; The dilemmas of French policing,' in Roger Hood and Norbert E. Courakis, (eds.), *The Changing Face of Crime and Criminal Policy in Europe*, Oxford, 1999, pp. 67-87).

When the controlled delivery problem surfaced, the two ministries (Budget and Justice) had been discussing this issue for nearly one year without any progress: the Budget department wanted customs officers to be able to cumulate criminal investigation powers with their traditional ones, while the Justice Ministry refused this and would only accept that a limited number of officers be granted these if they relinquished their customs powers and submitted to judicial supervision, which in turn was refused by the Budget Ministry.

In this context, the case against the jailed customs officers, whom the Budget was eager to clear, was to give the Ministry of Justice an opportunity to turn the matter to its advantage.

A Close-Up View

A look at the course of events shows that the French government did not intend to legalize controlled deliveries but was forced to do so under the pressure of unexpected events and the scandal which ensued.

I cannot go into the details of the discussions between the different ministries involved, or of the parliamentary debates (extremely brief: three hours for the *Assemblée* and one hour for the Senate!). Suffice it to say that in the end, specialized judicial police and gendarmerie officers and selected customs officers were granted the right to set up controlled deliveries aimed at drug traffickers or their accomplices, under the authority of a public prosecutor or an examining judge.

In doing so, they were allowed to acquire, detain, transport and deliver illegal drugs or raw materials or equipment needed for producing drugs, or funds originating from these activities; they might also provide the traffickers with legal means, transport, storage or communications. Technically, these are all criminal offenses, but the officers were legally excusable and thus not prosecutable for these, as long as their dealings did not induce the suspects to commit their own offenses (the traditional French conception of legitimate entrapment was thus retained.)

The fact that these policing operations were to be supervised by a public prosecutor or an examining judge is quite in keeping with the French legal tradition. As Hodgson explains,[11] in France, as opposed to the Anglo-Saxon tradition, the judiciary plays a role in the investigative phase prior to the criminal trial. Although the police has some degree of autonomy and is allowed to undertake investigations on its own initiative,[12] it is legally subject to the authority of the public prosecutor, to whom it is accountable for its investigations and who then decides whether or not to prosecute. In the most serious or complex cases – and this is in fact compulsory for 'crimes'[13] – the public prosecutor may hand the affair over to an examining judge, who has extensive investigating powers. It is he, then, who directs the police officers in charge of the investigation.

---

[11] Hodgson, 'The police, the prosecutor and the *juge d'instruction...*'

[12] Its coercive power varies, however, depending on whether the offense may or may not be viewed as flagrant.

[13] French criminal law divides offenses into three categories, on the basis of increasing seriousness: *contraventions* (misdemeanors); *délits* and *crimes*, judged in different courts and entailing more or less harsh sentences.

These arrangements did not – and in fact still do not – apply to the customs department, which came under specific legislation giving it extended powers of investigation and constraint without subjecting it to judicial control. Conversely, however, when customs officers conduct investigations, leading them to seize illegal substances or mete out fines, this is not recognized by the criminal justice system. The outcome is that when customs feels it has turned up a criminal offence which should be prosecuted as such, and not simply a breach of customs or fiscal regulations, it must transfer the case to the justice system which will do its own investigating and then decide whether or not to prosecute. Whence the tendency for customs to postpone police (or gendarmerie) action and its judicial corollary as long as possible in cases where the offence undeniably falls within both the customs and the criminal domain, as in that specific form of smuggling represented by drug trafficking. This is what caused its judicial troubles in 1991.

But what these events reveal, as well, is that where the fight against drug trafficking is concerned, the police – and apparently, to a lesser extent the *gendarmerie* – also operate without systematically informing the public prosecutor's office. Legally, 'monitored' deliveries – there was no question of 'controlled' deliveries at the time – were only regulated by in-house Ministry of Justice instructions dating back to 1984 and aimed at public prosecutors, which instructions demanded that they resort to a specialized National Police service disposing of the necessary information and means – the Central Bureau for the Repression of Illegal Drug Trafficking (OCRTIS) – for the implementation of this type of operation. However, it is difficult to determine the extent to which the public prosecutor's office actually controlled use of this technique, in spite of the emphasis placed by this ministerial order on the fact that it should 'fully act as coordinator' and on the obligation for the OCRTIS 'to scrupulously inform the various courts involved, and obtain their consent.'[14] The new texts were much more explicit on this point.

At first glance, then, the 19 December 1991 act may look like an operation where everyone comes out winning: both the customs department and the police gained legal recognition of previously questionable practices (and the indicted customs officers were amnestied), while the public prosecutor's office (which used to show deep mistrust towards customs) was explicitly entitled to overlook those practices and for the first time, the doings of customs officers. More broadly speaking, it would seem that undercover police and customs operations would be more strictly regulated, and therefore easier to control, thus possibly reinforcing the rights of the defense, representing an advance in accountability. All in all, the Justice department was able to use the scandal to its advantage: the move of a principled examining judge opened a window of opportunity, which the ministry seized to establish, for the first time, a modicum of control over an agency which until then had been able to function completely on its own, and to reinforce its control on the other policing institutions.

However, one striking feature of the whole process is that the Ministry of the Interior, although it was benefiting from the new provisions since they were likely to secure the legality of its own police operations, was strongly opposed to the legalization of controlled deliveries, and experienced the outcome of the discussions as a setback, for several reasons. Firstly, the new act seemed to encroach on the

---

14   Circ. CRIM 84-15 E2/10-09-84 dated September 17, 1984.

operational autonomy of the police; secondly, it legitimated what was perceived as an intrusion of customs on its territory, and above all, it deprived the police's central narcotics office (OCRTIS) of its pre-eminent position, since it ceased to be the central clearinghouse for anti-drug operations, and was put on the same level as the central customs investigative office (DNRED). Lastly, this was the second defeat for the Ministry of the Interior, since it had already suffered a similar setback from the Budget and Finances ministries the previous year (1990), when it tried to establish itself as the main actor in the fight against money-laundering through controlling the banking system.

Policing Methods, Between Legal Fiction and Concealment of the Facts

In his seminal work, *Undercover. Police Surveillance in America*, Gary Marx states that: 'The formal investigation may be a laundering operation so that improperly obtained results can be publicly offered; because the initial evidence came from an informant who was promised he would not have to testify or whose credibility as a witness could be easily challenged; or because the information may have been gathered properly but in a way that the authorities do not wish to have revealed.'[15] Here we have the crux of the dilemma of using undercover techniques, which results in all sorts of oscillations between reality and fiction.

The 19 December 1991 act introduces a 'legal fiction,' then,[16] since customs officers, gendarmes and police officers who act in ways which would constitute offences if committed by anyone else are exonerated of any criminal responsibility provided their motives are exempt of any criminal intent and provided, further, that they respect some provisos.

There is nothing exceptional about this legal fiction as such, since the totality of police and customs law consists of habilitating specific agents to do things that are prohibited to ordinary citizens.[17] More generally, this type of reconstruction is the very

---

[15] Gary T. Marx, *Undercover. Police surveillance in America*, Berkeley, 1988, p. 87.

[16] In the sense of a 'conscious denial or warping of natural reality by the jurist who constructs law' (according to Jean Dabin's definition, quoted by André-Jean Arnaud, *Dictionnaire encyclopédique de théorie et de sociologie du droit*, Paris, V° Fiction, 1993, p. 259), or of 'a lie creating law by contravening material or juridical reality' as Guillaume Wicker puts it (in Denis Alland and Stéphane Rials, (eds.), *Dictionnaire de la culture juridique*, Paris, V° Fiction, 2003, p. 717). A 'legal fiction' is thus a legal stratagem devised to reach or avoid certain legal consequences of a given factual situation.

[17] In countries with a written code of law in any case. When Michel Charasse, Minister of the Budget and well known for his sharp statements, defended 'his' customs officers, saying 'Customs has been doing that for ages (monitored and controlled deliveries) (…) and all of a sudden we discover that they are not covered by French law. But there is no law that explicitly prohibits them, and there is also a rule that should not be forgotten: everything that is not prohibited is allowed' (*Le Monde*, 24-25 March 1991), he necessarily knew that what he was saying was juridically outrageous.

essence of law, which is entirely 'fictive' in this respect.[18] Nonetheless, the distance separating this fiction from the legally retranslated facts may vary considerably.

Prior to the 19 December 1991 act, the officers involved, aware of their legally ambiguous situation, would disguise their doings. A drawn-out operation involving the manipulation and payment of informers (who miraculously succeeded in evaporating when the police arrived) and sometimes even their infiltration (or that of officers themselves) in criminal networks, or again, involving doing some favor or supplying some resource for traffickers came out in the end, as mentioned earlier – and above all was registered in the investigations reports – as a 'routine check' that unexpectedly hit the jackpot.

We were in the realm of pure and simple fiction, then. This was not the use of theoretically reprehensible means authorized under specific circumstances, but their outright concealment, more or less covered by the justice system as long as no scandal was entailed. The ends justified the means, as long as there was patent evidence of an offense. The question of whether the principle of fairness of evidence was respected might of course be raised, but French law has never been particularly exacting on that count, and the *Cour de Cassation* was notoriously loath to invalidate proceedings. As two eminent specialists put it: 'the invalidation suit is a type of suit that legislators (…) and judicial practice do not "like" and do not encourage', for 'the entire spirit of regulation (…) is restrictive, so as not to save a person suspected of having committed an offence by having the proceedings nullified.'[19]

One might have thought that the 1991 reform would instill greater transparency, and perhaps even honesty in the police dealings it covered, upholding the rights of the defense, especially through the obligation – imposed by the new legislation – to obtain an authorization from the public prosecutor's office prior to any infiltration operation; Subsequent developments were to show that this was not the Justice department's main consideration. Concern with both protecting infiltrated agents and maintaining effectively punitive penal action soon prevailed, both in ministerial orders and in case law.

Physical Security of Infiltrated Agents and Legal Security of the Procedure: What May be Said in a Criminal Procedure?

In French law, legislation is regularly completed by enforcement measures issued by the government, specifying the manner in which the legislative acts are to be implemented. Without these regulations laws usually remain dead letters, so that by postponing them the various ministries involved may effectively empty of its contents a law to which they are opposed. In the present instance, there was an emergency and all four ministries involved – the Budget, Justice, the Interior and Defense – all hurriedly agreed on the enforcement texts, sometimes attempting to introduce

---

[18] As Marie-Angèle Hermitte, 'Le droit est un autre monde,' *Enquête*, 1998, 7, p. 17, says, 'juridical constructions are characteristically extremely abstract and set their initial object at a distance. Law does not aim at reality, even less at truth, it reinvents another world.'

[19] Serge Guinchard and Jacques Buisson, *Procédure pénale*, Paris, 2000, p. 1247.

measures in the regulations that they had not been able to obtain through the legislation.[20]

The main text here is an instruction dated 14 April 1992, written with great care, as shown by the seven successive versions drafted between mid-February and mid-April 1992. During that gestation period it was thoroughly examined by the Justice Department's DACG, in collaboration with the other administrations involved.

This 8-page instruction was divided into two parts. The first described the new legal arrangement, the reasons for its creation and the objectives of the act. Part two, devoted to its implementation, specified the requirements to be met by monitored deliveries and infiltration operations. In the case of monitored deliveries it recalls that the judicial authority must be informed in advance and must make sure that the legal requisites are fulfilled, so as to give the necessary instructions and arrange the relations between the different services involved. As for infiltration, it recalls that the operation must be explicitly authorized by the judicial authority, must not constitute an entrapment and must pertain to legally defined offenses.

In practice, these formalities mean that the soliciting agencies must demonstrate that a particular operation is absolutely necessary and may be interrupted at any time without endangering the security of the agents involved, and must give a detailed description of how it will take place, with the identity of the latter.

The main difficulty inherent in infiltration is that the principle of fairness of evidence interferes with two concerns, different in nature but converging in their effects. First there is the desire to avoid having the results of long, complicated operations, difficult and often dangerous to implement, called into question, or of having policing techniques publicized, even if they are legal. It is a fact that when an infiltration, even a perfectly legal one, is revealed, it supplies arguments for the defense, which will attempt, sometimes successfully, to demonstrate that there was entrapment and not simple infiltration, obliging the services and agents involved to justify their action. The second concern is with protecting the agents, and eventually their entourage. The fact that they have a legal excuse does not solve the problem. It does provide legal security, but by definition exoneration from penal responsibility only works after the fact, once their role is revealed, and provided the judges do not uncover any acts not covered by the legal provisos. But in any case, their identity will have been revealed, thus exposing them to the eventuality of retaliation by traffickers or their accomplices. Both concerns encourage dissimulation of the true nature of the operations, a temptation which the enforcement instructions do not avoid.

In its initial version the instructions required not only that the public prosecutor be informed of the identity of the agents to be infiltrated, but that it deliver an individual authorization, limited in time, for each person, specifying the acts and places involved. This document was to be used, if necessary, to establish an excuse exonerating the agent from any criminal prosecution. This draft also stated that the infiltrated agents would not participate in any way in writing up the criminal files, and that every attempt should be made to avoid mentioning their identity inasmuch as 'the

---

[20] For instance, in a last minute offensive, the Ministry of the Interior vainly attempted to have the OCRTIS reinstated in its earlier prerogatives.

charges accumulated against the traffickers do not rest on the testimony of those agents.'[21]

The final version, on the other hand, no longer required an individual authorization, nor did it mention the writing of case files, whereas it maintained the need to have the identity of the agents communicated to the public prosecutor. However, it made it clear that this authorization would not constitute a procedural document and would have no effect on the validity of the prosecution.

The question of formal authorization had already been raised during the parliamentary debate. In opposition to those who wanted the law to specify the need for a compulsory *written* authorization, the government imposed its position, which was that this formality had the disadvantage of revealing the identity of the infiltrated agents to all parties.

The objection was raised again by some of the judges involved in drafting the instructions, who felt that the principle of fairness of evidence required that the request for authorization be included in the legal file, but this in-house discussion had the opposite effect. Whenever the infiltrated agents were not indicted and therefore had no need for an excuse, or again, when they themselves had not recorded the offense, there was no need to reveal their identity, and it was hoped that the investigating services would take all proper precautions in this respect. In fact, the drafters of the instructions firmly believed that the case files should not even mention the intervention of these agents, if this was not required for the manifestation of the truth. Indeed, what point was there in divulging 'the details of the operation when there is flagrant violation or a confession that sufficed? The whole problem is to have the instructions indicate this, without saying it', as one note in the archives bluntly states.

Consequently, according to the DACG view, the authorization would only be shown if the infiltrated agent was indicted, which was the very purpose of the law. Any other position would require that the consequences be shouldered and the infiltrated agents and their family be physically shielded (a task deemed impossible, in practice), and at the same time would run the risk of having the whole operation fall apart as soon as a lawyer stepped in, and of having the defense attorney systematically make use of the excuse of entrapment.[22]

From the viewpoint of the judicial and police authorities, then, the new legislation was definitely not intended to improve the transparence of policing operations. Quite to the contrary, it had to be made clear to the various services that they should make every effort to conceal the true nature of the operation as effectively as possible in the file sent to the court. They should therefore reconstruct the facts, as they did previously, doing the utmost to prevent the accused themselves from realizing how they had been identified and arrested. After some hesitations, the courts were to back up this attitude.

---

[21] DACG/SDLC, n° 1468-19/2, DG.239, February 20 (1992) draft.

[22] DACG/SDLC, n° 1468-19/2, sub-folder February 20 (1992) draft. Consultations on the 'narcs instructions project,' handwritten notes dated February 27, 1992, February 26, 1992 and March 3, 1992.

A Hesitant Case Law

To what extent did case law uphold these new legal formalities, especially the need for judicial authorization, and what were the consequences for the police and customs forces and for individuals indicted in cases involving a monitored delivery or infiltration?

The debate – the minute technicalities of which cannot be discussed here – revolved around the following issue: does the authorization required by the new law represent a substantial formal obligation, non-respect of which should result in the pure and simple voiding of the procedure, or is it an administrative act involving the internal relations between the justice department and its auxiliaries – police and customs officers – non-respect of which may of course entail administrative sanctions for the guilty agents, but would not interfere with the legal validity of the operations and therefore could not be mentioned by the accused in an attempt to invalidate the suit?

Interestingly enough, in this domain which touches directly on the rights of the defense, the Criminal Chamber of the *Cour de Cassation* – the highest court in criminal affairs – took two diametrically opposed positions, one after the other. Its about-face certainly affected practices and considerably reduced the impact of what was presented during the parliamentary debate as a fundamental clause.

The first commentators of the law emphasized the absolute necessity for the public prosecutor to authorize the implementation of the excuse, and felt that the lack of a *written* authorization – actually not explicitly called for in the law – should lead to the invalidation of operations conducted by the police or customs officers. They felt that this position was most favorable to the rights of the defense and more in step with article 6 of the European Convention for Human Rights[23] and with the case law of the European Court of Human Rights inasmuch as, unlike the other solution, it did not entail the need to conceal part of the procedure and made it possible for the investigator to submit a clear case to the court. This controversy reflected the discussions raised during the parliamentary debate, and subsequently within the DACG, during the drafting of the enforcement instructions, as we have already mentioned.

However, some courts had taken the opposite position and refused to nullify unauthorized procedures, and for a while the *Cour de Cassation* and the lower courts diverged repeatedly on this issue. At first, between 1995 and 1997, the *Cour de Cassation* took several decisions favoring the stance that without explicit authorization by the public prosecutor the procedure is void, and most commentators therefore felt that this position was clearly established. Then all of a sudden, in 1998, the Court began to adopt the opposite attitude, reducing authorization to a simple formality that should not affect the trial. The commentators were all the more astonished since the

---

23 Especially article 6-3 a and d: '(a) to be informed promptly, in a language which he understands and in detail, of the nature and cause of the accusation against him'; '(d) to examine or have examined witnesses against him and to obtain the attendance and examination of witnesses on his behalf under the same conditions as witnesses against him.'

Court refrained from detailing the reasons for its reversal of opinion.[24] From then on the goal of punishment prevailed over the rights of the defense, the (implicit) argument being that criminal acts had unquestionably been committed, even if the way they had been uncovered might be questionable.[25]

Even if the guilty agents were still answerable to a court or to their administration for their actions (by definition not covered by the excuse represented by authorization by the public prosecutor) and if the procedure was threatened with invalidation for entrapment if their operations were deemed to have effectively caused the offenses to be committed, we are justified in considering that controlled deliveries are no longer controlled by the court, since the chances of a civil servant being prosecuted for having committed a procedural error rather than for a downright dishonest act are minimal.

In short:

– According to present case law, the fact, for police and customs officers, of having set up a controlled delivery operation unknown to the public prosecutor's office does not intrinsically constitute an entrapment for the indicted individuals, provided the operation did not cause the latter to commit any offenses and does not constitute a breach of the rights of the defense; consequently, this situation does not cause the procedure to be invalidated.[26]

– Police and customs dealings are not covered by any excuse, as they would be had they been given the said authorization. They are therefore liable to prosecution as accomplices to drug trafficking. This is a purely hypothetical case, however. Apparently, aside from the customs officers mentioned above, there is no known case in which a police provocation led to the prosecution of its agents. The unprecedented nature of their indictment explains why the customs cases were so disturbing, and the normal course of events, involving impunity, was reinstated when the officers were amnestied.

---

24 The way in which rulings are written by the *Cour de Cassation* differs completely from the styles of writing adopted in common law countries. The writs are often very brief, formulated in an elliptical, allusive style, and do not delve into the arguments leading to the particular decision. Similarly, there are no statements by the minority. When the Court wishes to make its reasons known it may authorize publication of either the closing speech of the prosecuting attorney or the report of the judge who prepared the decision. In the present case this occurred for the Court's first decision in 1995, but it made no attempt to explain its reversal in 1998 through those channels.

25 In one and the same case, for instance, the following episodes occurred: a court of appeals refused to invalidate a procedure for lack of authorization and this ruling itself was voided by the *Cour de Cassation* in 1997. At the time, the latter was defending the opposite position, as mentioned above. In such instances, the case is referred to another appeals court to be reexamined, and the second appeals court took the same stance as the first one. Now, when the ruling was sent back to the *Cour de Cassation* in 1999 it was not nullified that time because in the meanwhile the Court had revised its own position and therefore corroborated the challenged ruling. Here we have two perfectly contradictory decisions by the same court in the same case at a fifteen-month interval!

26 Conversely, the existence of an authorization does not prevent the courts from determining whether there was entrapment in the legal sense of the term: that is, incitement to commit an offence.

– In a situation of this sort, however – and independently of any criminal prosecution – disciplinary sanctions may also be inflicted on the agents involved by their respective administrations or by the judicial authorities, based on their control over such agents (and especially on their power to withdraw capacitation). The threats menacing these agents when they have no authorization from the public prosecutor therefore seem to be sufficient to incite them to respect the law. One would even think that the risk of being sanctioned personally would be more dissuasive than the fear of having a procedure go to naught. However the very existence of this kind of case law proves that this is not necessarily the case, and there is no proof that such control is effectively exerted.

In the last analysis, our assessment of this issue is balanced: if we refer to the explicit goals of the Ministry of Justice – reinforcement of the authority of the public prosecutor's office over the police and customs services – we find that the legislation and the attendant instructions clearly give public prosecutors adequate means of control, and the courts, in their interpretation, hand over the ultimate responsibility for heading judicial policing operations to the latter. The situation of people indicted following operations of this type is completely different. The fact that police and customs officers were given greater leeway was not counterbalanced – except in the initial period with its hesitant case law – by better legal protection of the targets of policing operations (except indirectly, if we consider that it was up to the public prosecutor to decide whether or not to authorize a controlled delivery).

Here we see the ambiguous consequences of pragmatic law-making, intended both to authorize and to control a particular policing technique, depending on whether emphasis is placed on control or on consent. The intention of the legislator, traditionally referred to in juridical interpretation, is of little help here since this intention itself is profoundly ambiguous and, as we have seen, susceptible of divergent analyses.

Spiraling Legalization

Some years ago Jean-Paul Brodeur, a reputed Canadian criminologist, expressed a 'sociological law' which stated that whenever a contradiction arises between police practice and legality, it is usually the law which is modified, not the practice.[27] This points to a specific 'police' way of considering the law, which is intrinsic to police culture.

Police officers (including customs officers) have a specific relationship with the law: although in our present society (especially in welfare states) very few activities remain unregulated, the police's relationship to law is not comparable to that of other craftsmen. In most cases, a craftsman can violate the laws or regulations pertaining to his craft without jeopardizing the quality of his work, which is in fact ruled by other norms. It is therefore legitimate to study the possible discrepancy between professional norms and legal norms pertaining to a particular profession.

The case of the police is different insofar as its existence is unconceivable outside of law: the police is legally instituted, legally habilitated to enforce the law and

---

[27]   Brodeur, 'La police...'

consequently to produce law. In principle, for a police officer there should not be any hiatus between professional norms and legal norms, *i.e.* between what he ought to do as a good policeman and the prescribed legal framework of his work. Now, we all know that such is not the reality, as is amply demonstrated by the amount of research devoted to police discretion.[28]

Thus, from the perspective of the police, the law is something very ambiguous because it simultaneously enables, protects and coerces.

Law is also problematic for police officers because it is the only legitimate language of the criminal justice process; as shown by many studies, mastering legal technicalities is a necessity if one wants to turn an event into a successful case (which is basically what detectives do).[29] Richard Ericson wrote: 'Retrospectively, detectives make official accounts of their actions which conform with what they think the rules say should have been done in the circumstances.'[30] However, in doing this they rely more heavily on experience, traditions and their own recipes than on law itself, and are therefore clearly at a disadvantage by comparison with magistrates or defense lawyers, who by training are much more capable of manipulating legal concepts.

Hence, two competing tendencies are constantly present in both the profession and the institution of policing: a tendency towards internal codification and legalization born of both bureaucratic compulsion and the will of the police to cover their tracks; and a reaction, in the name of efficiency, characterized by a desire for autonomy, flexibility and personal discretion. These opposing tendencies ensure a dynamic which engenders a continuous succession of legalizations and new illegalities.

A few years ago, together with Dominique Monjardet,[31] I proposed a 'model' describing the dynamics of police illegalisms, based on a study of undercover dealings. We had shown that these could be described by combining two independent dimensions:

– The first dimension is the degree of internal formalization within a given police agency: it varies from a complete lack of internal rule leaving the matter to the officer's personal discretion, to a very explicit and formal set of rules prescribed for the whole agency (which may be kept secret); intermediary situations are also possible, police action being subjected to an unwritten custom which may be proper to a specific division or unit within the agency.

– The second dimension pertains to the legal status of a given method, which may be strictly forbidden in law or completely legal. Here again we have intermediary situations, as when a given method has not yet been subjected to a legal test in court.

Based on these 2 dimensions, we proposed a four-stage model, as shown in the following diagram:

28   See for instance: Joseph Goldstein, 'Police discretion not to invoke the criminal process: low-visiblity decisions in the administration of justice,' *The Yale Law Journal*, 1960, 69, pp. 543-594; Jerome H. Skolnick, *Justice without Trial. Law Enforcement in Democratic Society*, New York, 1966; Richard V. Ericson, *Making Crime. A Study of Detective Work*, Toronto, 1981.
29   David Dixon, *Law in Policing. Legal Regulation and Police Practices*, Oxford, 1997, chap. 7.
30   Ericson, *Making crime…*, p. 16
31   I am drawing here on Monjardet and Lévy, 'Undercover policing in France…'

- illegality without internal regulation,
- administratively codified illegality,
- legalization,
- violation of a newly established rule and starting of a new cycle of illegalism.

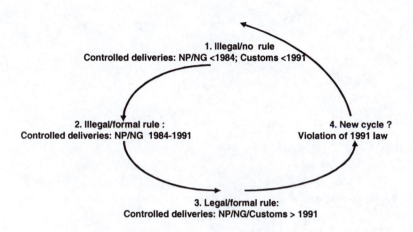

Figure 8.1 The spiral of legalization of police activities

In our case, this model does hold for monitored deliveries (the low intensity surveillance method): we have a passage from a situation of illegality (or at least of dubious legality) more or less mitigated by internal rules to a situation of lawfulness. It also holds for controlled deliveries organized by the police and gendarmerie. But regarding controlled deliveries organized by customs (*i.e.* infiltration), though, the intermediary stage seems to have been more or less short-circuited, at least until March 1991 (*i.e.* when judicial problems surfaced): this is all the more noticeable as it occurred in the wake of a scandal which might have weakened the position of the customs department.

*

In a very influential article, Doreen McBarnet once wrote that, despite all the rhetoric, due process was '*for* crime control.'[32] There is much in our case to confirm this view, especially if one takes into account the court decisions regarding the 1991 law. But seen in a broader perspective, the 1991 law has at least set the foundations for

---

[32] Doreen J. McBarnet, 'Arrest: the legal context of policing,' in Simon Holdaway, (ed.), *The British Police*, London, 1979, p. 39.

stronger judicial supervision of customs and police undercover operations and thus has a more positive side: from the citizen's point of view, once we admit that some degree of police discretion is unavoidable, even partially controlled discretion should be preferred to uncontrolled discretion.[33]

---

[33]   Dixon, *Law in policing...*, p. 300.

PART IV
REPRESENTATIONS OF
CRIMES AND CRIMINALS

Chapter 9

Private Crimes and Public Executions: Discourses on Guilt in the *Arrêts Criminels* of the Eighteenth-Century Parliament of Paris

Pascal Bastien

Introduction

In her book entitled *Private Lives and Public Affairs: The Causes Célèbres of Prerevolutionary France*, Sara Maza offers an excellent analysis of the literary and rhetorical aspects of the *mémoires judiciaires*. Though essentially ephemeral, this literature nonetheless constituted an authentic means of communication that was designed to enlighten public opinion, 'the tribunal of the people,' not only in judicial terms but also in political ones. For historians of criminal justice, Maza's study opens up perspectives and provides new avenues of reflection that differ widely from the methods generally employed by researchers of judiciary archives.

It is with this new perspective in mind that I now wish to examine another form of so-called ephemeral literature, the *arrêt criminel* (criminal court judgment.) As in the case of the *mémoire judiciaire*, peddlers distributed copies of these documents in the streets, but *greffier* (court clerk) also read them aloud during the spectacle of execution. On occasion, they could even be found posted on the walls of public places. There were thus many avenues of consumption for the *arrêt criminel*: sometimes it was heard by the crowd when the *greffier* read it aloud, at other times a private reader could procure one through anonymous channels. Using the example of a particularly scandalous legal case involving Antoine-François Derues, I would like to describe the evolution – analogous to the one S. Maza observes in the *mémoires judiciaires* – of the narrative structure of these criminal court judgments, which were printed by order of the Parliament of Paris. Much more than boilerplate forms – despite their legalistic style and certain fixed formal phrases – the *arrêts* evolved into a complex series of texts whose rhetoric was designed to excite public opinion against the opposing attorneys. In response to the vogue of the *mémoire judiciaire*, the authors of these texts sought to reverse growing criticism towards the judicial system by justifying, with the aid of an 'authentic' account of the facts at hand, the judge's decisions.

In order to demonstrate precisely how the *arrêt criminel* progressively established itself as the mirror image of the *mémoire judiciaire*, I shall divide my argument into three parts: 1) following on Maza's methodology, I will first set forth the elements necessary to the understanding of the case of Antoine-François Derues. The 'exemplary' death of this notorious Parisian poisoner, broken at the wheel in May 1777, inspired an outpouring of literature at the very least equal to that involving Cartouche and Mandrin; 2) based on this example, I will discuss various mutations in the rhetoric of the criminal court judgment beginning in the middle of the century; 3) finally, I will return to the analysis of the Derues case, citing the various leaflets that circulated in Paris following the execution. These were meant to counteract the prevailing opinion that a miscarriage of justice had occurred and that an innocent victim had unjustly been sentenced to death.

The Case of Antoine-François Derues (1777)

From 11 April 1777, when the investigation opened, until the conclusion of his trial on 5 May, the grocer Antoine-François Derues, charged with poisoning, obstinately refused to admit that he was guilty. In legal terms, this did not in itself pose a problem, since the principle of the *intime conviction* of the judge had long since prevailed over the necessity of obtaining a true confession.[1] It was rather Derues' air of complete and utter resignation during the entire ritual of the execution that had aroused sympathy. It would therefore require considerable effort for the authorities to portray him, within the *arrêt*, as an authentic and fearsome criminal:

> The public papers gave an account of the execution of Derues, this Herostratos reborn, the enormity of whose crimes would win him the sort of immortality indeed associated with great assassinations; *but they made no mention of the revolution that has transpired in the people's minds since his death.* The following day, the people bought his ashes and bones; *they wept for the demise of a villain who the night before they would have torn to pieces themselves* had they been authorised to carry out his execution. *The force of the condemned man's conviction, his gentleness, even his religious sentiments, offered a truly astonishing spectacle.*[2]

Two sources permit us to follow the Derues' affair at the same rate as that experienced by his contemporaries: the journal penned by Siméon-Prosper Hardy, whose tireless commentary of the events in Paris spans the second half of the eighteenth century,[3] and the anonymously written *Correspondance secrète et littéraire*, published in London as early as 1786.[4]

By 29 March, the day Hardy first mentions the name of Derues, the rumors regarding the case had been circulating in the capital for nearly twenty days, and Derues had already been incarcerated in the prisons of the Grand Châtelet for more than a week. On 21 March, by order of the Lieutenant of the Police, he had been arrested and imprisoned on suspicion of his role in the disappearance of the wife and

---

[1]   Michel Porret, *Le crime et ses circonstances. De l'esprit de l'arbitraire au siècle des Lumières selon les réquisitoires des procureurs généraux de Genève,* Genève, 1995.

[2]   *Annales politiques, civiles et littéraires du XVIIIème siècle,* 1777, vol. 2, pp. 218-219. Emphasis mine.

[3]   Bibliothèque nationale de France (B.N.), french manuscripts 6680-6687, *Mes loisirs, ou Journal d'événemens tels qu'ils parviennent à ma connaissance,* 8 volumes in grand-folio, 4158 pages.

[4]   *Correspondance secrète, politique et littéraire,* London, 1786-1789, 9 volumes.

son of Monsieur de Lamotte, whose estate in Buisson-Soëf, near Villeneuve-le-Roi, Derues had previously offered to buy for the sum of 150,000 *livres*.

Derues became a veritable item of curiosity. His stubborn refusal to declare his guilt despite mounting evidence against him (the two bodies were discovered on 23 April) made him a bewildering character, and consequently one that was particularly monstrous. 'We could find upon his face no sign of alteration, either when confronted with the crime or during the interrogations,' stated the *Correspondance secrète*.[5] 'The more one interrogated him and heard his reasoning,' wrote Hardy on 23 April, 'the more one came to regard him as an incomprehensible and altogether extraordinary creature.'[6] In his 27 April entry, the bookseller underlined the suspect's cold bloodedness and his 'singularly possessed art of playing the bigot.'[7] 'The high esteem and veneration' he had earned from Parisians, as from all the inhabitants of Villeneuve-le-Roi, 'who regarded him as a saint,'[8] shocked observers convinced of his guilt. Louis-Sébastien Mercier, in an entry entitled 'Place de Grève' in his *Tableau de Paris*, testifies to the magnitude of the Derues' affair, as he waxes indignant about ['Derues'] cold intrepidity and the calm courage of hypocrisy'[9] to which Mercier had borne witness. Even when he was sentenced to death on 30 April, Derues 'was himself, or feigned to be, quite blindly confident, thinking that his case would receive a pardon.'[10] On 5 May, shortly after hearing the Parliament confirm the decision, the popular fascination with this individual grew to such a level that Derues had to be transferred from the Châtelet to the Chamber of the Édit du Palais at four o'clock in the morning so that the curious could come and see him with their own eyes. 'All the honest people who asked to see him were admitted in groups of six until about nine o'clock in the morning, but when the numbers became too considerable, no one was allowed to enter save the lawyers or crown prosecutors.'[11] The conversation he made with those who came to observe him either surprised or angered the witnesses. The anonymous author of a diary preserved at the *Bibliothèque historique de la ville de Paris* observed Derues at the Palace: 'I saw the villain Desrues [sic], I was taken aback with strong emotion on his countenance: his features appeared composed, his mien hypocritical and submissive, and tranquil.'[12]

On 5 May, the Chamber of Tournelle confirmed the sentence of the Châtelet and ordered it to be carried out the following day.[13] In the *arrêt criminel* we read that Derues was 'to make his *amende honorable* (his full apology) in front of the main portal of the

---

5   *Correspondance secrète…*, 1786-1789, p. 325.
6   B.N., French manuscript 6682, p. 351.
7   *Ibid.*
8   *Ibid.*, p. 353.
9   Louis-Sébastien Mercier, *Le tableau de Paris*, Paris, 1994, vol. 1, p. 714.
10 B.N., French manuscript 6682, p. 354.
11 *Ibid.*, p. 355.
12 Bibliothèque Historique de la Ville de Paris, manuscript 697, *Journal d'un Parisien anonyme, années 1777-1784 et 1787*. The manuscript is in very poor condition; the folios dispersed and certain leaflets lost. Page 101 is torn in such a way that the heading of the 6 May 1777, concerning the execution of Derues, is missing although, curiously, the 5 and 7 May headings are intact. It is the only page in the manuscript that has been torn.
13 The minutes of the proceedings are conserved at the Archives Nationales de France, Y-10375, Y-13299, X^{2b}-1364, X^{2b} 1365 and X^{2b}-1366.

Cathedral of Paris (Notre-Dame de Paris), to which he shall be driven by the Executioner in a tumbril marked in front and in back with the words: *Empoisonneur de dessein prémédité* (Premeditated murder by poisoning) [...]; this done, [he] will be taken to the Place de Grève where, on a scaffold which shall be erected for this purpose, he shall have his arms, legs, thighs and stomach broken by the aforementioned Executioner and immediately thrown onto a burning stake which, for this purpose, shall be erected at the foot of the said scaffold, his body reduced to ashes, and his ashes thrown into the wind.'[14]

Ritual, Text and Criminal: The New Judicial Rhetoric of the *Arrêts*

Putting aside the question of Hardy and his judges for a moment, let us examine the larger context of the forms and practices of the *arrêt criminel* in the eighteenth century.

The *procès-verbaux* (transcripts) of execution of the Parliament of Paris, which deal with punishments carried out in the capital during the eighteenth century, are classified under the number X[23] 1333-1334 in the Archives Nationales. Though only partially preserved, as a whole they paint a picture of a ritualized procedure, structured by the reading of the judgment, which, through careful word play, both offered an interpretation of the drama and guaranteed the legitimacy of the punishment. The itinerary of the procession leading to a prisoner's execution was deliberately punctuated by the reading of the sentence: at least twice during the trip, upon leaving the prison and then immediately preceding the execution, the executioner formally called for silence and the *greffier* solemnly read the *arrêt*; each additional halt during the procession meant that the reading began anew.

The Arrêt *in Lieu of the Spectacle*

On 27 April 1770, mentioning in his *Journal d'événements* the execution of Jacques-Martin Bouvier for breaking and entering, Hardy notes that 'it was the first capital execution of the year inside Paris, an event unseen for ten years.'[15] Twelve years later, on 20 December 1782 he wrote the following passage in regard to Jean-François Leclerc, a dealer in second-hand goods, also hanged for breaking and entering:

> The more sensitive souls were glad to see that no one had been put to death in the city of Paris since Tuesday, April 24, 1781. Already they had begun to hope that the present year, 1782, would be free of such things, and the only year perhaps since the birth of the capital during which *we would see no person condemned to death*; when they heard the peddlers selling the *arrêt* mentioned in the present article.[16]

---

14 B.N., F-23675 (733.)
15 B.N., French manuscript 6680, p. 324.
16 B.N., French manuscript 6684, p. 249. Emphasis mine.

Finally in his 31 December 1788 entry the bookseller noted the astonishing disappearance of capital punishment inside the walls of Paris.

> One observed, quite probably for the very first time in the existence of the city of Paris, that neither within the city walls, nor in the surroundings, had there been any sort of punishment whatsoever concerning the death penalty. Far from such a singular event being something which, in my opinion, could be omitted or passed over in silence, I thought it my duty to make mention of it here and with it close the present year.[17]

The sight of punishment in Paris had progressively ceased to integrate itself into the daily life of the inhabitants of the capital. Although, as Hardy suggested (and as the judicial statistics confirm),[18] the execution of non-capital punishments continued to be a familiar scene up through the end of the *Ancien Régime*, capital punishment was slowly excluded from the turbulent daily life of the city. The judicial power adopted new means of making itself felt, confirming its existence through its very absence.

The '*Arrêts de la Cour du Parlement*' deserve a particularly attentive reading, since they had the power to freeze, and, as it were, perpetuate a decision made by the courts; the carrying out of the sentence could incorporate the decision through the instantaneity of its corporal language. The *arrêts* printed from the sixteenth to the eighteenth centuries by order of the Parliament of Paris, which reproduce the handwritten minutes of the judgments of Tournelle, can be found in the series X[2b] at the Archives Nationales. As Yves-Marie Bercé and Alfred Soman both caution, it would most certainly be misleading to evaluate the judicial activity of the Parliament exclusively by the judgments which the jurists printed in leaflet form or as part of a compendium. 'We would effectively only perceive the image which the courts of law wished to give of themselves in the eyes of public opinion.'[19] Yet it is exactly this perspective – that of understanding 'the image which the courts wanted to project' – that I would like to explore. I shall approach the analysis from two angles: 1) I shall trace, and explain, the growth in the number of *arrêts* published in Paris during the eighteenth century, and 2) attempt an interpretation of the radical evolution of the discourse of punishment which the *arrêts* propagated within the course of this same period.

---

[17]   B.N., French manuscript 6687, p. 189. Emphasis mine.

[18]   Gérard Aubry, *La jurisprudence criminelle du Châtelet de Paris sous le règne de Louis XVI*, Paris, 1971; Dominique Muller, 'Magistrats français et peine de mort au XVIIIème siècle,' *Dix-huitième siècle*, 1972, 4, pp. 79-107; Richard Mowery Andrews, *Law, Magistracy, and Crime in Old Regime Paris, 1735-1789, 1: The System of Criminal Justice*, Cambridge, 1994. Robert Muchembled also insists on this period in *Le temps des supplices. De l'obéissance sous les rois absolus. XVème-XVIIIème siècles*, Paris, 1992, pp. 187-224.

[19]   Yves-Marie Bercé and Alfred Soman, 'Les Archives du Parliament dans l'histoire,' *Bibliothèque de l'École des chartes*, 1995, 153, pp. 259-260.

Table 9.1 *Arrêts criminels* printed by order of the Parliament of Paris (1711-1790)

Years	Number of *arrêts*
1711-20	5
1721-30	112
1731-40	85
1741-50	66
1751-60	220
1761-70	416
1771-80	609
1781-90	307
Total	1,820

Source: Bibliothèque nationale de France, F 23672 to F 23676.

A study of the collection of more than 1800 *arrêts criminels* printed by order of the Parliament of Paris between 1711 and 1790[20] enables the historian to conclude that there was an undeniable growth in the number of *arrêts* during the period, an increase which can be seen most clearly within two major breaks observed in Table 9.1. In the first decade of the corpus (1711-1720), the small number of *arrêts* reveals that their publication during this period was exceptionally low. However, in the decade immediately following, an important modification of the trend occurs. The execution, in November 1721, of Louis-Dominique Cartouche, the man behind the most tremendous criminal scandal of eighteenth-century Paris, provoked a marked increase in the number of *arrêts* issued. A long period of collective insecurity, brought to light by Patrice Peveri in regard to the Parisian environment,[21] then followed. The serial executions of 350 of Cartouche's accomplices in person, and as many in effigy, would thus seem to constitute some sort of 'judicial catch-up,' a phenomenon that seems to have been echoed in the increased number of these documents printed between 1721 and 1730. Jean Buvat, the king's librarian, gave an account, in his *Journal de ce qui s'est passé de plus considérable pendant la régence,* of the mass executions of the brigand's collaborators in Paris. 'They continued to execute each week eight or nine of them on the wheel and the gallows,' he wrote in July 1722. Over the following months, Buvat noted the publication of the *arrêts criminels* that accompanied the repression: 'On the 29th [of August 1722] an *arrêt* of the Parliament was published, condemning thirty-seven thieves in the company of Cartouche; the 2nd of September, another one from the same Parliament was printed, condemning thirty-three of his accomplices, some to the gallows, others to the whip and to be branded with a hot iron rod; on the 9th, the Parliament condemned eighty-five of Cartouche's accomplices.'[22] Between 1721 and 1724, forty-eight *arrêts* concerning the brigand's gang, 43 per cent of the total produced during the entire decade, accompanied the executions. The sudden increase

[20] B. N., F 23671 to 23676.
[21] Patrice Peveri, 'Cette ville était alors comme un bois… Criminalité et opinion publique à Paris dans les années qui précèdent l'affaire Cartouche (1715-1721),' *Crime, Histoire et Sociétés/Crime, History and Societies,* 1997, 1-2, pp. 51-73.
[22] B. N., French manuscript 10284, pp. 2127 and 2130.

in the issue of the *arrêts* during this extremely brief period marked the beginning of a phenomenon which was to explode during the decade of 1751-1760. During this time, there were 220 *arrêts* published, in comparison with the 66 judgments published in 1741-1750. There were then 416 printed between 1761-1770 and 609 between 1771-1780. While there certainly was a significant decrease in the numbers of *arrêts* printed during the final decade of the *Ancien Régime*, they still contribute 16.9 per cent to the whole, with 307 *arrêts* printed between 1781-1790. Thus, from 1722 onward, and more especially beginning with the period spanning 1751-1760 (during which, incidentally, there was no criminal case as scandalous as that of Cartouche), the *arrêt* seems to be a form of communication that was more and more employed by representatives of royal justice. Barbier, the well-known eighteenth-century attorney, commented on the interest the people had in the publication of these judgments in his diary: in June 1753, a judgment condemning two books was distributed in the streets of the capital: 'It has been a long time since we have not heard an *arrêt* of the Parliament announced in Paris; *consequently, a great many were sold.*'[23]

This increase in the number of *arrêts criminels* printed represents a break with the communications policy previously followed in Tournelle. It is perhaps not unrelated to another ruling of the Parliament, registered 26 May 1713, which authorized the printing of all *mémoires judiciaires* signed by lawyers or prosecutors with no prior permission required.[24] One of the greatest paradoxes of the conflict between the powers of justice and those being tried is that the *mémoires judiciaires* and the *arrêts criminels* – respectively written in defense of the accused and of the accusers – are both part of the same dynamic of seeking supremacy through appeals to the court of public opinion. Similarly, in its bid to assume a dominant position in the political framework, the Parliament of Paris developed various modes of contestation that were related in a certain sense to the printing of the Tournelle judgments observed in Table 9.1: admonishment of the king, formerly circumscribed as *secret du roi*, together with the controversy over the denial of last rites in 1750, the institutional conflicts caused by the easing of restrictions on grain trade in 1760, and, finally, the anti-fiscal campaigns preceding the coup lead by Maupeou in 1771, shattered the rule of silence and provoked a wave of *arrêts* successively quashed by the king's Council. During this time, the Parliament was quite clearly taking on a political role of unprecedented scope and changing the existing political givens.[25] In this sense, the circulation of *arrêts* clearly expressed the Parliament's increasing will to rally round those accused: progressively establishing itself as the mouthpiece of a newly emerging public opinion, was it not in the best interest of the Parliament to impose upon this burgeoning opinion its own vision of justice? The fact that the spectacular growth in the printing of *arrêts* continued following the return of the Parliament of Paris from its sixteen-month exile

---

23 B. N., French manuscript 10290, p. 93. Emphasis mine.
24 Lucien Karpik, *Les Avocats. Entre l'État, le public et le marché, XIIIème-XXème siècles*, Paris, 1995, p. 126.
25 Keith M. Baker, *Inventing the French Revolution: Essays on French Political Culture in the Eighteenth Century*, Cambridge, 1990; Jeffrey Merrick, *The Desacralization of the French Monarchy in the Eighteenth Century*, Baton Rouge, 1990.

(May 1753-August 1754) in Pontoise[26] perhaps manifests the will of the courts of justice to shatter the silence imposed on them up until then, voicing an opinion that was guaranteed to have an effect in the publishing network.

An Alternative Rhetoric

Nevertheless, the visibility of the activities of Tournelle was not enough to entirely transform judicial discourse: it was the means of its diffusion but it did not transform. Sarah Maza has done more than simply uncover the vogue for, and the editorial dynamism of, the *mémoires judiciaires*; she has also traced the transitions of their literary genre. If the corpus of *arrêts criminels* published by the Parliament represented an increase in the practice of printed publicity, one can equally consider it as a new stage in the conventions of the punitive discourse. To show what I mean more clearly, let us return to the Derues' case. We last left Derues on 5 May, the day on which the death sentence imposed on him was upheld on appeal by the magistrates of the Parliament of Paris.

Though delivered without the accused having ever confessed, the judgment did not manage to produce one. 'Right unto the last moment he confessed nothing,' the author of the *Correspondance secrète* related. 'This man conserved his mask of hypocrisy to his dying breath, talking unceasingly of God, of his innocence, saying he forgave his Judges for unjustly condemning him to death.'[27] Though tortured, as Hardy reported, 'he protested having ever held, sold, or prepared any poison, declared to be not at all the author of the deaths of those persons which he was accused of poisoning and assured that they died natural deaths, assurance he perversely upheld the whole duration of the torture.'[28] It was around three o'clock on the afternoon of the 6th that Derues left the prisons of the Grand Châtelet, escorted by the executioner and the confessor, and began his final journey that led up to the scaffold.

In his 6 May entry, Hardy recorded the last moments of the condemned man with precision. During the entire ritual of execution, for the point of view of the author as well as for the crowd attending the event, the convicted man deserved, and was given, more attention than the punishment; the body, the gestures and the reactions of the culprit constituted the center of interest in the ceremony of punishment. 'Through a prodigious multitude of spectators,' the convoy journeyed from the prisons of the Châtelet to the square of Notre-Dame Cathedral, so that the *amende honorable*, the public confession of the crime, could be pronounced. On his knees, before the court clerk could begin the reading that the condemned was then to repeat, Derues 'proteste[d] once again his innocence, and cried out that though his body belonged to justice, he hoped that God would have his soul.'[29] Hardy, who was probably an eyewitness to the execution, added that '[Derues'] pallor was extreme but his countenance cold and silent, to the point where it did not seem easy to guess the many movements that might be agitating his soul in the face of the dreadful

---

26   Clarisse Coulomb, '"L'heureux retour." Fêtes Parlementaires dans la France du XVIIIème siècle,' *Histoire, Économie et Société*, 2000, 19, pp. 201-215.

27   *Correspondance secrète...*, 1786-1789, p. 358.

28   B.N., French manuscript 6682, p. 356.

29   B.N., French manuscript 6682, p. 357.

circumstance in which he found himself.' Climbing once again into the tumbril, Derues was at last taken to the foot of the scaffold at the Place de Grève, where he decided, according to the custom granted those condemned to death, to go into the Hôtel-de-Ville. He remained there for more than three hours 'but came no closer to giving a confession.' Finally, he returned to the Place de Grève, 'after saying himself that this thing must be finished.' The author of the *Correspondance secrète*, despite his belief that the condemned man was guilty, wrote that 'one might have thought that he was looking upon one of our early Christians walking to his execution when [Derues] came down from the Hôtel de Ville.'[30]

According to Hardy, the printed *arrêt* was sold during the execution.[31] Eight pages long instead of the usual four, the narration of the crime appears all the more important in that it is fully presented two times: once to indicate the charges, a second time to give the wording of the contents of the *amend honourable*. Keeping in mind this unusual element (the counts of indictment and the *amende honorable*), if we quantify the attention given to the crime in terms of the number of words, we arrive (with 2,173 words out of 3,692) at 59 per cent of the *arrêt*. More than half of it is dedicated to the description of the crimes of the condemned. In addition, the *Journal de Paris* published an excerpt of the sentence in its 7 May edition: there the crime was stated only once, but in its entirety. The reading of the *arrêt* having been done three times by the clerk during the course of the ritual – upon leaving the prisons of the Châtelet, before the Notre-Dame Cathedral, and at the Place de Grève – the spectators would have been in a position to hear it no less than six times.

Although it remains largely unstudied by historians of justice, the question of the reasoning behind a court's judgment, which forms an inherent part of the larger question of jurisprudence, opens up the problem of the sacredness of power under the Ancien Régime. Article 15, chapter 5 of the law of 16-24 August 1790, decreed by the *Assemblée Constituante*, stipulated that from henceforth 'the results of the facts recognised and established by the preparatory inquiry, and the grounds on which the judgment is decided, shall be made public.'[32] What did people understand by 'the grounds of a decision' and in what way did the use of the *arrêts* by the Parliament dispense or not with the need to justify a sentence pronounced by Tournelle?

From the time of thirteenth-century lawmakers to that of the jurists of the eighteenth century, legal doctrine had always been stood against discussion of the reasons for judgments. Historians of law who have worked on this question[33] have

---

30 *Correspondance secrète…*, 1786-1789, p. 359.
31 A transcription of the *arrêt*, in French, can be found in the appendix of this study.
32 See Bernard Schnapper's recent analysis of the law texts of the *Constituante*, 'Les systèmes répressifs français de 1789 à 1815,' in Xavier Rousseaux, Marie-Sylvie Dupont-Bouchat and Claude Vael, *Révolutions et justice pénale en Europe. Modèles français et traditions nationales (1780-1830)*, Paris, 1999, pp. 17-35.
33 Corinne Bléry, 'L'obligation de motiver les décisions de justice était-elle révolutionnaire en 1790?,' *Histoire de la Justice*, 1991, 4, pp. 79-97. This article studies the legal practice only through the juridical theory and, strangely enough, Bléry never consults the judicial archives to support her thesis. See also Tony Sauvel, 'Histoire du jugement motivé,' *Revue du droit public et de la science politique en France et à l'étranger*, 1955, 71, pp. 5-53; and Philippe Godding, 'Jurisprudence et motivations des sentences du Moyen Âge à la fin du XVIIIème siècle,' in

underlined that from the moment when judicial proceedings became written and secret, the expression '*pour les cas résultant du procès*' (on grounds brought to light during the trial), still in use at the end of the eighteenth century, was adopted in order to exempt the judges from having to inform the public of the reasons for a condemnation or an acquittal. 'The judges' conscience,' Jean-Marie Carbasse has recently written, 'such as it manifests itself throughout European history, appears as a ground where transcendence and human reason met.'[34] It is at this junction between the sacred power to judge and the rational procedures of human justice that the motivation behind the judgments finds all its ambiguity.

This right to withhold the reasons behind a judgment was generally defended according to three principles:

– The absence of the motivation of a sentence prevented a party from being able to contest an *arrêt* because the cause of the legal action remained unknown;

– Moreover, it forbade a decision from becoming precedent that would bind the judges against their will to previously pronounced judgments;

– It confirmed the independence and the sacred power of the judge, since the magistrates were accountable to no one regarding their decision, neither to those they condemned, nor to those on trial, nor even to the king.[35]

Several rulings of the Parliament of Paris (1640, 1656, 1676, 1732), binding the courts within its jurisdiction to always justify their decisions, often cited in the law manuals of the eighteenth century,[36] established an incontestable hierarchy between the lower courts and the supreme courts. The decisions of the first instance thus had to be defended, though the judges of the lower courts were obliged, to a much lesser degree, as we shall see, to legitimize their decisions.

What exactly is a judgment containing legal arguments? Tony Sauvel defines it as an 'exercise in persuasion,'[37] a piece of judicial rhetoric seeking to rally the reader to the decision of the magistrates. However, the reality under the *Ancien Régime* was much less precise: legal argument was generally limited to a description of the offenses. Admittedly, any attempt to structure and manipulate the legal arguments in a judgment ended up being extremely difficult, since between 1) the complete absence of any reasoning, 2) the elementary description of the crime and 3) the 'detailed' account of the criminal acts, there was often a considerable distance. These problems were all the greater in that the judgment was drafted in the most arid legalistic style, in which procedural details could make up a large portion of the judgment without the author ever formulating a legal argument justifying the court's decision. The example of the *arrêt* pronounced against Robert-François Damiens is an obvious one: in addition to the customary juridical formulae, the text includes the names of every witness interrogated, the description of a suspect who failed to appear in court, and a

---

Chaim Perelman and Paul Foriers, (eds.), *La motivation des décisions de justice*, Bruxelles, 1978, pp. 37-67.

[34] Jean-Marie Carbasse and Laurence Depambour-Tarride (eds.), *La conscience du juge dans la tradition juridique européenne*, Paris, 1999, p. 15.

[35] C. Bléry, *art. cit.*, p. 81.

[36] Such as those written by Daniel Jousse, *Traité de la justice criminelle de France*, Paris, 1771, 2, p. 650, and Pierre-François Muyart de Vouglans, *Instruction criminelle suivant les lois et ordonnances du royaume*, Paris, 1762, 2, p. 659.

[37] T. Sauvel, *art. cit.*, p. 6.

list of the decrees, minutes of the proceedings, interrogations, continuing investigations and requests which comprised the pre-trial investigation.[38] Cumbersome legal formulas surrounded a hermetical procedural accounting to produce a conscientious description of the formalities of the investigation. This accounting should not however be confused with the legal argument for the sentencing, whose objective was not to prove the guilt of the condemned man, but rather to designate a crime to correspond to the punishment given.

It seems clear that between 1760 and 1790 at the latest, all lower courts of the Parliament of Paris were obliged to indicate the crime for which the conviction had been pronounced: and at least a minimal description of the crime ('theft,' 'assassination,' 'rebellion against justice,' 'insolence,' etc.) was to be added to or replace the existing phrase *'pour les cas résultant du procès.'*

Throughout this period, the *arrêt* never strayed from the unchanging form and logic of its narrative. The description of the plaintiffs and of the prosecutors, at times abridged, at others fully appended, was made, followed by their surname, given name and occupation. The decision rendered by the court of first instance and the announcement of the appeal procedure preceded the brief expression *Tout considéré* (all considered), which split the text into two parts. It was in this second section of the text that the final verdict, if different from the first ruling, would be cited. If there was sufficient legal argument contained in the judgment of the lower court and the nature of the crimes was stated in the first part of the text, the court of Tournelle did not repeat the recital of the offenses of the convicted person in its *arrêt*. Instead, it merely indicated whether the trial had been 'well' or 'poorly' presided. The *arrêt* generally ended with the order of the Parliament to publish, post and print the text, followed by the date of the final decision.

Beyond reeling off the array of statistical information that an inventory of the corpus can provide, is it possible to go beyond the question of the quantitative increase in printed judgments, as demonstrated in Table 9.1, to a discussion of the *qualities* of the discourse they put forward? In other words, rather than the serial treatment of crime and punishment to which an analysis of the minutes of the Parliament has accustomed us, is it possible to recognize in the *arrêt* something other than mere discursive repetition? Because the text of the *arrêts* was written in conventional legal jargon, the documents have never previously been subjected to a rigorous discursive analysis.

It would be a mistake to assume that these documents were no more than a set of sclerotic formulae whose content remained frozen between the second half of the seventeenth century and the end of the *Ancien Régime*. For example, in the early eighteenth century, the phrase *'pour les cas résultant du procès'* was used as the sole legal argument. Although in theory it simply designated the crime in question, in fact it imposed a vision of punishment and retribution on the reader that was much more striking than that of a transgression. In this fashion, the sentence was presented by the authors as an implacable judgment whose foundation was the weight of authority rather than the specific crime. 'The said [name of accused] *on the grounds brought to light by the trial* was condemned,' to be hanged, placed in iron shackles or banished, for a crime depicted in the most simple terms: 'household theft,' 'pimping,' or 'violence

---

[38] B.N., F 23674 (10.)

toward police on duty.' However, this narrative style of the *arrêt*, sometimes silent with regards to the particular crime, which was at other times appended to the counts of indictment, was progressively transformed over the course of the eighteenth century.

The development of narrative content within the *arrêt* can be most clearly detected if we divide the section of the judgment which states the crime of the condemned person into three categories. The first part, the 'minor narrative,' states very briefly the type of crime being punished, generally preceded or followed by the mention 'on the grounds brought to light by the trial.' A second part, the 'intermediate narrative,' supplements the simple indication of the crime with at least one or more aggravating circumstances. The third part, the 'major narrative,' abandons the traditional listing of the crime in order to describe the guilt of the alleged criminal with an extremely precise description of the different transgressions, as in the case of the *arrêt* rendered against Derues.

This division into three narrative categories freezes the discursive cycle of the *arrêt* into a document which corresponds to Tony Sauvel's interpretation of the purpose of the legal decision, that is, according to Sauvel, to formally present or argue a decision is to *persuade* the reader of the legitimacy of the conviction it entails. Thus, though perhaps unnecessarily, Parisians learned that Marc Troupeau, condemned to the wheel on 18 August 1777, had not only 'entered during the night of 29 August 1776, the house and domicile of (...) the widow Chereau, had climbed over the walls of the courtyard of the aforementioned widow, [had gone] over to the bed where she lay in the deepest slumber and [had thrown] himself at her, [but that he had also] put one hand to her throat and the other to her mouth to smother her and this with such violence that he caused the last two of her teeth to fall out, and in such a manner that he left the aforementioned widow all covered in blood and without movement, thinking her dead.' If not to be persuaded, did Parisians truly need to learn that in August 1766, Simon Chorat had assassinated his wife 'with *cruelty and ferocity*, breaking his rifle over her body, dragging her by her hair, giving her many kicks, and *in a word rained so many blows upon her during several hours*, sometimes outside the house, sometimes within, that she died of it; of having even brought *savagery and irreligion* to the point of becoming *insensible* to the reproach of several persons, and to the pleas of the said Daoust [his wife], who begged him for pardon and to spare her life, and beseeched him to fetch her a man of God so as to confess, *despite all of which he continued in his mad rage [to rain on] his blows?* [39] Such a recitation was indeed necessary, however, if the magistrates were anxious to convince the populace that their judgment was imperative and legitimate, not founded on faulty judgment but of course on the urgent need for true and exact justice.

Indeed, the purpose of this new linguistic format was to make clear that the convicted man was *intentionally* responsible for his criminal acts. Eric Walter's study of the La Barre case and public opinion in 1766 reveals in passing the evolution of the 'journalistic' exercise, which would replace the detailed account of the execution in use in the first half of the century,[40] by the verbatim reprinting of the full text of the

---

[39]   B. N., F 23674 (946.)
[40]   Robert Favre, Jean Sgard and Françoise Weil, 'Le fait divers,' in Pierre Rétat and Jean Sgard, (eds.), *Presse et histoire au XVIIIᵉᵐᵉ siècle. L'année 1734*, Paris, 1978, pp. 199-225.

arrêt, 'which thus began its long career in the press.'[41] It was this practice that the *Journal de Paris*, the first daily newspaper in France, introduced[42] during the first six months of its existence in 1777 (interestingly enough, on the 29 January in the same year, it had been forced to cease publication of its judicial column).[43] The recounting and spinning of the criminal event in the text of the *arrêt* argued in defence of the severity of a sentence and underlined the justice of the punishment inflicted. Expressed in the most rudimentary language, purged of the complicated traditional legalistic style, the argument anthropomorphized the 'Criminal' with a vocabulary of disobedience from which all nuance was removed.

Table 9.2 The narrative content of the *arrêt*

Years	Minor narrative	Intermediate narrative	Major narrative	Total
1721-30	58	43	11	112
1731-40	45	30	10	85
1741-50	36	24	6	66
1751-60	115	73	32	220
1761-70	143	171	102	416
1771-80	142	188	279	609
1781-90	30	81	196	307
Total	569	610	636	1,815

Source: Bibliothèque nationale de France, F 23672 to F 23676.

As early as the 1750s, we can clearly observe the growing use of the major narrative in the *arrêts*. Table 9.2 shows the evolution of the narrative section within the *arrêts* printed from 1721-1790. From 1751 onwards, when, as we have noted, there was once again a large jump in the number of judgments printed, there is a clear inversion of the customary narrative practice. Significantly, the use of the intermediary narrative jumps from 33 per cent to 41 per cent between 1751 and 1770, signalling an increase in the use of details to describe the crime – it apparently represented a transitional practice during this period. The number of intermediary narratives then regresses, at first dropping down to 31 per cent, and finally to 26 per cent, between 1771 and 1790. This opposing trend is part of an increasingly pronounced tendency to abandon brevity in legal judgments. The antithesis of the two narrative antipodes reaffirms the changing nature of the process. Thus, whereas in each decade between 1751 and 1790 the rate of inclusion of the minor narrative drops dramatically (from 52 per cent to 34 per cent, then to 23 per cent, and finally to 10 per cent), the proportion of the overall text which the major narrative occupies increases decidedly,

---

41 Éric Walter, 'L'affaire La Barre et le concept d'opinion publique,' in Pierre Rétat, (ed.), *Le journalisme d'Ancien Régime. Questions et propositions. Table ronde CNRS, 12-13 juin 1981*, Lyon, 1982, p. 363.
42 See, for example, the May 7, 1777 edition, which published a large excerpt of the *arrêt* (in major narrative) pronounced against Antoine-François Derues.
43 Jean Sgard, *Dictionnaire des journaux, 1600-1789*, Paris, 1991, 2, p. 619.

passing from 15 per cent to 25 per cent, 46 per cent and then to 64 per cent of the total length of the *arrêts*. From 1750 onward, elaborating on a practice that had been rather exceptional up until that point, the magistrates broke with existing penal rhetoric with an argument written in an entirely new vocabulary whose discourse was aimed at those on trial.

The evolution of the type of narrative employed thus closely paralleled this shift in the number of *arrêts* printed. The progression of the major narrative was thus part of an evolving 'zone of public contestation' that Habermas and other historians of public opinion have studied.[44] Beginning in the late 1750s, royal edicts attempted to explain and justify government policy with increasingly lengthy and more detailed preambles. Conversely, the Parliament took sides against the king and its Council by means of the repeated publication of *arrêts*. The Parliament was directly responsible, by its printing of *arrêts* opposed to the papal bull *Unigenitus*, for bolstering the emerging political conscience of the population.[45] Through the use of the major narrative, the *arrêt* transformed the subject of a private dispute into an enemy of the public. Simultaneously, the growing flood of *mémoires judiciaires*, particularly from the 1770s onward, that were distributed or sold in Paris for the purpose of decrying the archaic administration of justice and tyrannical judiciary, apparently constituted, as I have previously suggested, an extremely important factor in the development of the new judicial rhetoric concerning criminal judgments. Admittedly, it is difficult to determine whether *mémoires* and *arrêts* reached the same public or, following a categorization no doubt greatly oversimplified, whether one should classify the documents respectively as 'scholarly' and 'easy' reading. The parallel increase in both types of publication seems nevertheless to point to a considerable broadening of the readership or, at the very least, the increasingly manifest will of lawyers to propagate, through either one intermediary or the other, the legal culture that they wanted to defend. At the heart of public debate in the Capital, engaged in by a population that was becoming more and more literate, was the *arrêt criminel*, an inexpensive little pamphlet that, once no longer restricted to the limited audience of lawyers, became increasingly central as the 'site' of an enlarged public sphere where the stakes were increasingly high.

The comparison of the *canard* (broadsheet) and tragic literature of the period has proven beyond a doubt that a correlation exists between these two types of editorial enterprises. Frequently, entire excerpts from the first were reproduced in the stories of the second, the substitution of names often sufficing in order to entirely comprise, without any further dissembling, the text printed in the broadsheets.[46] Anne de Vaucher Grivaldi, apparently unfamiliar with the legal style used in the criminal judgments of the seventeenth century, misinterpreted a description of the punishment of a male witch condemned to the stakes as part of an elaborate baroque literary

44   Jürgen Habermas, *The Structural Transformation of the Public Sphere: an Inquiry into a Category of Bourgeois Society*, Cambridge, 1989. The bibliography regarding the notion of public opinion in pre-Revolutionary France is immense; one may profitably refer to the one found in the book by Vincenzo Ferrone and Daniel Roche, *Le Monde des Lumières*, Paris, 1999, p. 601.

45   Catherine Maire, *De la cause de Dieu à la cause de la nation. Le jansénisme au XVIIIème siècle*, Paris, 1998, pp. 401-404.

46   Maurice Lever, 'De l'information à la nouvelle : les 'canards' et les 'histoires tragiques' de François de Rosset', *Revue d'Histoire Littéraire de la France*, 1979, 79, pp. 577-593. See also Robert Muchembled, *Une histoire du diable. XIIème-XXème siècles*, Paris, 2000, pp. 186-188.

process. On the contrary, it was the transcription, word for word, of a judgment that was anything but atypical.[47] The legalistic style of the *arrêts* unquestionably influenced that of tragic literature; indeed, certain broadsheets didn't even bother to hide that they quite openly and directly borrowed the body of their 'authentic and most extraordinary' story from the text of the criminal judgments.[48] Why then, conversely, can we not judge the influence of eighteenth-century writers of tragic literature, such as Prévost or Baculard d'Arnaud, on the major narrative? 'The tales about the living dead, the taste for the morbid, the lugubrious anecdote, all of these methods of portraying the world are important in the second half of the eighteenth century and propose to the imaginary collective the layout of the Gothic novel.'[49] It seems that the tendency toward excess characteristic of the *arrêt* was often a borrowing from a dramatic writing process that no longer had anything to do with court diplomacy. Instead of judges tormenting criminals through corporal punishment replete with exposed flesh, oozing blood and terrible cruelty, signs of baroque overkill on the 'doctrine of fright'[50] that were still in vogue with jurists toward the end of the *Ancien Régime*, the second half of the eighteenth century featured a shift in the basis of repressive justice to underlining the responsibility of the criminals. This shift, part of a politico-judicial strategy designed to shape the opinion of the Parisians, manifested itself on several fronts: firstly, in the nature of the text heard or read within the Parisian sphere; secondly, by the progressive withdrawal of executions from the urban environment, analogous to the transfer in the collective imagination brought on by the major narrative. The chronological approach to the study of the judicial system in countless works on criminal history has long since demonstrated that the number of death sentences receded sharply during that time, to be replaced by less defamatory punishments. Justice was every bit as present in the city (indeed more so) but clearly represented less of a mortal threat and was more indulgent than in the seventeenth century, which ruled by the stake and the gibbet.[51]

Toward the 1750s and 1760s, at the exact moment when criticism against the justice system started to be heard within the Parisian intellectual circles and the major narrative of the judgments started to oppose these criticisms, magistrates began to send the condemned back to their courts of first instance, thereby evacuating the

---

[47] Anne de Vaucher Gravili, *Loi et transgression. Les histoires tragiques au XVII*^(ème)^ *siècle*, Lecce, 1982, p. 75.

[48] *Relation véritable et des plus remarquables qui ait jamais paru dans le siècle où nous sommes,* **le tout tiré sur la sentence de mort rendue par le bailliage de Laon en Laonnois,** *des 11 et 18 du présent mois de juillet 1750, qui condamne une bande de 35 bergers à être tant rompus que pendus* (Being the veritable and the most extraordinary tale that has ever been told in our century, **all taken from the death sentence rendered by the bailiwick of Laon in Laonnois,** the 11th and 18th of the present month of July, 1750, which condemned a group of 35 sheepherders to be broken and hanged), B. N., ms. Fr. 21730, f° 129 (printed text added to the manuscript). Emphasis mine.

[49] Antoine de Baecque, *La gloire et l'effroi. Sept morts sous la Terreur*, Paris, 1997, p. 18.

[50] Michel Porret, 'Effrayer le crime par la terreur des châtiments' : la pédagogie de l'effroi chez quelques criminalistes du XVIII^(ème)^ siècle,' in Jacques Berchtold and Michel Porret, (eds.), *La peur au XVIII*^(ème)^ *siècle : discours, représentations, pratiques*, Genève, 1994, pp. 45-67.

[51] Robert Muchembled, *Le Temps des supplices. De l'obéissance sous les rois absolus. XV*^(ème)^-*XVIII*^(ème)^ *siècles*, Paris, 1992, pp. 197-202.

execution of sentences, which previously had been almost exclusively carried out within the walls of the Capital, towards the original site of the crime. There no longer was the need for such continuous displays of authority: even as capital punishment slowly moved away from the Parisian urban milieu, the *arrêts* affirmed and rendered visible the exercise of royal justice, banishing the spectacle of punishment but in no way sacrificing its omnipresence nor its exemplary nature. 'While the peddlers advertised the aforesaid *arrêt* in Paris, the execution took place in Bondy,'[52] Hardy wrote in 1779 regarding the death of a highwayman. From lack of means or will to embark upon a true reform of the penal system, which would have completely undermined the foundations of the symbolic interlay between justice and the trial, the judges made the decision to disperse with a spectacle which presented in too concentrated form the hostile odour of tyranny, abuse, and cruelty.

The private and public reading of the *arrêt* placed the criminal within a Manichean moral system by forcing him to assume, *alone*, the responsibility for his condemnation. It did not allow considerations for criminality on economic or emotional grounds. Even as royal justice progressively lost its status as the all-knowing and all-encompassing arbiter of Good and Evil, the argument by major narrative in the *arrêt* seems to have imposed itself as a *rational assessment of the judgment*. Paradoxically, in setting itself up against a weakened royal authority, it was really against the foundations of its own sacredness that the Parliament – which rendered the king's justice – acted. In this sense, it is important to understand the existence of a shift from the notion of *raison d'État* towards that of *salut public* (public safety).[53] It was surely part of this fundamental transfer of political practice that the development of the major narrative, justifying and motivating the court's decisions and concentrating public opinion on the *responsibility* of the criminal, inserted itself.

The Multiplication of *Arrêts* as Proof of Guilt

The Derues' affair demonstrates how the attention the Parliament paid to justifiying its criminal judgments bordered on excess. In its role as the people's tribune, the Parliament could not allow doubt regarding the rightness of its decisions to invade; owing to the particular circumstances of the case in question, the Parliament was forced to resort to devices other than the *arrêt criminel* alone.[54] Hardy wrote in his 7 May entry that Derues 'finished as he had begun, that is to say, without them being able to pull any confession whatsoever out of him [and] persisted in denying that he was guilty as accused on the count of poisoning.'[55] His public declarations of innocence accompanied the same pious resignation he had shown the whole length of his execution, and shook popular belief that he was guilty. The execution further

[52] B.N., French manuscript 6683, p. 107.
[53] Marcel Gauchet, *Le désenchantement du monde. Une histoire politique de la religion*, Paris, 1985.
[54] Hans-Jürgen Lüsebrink makes a complete inventory of these other devices in *Kriminalität und Literatur im Frankreich des 18. Jahrhunderts. Literarische Formen, soziale Funktionen und Wissenskonstituenten von Kriminalitätsdarstellung im Zeitalter der Aufklärung*, München-Wien, 1983.
[55] B.N., French manuscript 6682, p. 358.

deteriorated public confidence in his guilt: the 'mental revolution'[56] had become too important. 'Some,' wrote the author of the *Correspondance secrète*, 'as there are always those who like to complain, found that the law had been betrayed in condemning to death a man who stubbornly denied his crime and against whom no valid proofs were found.'[57] Hardy confirms this evolution in voicing his own opinion: 'A great number of fools, ignoramuses or people disposed to prejudice against magistrates, grumbled against the rigor of the judgment pronounced and executed on Tuesday the sixth of the same month.'[58] The Parliament judges could not lightly consider the possibility of a new judicial disgrace after such tremendous scandals as Calas or the Chevalier de La Barre.

Three days after the death of Derues, Hardy reported that the magistrates had begun to take certain preliminary measures. 'The judges, in order to prove their full and entire justification by enlightening all those who prided themselves on their uprightness, intelligence and the good will to improve themselves, felt the need to give the public a general account of the procedures. (…) This account, entitled *Détails historiques et véritables des manœuvres abominables et des crimes atroces commis de dessein prémédité par Antoine-François Desrues*, was distributed in various quarters by the peddlers, and could not but produce a very good effect, for it was not possible after having read it to believe Desrues innocent.'[59]

It has not been possible to find the '8 printed pages in-quarto format' published and printed by Cailleau. However, far from being unique, this document, which appeared 9 May, belongs to a sizable series of literary and iconographic works published in the weeks that followed the execution. These documents were exclusively devoted to recounting Derues' crimes; through them, he became the very incarnation of hypocrisy and vice.

The most complete text of the lot, which was blessed by at least four editions in 1777, was *La vie privée et criminelle d'Antoine-François Desrues; contenant les particularités de sa jeunesse, ses mauvaises inclinations, son insigne hypocrisie; et le détail des manœuvres abominables et des crimes atroces commis, de dessein prémédité, par ce scélérat, envers la Dame De Lamotte et son fils*. It apparently appeared for the first time in the initial days following the execution: the *Correspondance secrète* reports on it in a letter dated 17 May.

In this widely distributed text, no means was spared to construct Derues as a monster. Not only was he morally reprehensible, but he was also physically distorted: 'This monster was Hermaphrodite in nature; and it was at the age of 22 to 23 that

---

56   See note 2.
57   *Correspondance secrète…*, 1786-1789, p. 359.
58   B.N., French manuscript 6682, p. 359.
59   *Ibid.*, p. 359.

treatments were administered and an operation was performed on him, giving him the distinctive characteristic of the male sex.'[60] His whole body and his gestures were signifiers of his villainy.

> To picture this execrable monster, imagine a feeble constitution, a short stature (four feet three inches), an elongated face, pale, delicate and thin; almost no beard, a laugh like unto a Satyr's, a deep-set mouth, a perfidious eye; in a word, a villain. His round eyes, deep and piercing, somehow betrayed the perversity of his soul. He was above all strongly attached to covering himself with the hypocrite mask of false devotion, always surrounded by the saintly Books, speaking only of Religion, of God, of the Saints, of Paradise, and even daring, by the most sacrilegious of abuses, to participate frequently in our Holy Mysteries.[61]

Derues' actions foretold the tragedy of 1777 as early as his earliest childhood. At the age of three 'he already displayed these vicious inclinations'[62] and, despite the bodily punishments he received from his foster parents, he remained 'incorrigible.' In adolescence he became most accomplished in the art of deceit. He never failed, 'by his hypocrisy and the seductiveness of his language,'[63] to attract the goodwill of those around him. His false piety and his feigned devotion charmed the whole neighborhood; even his confessor was misled by his exemplary piety. 'Who could not be fooled? This scoundrel, to better hide his deception, carried with him two shrouds, to which were attached the Relics of Madame Chantal and a Medallion of Saint Francis of Sales.'[64] Afterwards, crimes followed, though they were never reported: he accused his brother of theft to better shine the light of honesty upon himself; very craftily he stole merchandise in the shop where he had served as apprentice-grocer, causing the business to go bankrupt; twice he openly proposed using poison to eliminate undesirable creditors. He blamed his thefts on innocent people who had disappeared without a trace (this detail naturally gave the author of the text reason to suggest a list of assassinations much longer than that which had sent Derues to the scaffold). The writer finally concludes Derues' story, after describing his unsuccessful attempt to put poison in his mistress' soup, by lengthily retracing the tragedy of the Lamottes: 'This anecdote, together with those which precede it, of which there can be no doubt, must well convince the Magistrates and the Public of the crime of poisoning committed by this villain, towards the Lady Lamotte and her unfortunate son.'[65] The word count is most telling: in his description of Derues and each of his gestures, the author uses the term 'hypocrite' 15 times, 'monster' 24 and 'villain' no less than 41 times.

Other texts appeared over the following year, always built around the assassinations of the wife and son of Lamotte. We can also read, in song form, the

---

60   B.N., Ln²⁷-6008, p. 8.
61   *Ibid.*, pp. 46-47.
62   *Ibid.*, p. 7.
63   *Ibid.*, p. 10.
64   *Ibid.*, p. 13.
65   *Ibid.*, p. 30.

Histoire tragique et moral d'un ci-devant épicier-droguiste faussaire et empoisonneur, which also insists on the hypocrisy of the criminal.

> *Et nonobstant des actions si vilaines,*
> *Il affectoit catholique maintien,*
> *Communiant de deux à trois fois semaines,*
> *Pour déguiser comme il étoit vaurien.*[66]

> And despite such villainous actions,
> He feigned Catholic posture,
> Receiving Communion twice or thrice weekly,
> To disguise that he was a scoundrel.

The printer published another song similar to the first during the same period: *Complainte historique et circonstanciée sur les cruautés commises par le nommé Derues, épicier-droguiste à Paris*,[67] where the crime is, once again, described in detail.

Another most interesting text, still published within the course of the same year, presents the inner workings of Derues' soul by means of a 'confession' written a few hours before his execution: *Vision, réflexions et aveux de Derues, trouvés dans sa prison, écrits de sa propre main*. Interspersed with brief citations from the Bible, it exposes the tormented religious confessions of a criminal who nonetheless stubbornly continued to dissimulate his guilt to human justice. Thus, the criminal writes:

> Yes, my God, I declare to you these iniquities which are known to you, so that I may be granted your mercy! I will confess them again to one of your Ministers, to accomplish your divine Commandments, which I have always feigned to scrupulously observe; but they of Human Justice will never tear from my mouth the confession of all my atrocities! Rather I shall endure the hardest tortures and torments! Yes, invincible sentiments will make me support them with a firmness which not even the aspect of death itself shall be capable of shattering![68]

The four printings of the *Vie privée et criminelle* attests without a doubt that these stories of Derues' crimes attracted a sizeable audience. A further anecdote recorded in the 11 September edition of the *Journal de Paris* testifies as well to the effectiveness of the editorial campaign against Derues, although this tragic tale is perhaps nothing more than the exaggerated echo of the active propagation of Derues literature: 'One woman, already sick it is true, was so shocked by the details of the Villain's crime that she became suspicious of her own complicity, and this impression alienated the unfortunate woman's spirit to the point where she threw herself out a window on the third floor.'[69] Finally, it may be recalled that Cesare Lombroso, in his renowned anthropometrical study, used the portrait of Derues published in 1777 as a demonstration of criminal traits according to his theory of criminological determinism.

---

66 B.N., Ye-24861, p. 2.
67 B.N., Ye-24861.
68 B.N., Rés 8-Ln[27]-6010, pp. 11-12.
69 *Journal de Paris*, September 11, 1777, p. 3.

Conclusion

It is clear that the published texts and engravings did not proliferate in response to the poisoning of the wife and son, but rather to Derues' repeated declarations of innocence: neither Damiens, condemned for regicide, nor Chabert, for parricide, were the subjects of such abundant tragic literature. As for the highwaymen Cartouche and Mandrin, there was never truly any doubt over their guilt. They were at times portrayed as courageous and generous men, at others mean and pitiless creatures, but they nonetheless always deserved punishment for their disobedience. In Derues' case, however, royal justice found it essential to prove with certainty the criminal's responsibility in order to renew its own legitimacy. A similar example, though much less ambitious in scale, can be traced back to 1755. It is the case of the widow Lescombat, accomplice in the assassination of her husband,[70] whose execution the lawyer Barbier reports with great interest. Though the execution of the sentence was delayed for several weeks due to her pregnancy, Barbier specifies that 'this woman, twenty-six or twenty-seven years old, is one of the prettiest women there is in Paris, *which causes compassion.*' The Marquis d'Argenson was of the same opinion: 'As she is the most beautiful woman in Paris and the most shapely, she has found many protectors in the court.'[71] She was finally hanged, *le visage voilé* (face covered), on 2 July 1755. Present at the execution, Barbier reported that 'they were selling the printed history of her crime in the streets, and her portrait, which is not as pretty as she truly was.' To this 'printed history,' which I was unfortunately unable to find, we can equally add the *Lettres amoureuses de la Dame Lescombat et du Sieur Mongeot, ou L'histoire de leurs criminelles amours,* which was published by Cailleau, and which recounts with a certain eroticism all the cruelty and diabolical power that she practiced on all those she frequented.[72] In this case as in Derues', sympathy for the condemned appears to spawn or orient an outpouring of tragic literature designed to uphold the authority of justice.

One might note that the rise of modern media took place around the same time as the phasing out of public punishments of deviants, which was replaced by less conscious modes of processing the notion of criminality. Guy Schattenberg suggests that the continuing fascination of mass media with crime and deviant behavior may serve to disseminate information about moral boundaries in the same way that public punishments once did.[73] The writing, printing and distribution of the *arrêt criminel*, sometimes joined by other peddled literature, may have formed an important part of a process that would not come to an end until the Assemblée Constituante's declaration of 1790 that all sentences required legal justification.

We have seen in the literary form of the *arrêts criminels*, as well as in the justice system's effort to convince public opinion of the culpability of Derues, that the

---

[70] Sabine Juratic, 'Meurtrière de son mari: un "destin" criminel au XVIIIème siècle? L'affaire Lescombat,' *Revue d'Histoire Moderne et Contemporaine,* 34, 1987, pp. 123-137.

[71] Marquis d'Argenson, *Journal et mémoires du marquis d'Argenson,* edited by E.J.B. Rathery, Paris, 1867, 9, p. 9.

[72] B.N., Y²-43360.

[73] Guy Schattenberg, 'Social Control Functions of Mass Media Depictions of Crime,' *Sociological Inquiry,* 1981, 51, pp. 71-77.

direction taken by punitive discourse profoundly modified the focal point of criminal justice. Punishment was displaced as a demonstration of Parliament's power, and directed towards the criminal himself, thus highlighting the responsibility of the convicted man. *Homo criminalis* was not only the invention of a reformative penal philosophy but also, perhaps especially, that of a desacralized and rationalized justice[74] looking to orient public opinion in its favor.

---

[74]   Frédéric Chauvaud (ed.), *Le sanglot judiciaire. La désacralisation de la justice (VIIIème-XXème siècles)*, Grâne, 1999.

Chapter 10

Rebels or Bandits?
The Representations of the 'Peasants' War'
in Belgian Departments under
French Rule (1798)[1]

Xavier Rousseaux

Historiography often reserves special treatment for uprisings, especially when they fail to attain their immediate objectives. Their subsequent treatment is inseparable from the commemorative process, what French historians have termed '*lieu de mémoire*': the traumatic event they represent for the concerned populations.[2] When the development of the historical account is also embedded in a context of State formation and emerging nationalism, the account of the 'original crime' even becomes inseparable from the context in which the memory is produced; it is instantly perceived as a conflict between 'victims' and 'aggressors.'

Such is the case of the 'Peasants' War' against the symbols of the French Revolution in the former Austrian Netherlands and the Principality of Liège, annexed three years previously by the French Republic, in October-November 1798 (the Brumaire-Frimaire months of the year VII of the French Revolution). The variety of qualifiers applied to these events denotes the rich political debate fuelled by two centuries of historiography: 'rebel uprising,' 'Belgian Vendée,' for supporters of the Revolution; 'Peasants' war' for Belgian historiography; pre-nationalist 'Boerenkrijg' in the Flemish version; war of the cudgels, 'Kleppelkrick' for the German-speaking people of Luxembourg; there was no lack of expressions to evoke the violent incidents of the Fall of 1798.

In order to understand the revolt and the subsequent construction of the nationalist myths, this chapter will draw on two main sources of information: (a) research conducted in the past fifty years about the birth and development of the myth of the 'Peasants' War' over two centuries,[3] and (b) an examination of new

---

[1] Translated by Nora Scott. I warmly thank Emmanuel Berger Ph.D student in history (UCL-CHDJ), for his help in carrying out this project and Nora Scott for the translation of this chapter.

[2] Pierre Nora, *Les lieux de mémoire*, Paris, 1984-1992.

[3] An overview of this work can be found in the publications produced for the 1998 Bicentennial. In particular the volumes edited by Luc François, *De Boerenkrijg. Twee eeuwen feiten en fictie*, Leuven, 1998, or Jan Goris, Fred Stevens, Karel Veraghtert and Marcel Gielis, (eds.), *Voor Outer en Heerd. 1798. De Boerenkrijg in de Antwerpse Kempen*, Turnhout, 1998. For a

sources, namely French military court trials of captured rebels, which have not been studied systematically until now.

Studying the repression of these uprisings by the courts presents two interests: first, it completes the figures usually given in the French military and administrative reports regarding the fate of those arrested; second, it introduces some complexity into the mythic account of the revolt. The judicial sources by themselves do not construct the nationalist myth of resistance against the French.[4] But, by interpreting the occupiers' policy in the light of the laws of the young revolution, they do contribute to creating the 'security' myth. Through the practice of the military courts, the French sought to turn the military victory into a political triumph by identifying the 'rebels' with the hated figure of the 'bandit.'

The 'Events': Historiography and Knowledge

In the past half-century, different lines of research, each highlighting a different set of documents have dealt with the Peasants' War.

Because they have involved *military* history, the study of these revolts initially focused on the analysis of the events themselves: the chronology and geography of the uprisings, the retreat of the troops and of the French authorities, the occupation and plunder of villages, followed by the intervention of columns of soldiers, *gendarmes* and French supporters (*colonnes mobiles*), the violent engagements such as those at Hasselt, Diest or Clervaux, and the crushing of the rebels by the army. Of course, this militaristic and nationalistic interpretation of history took place in a specific ideological and political context: the assessment of the place of the 'French' régime in the legitimization of the 'Belgian' State and nation, under construction since 1830.[5] I will explore this later.

---

synthetic overview, see Fred Stevens, 'La résistance au Directoire dans les départements réunis. La 'guerre des paysans' (octobre-novembre 1798),' in Philippe Bourdin and Bernard Gainot, (eds.), *La République directoriale*, Clermont-Ferrand, 1998, pp. 1025-1045. For a more detailed study, see Marie-Sylvie Dupont-Bouchat, Xavier Rousseaux and Fred Stevens, 'La guerre des paysans (1798). Mythes et réalités. Brigandage, révolte nationale ou croisade religieuse?,' in Laurence Van Ypersele, (ed.), *Imaginaires de Guerre: l'histoire entre mythes et réalités*, Louvain-la-Neuve, 2003, pp. 53-89.

4 The same reflection underpins my work on other cases of political-style repression, in particular the repression of 'unpatriotic behavior' following the First World War and that of collaboration after the Second World War. See Laurence Van Ypersele and Xavier Rousseaux, 'La répression de 'l'incivisme' en Belgique au travers de la presse Bruxelloise francophone et des procès de la Cour d'assises de Brabant (1918-1922),' in Van Ypersele, *Imaginaires de Guerre…*, pp. 253-302.

5 For more on this subject, see Philippe Raxhon, *La mémoire de la Révolution française. Entre Liège et Wallonie*, Brussels, 1996; Jean Stengers, *Histoire du sentiment national en Belgique des origines à 1918. 1: Les racines de la Belgique*, Brussels, 2000. Jean Stengers and Éliane Gubin, *Histoire du sentiment national en Belgique des origines à 1918. 2: Le grand siècle de la nationalité belge (de 1830 à 1918)*, Brussels, 2002.

Since the 1960s, a *social and economic history* has developed on the heels of the historiography of the end of the *Ancien Régime*.[6] The sociology of rebels was the first subject to claim attention: the identity of the leaders, the sociology of the followers, the geography of the hotspots and the 'cooler' regions. Likewise, the analysis of the causes of the revolt became more finely drawn. The immediate causes, in particular the Jourdan conscription law, formed part of an analysis of underlying economic, social or religious causes. The revolts came to be interpreted within several theoretical frames of reference: Marxist (as pre-revolutionary collective action), nationalist (as resistance against foreign interference), cultural (as linguistic and 'ethnic' conflicts), religious (as Catholic reaction against the secularization introduced by the Revolution).

The return of *socio-political* history finally situated the revolts in a deeper context.[7] The 'Belgian' revolt was integrated into the international context of revolutionary unrest: the Great Fear in the North, the Vendée uprisings, and the Chouan revolt in the West but also into the climate of a generation marked by twenty years of political insecurity that began with the outbreaks of resistance against the reforms of Emperor Joseph II in 1787 and 1789, what is known as the 'Brabant' revolution of 1789-1790,[8] and the Franco-Austrian war of 1792-1794.

Finally, historians are now stressing *'conceptual'* confrontation: the clash between an originally Absolutist State and local communities jealous of their freedoms, the opposition between 'traditional liberties' and Liberty, transmitted by the revolutionary armies and inspired by the Enlightenment bourgeoisie.

Two methodological principles characterize the new historiography. First, the multiplicity of viewpoints: this approach takes into account sources from above and local sources, the viewpoints of the French, the rebels, the supporters of the regime, the opponents and those who were neutral. This perspective also acknowledges the fact that the creation of the historical myth is contemporaneous with the events themselves, rather than created later. Second, the inextricable mix of event and representation: the idea that every discourse is grounded in fact, and every fact is reported through discourse; every crime has a text, every text has a context. This applies not only to discourse after-the-fact, but to the understanding of the conflict itself. 'War' is not only physical, it is ideological, too.

---

[6] In particular the work of Albert Soboul, (ed.), *Voies nouvelles pour l'histoire de la Révolution française*, Paris, 1978; Jacques Godechot, *France and the Atlantic Revolution of the eighteenth century, 1770-1799*, London, 1973; François Furet, 'New work on the Old Regime and the French revolution,' *Journal of Modern History*, 2000, 72-1, pp. 1-182 (a special issue in honor of François Furet).

[7] Michel Vovelle, *La découverte de la politique. Géopolitique de la révolution française*, Paris, 1993.

[8] Luc Dhondt, 'Les processus révolutionnaires et contre-révolutionnaires en Belgique, des réformes de Joseph II à la réunion à la France (1780-1798),' in François Lebrun and Roger Dupuy, (eds.), *Les résistances à la Révolution. Actes du colloque de Rennes*, Paris, 1987, pp. 273-283; Luc Dhondt, 'De conservatieve Brabantse omwenteling van 1789 en het proces van revolutie en contrarevolutie in de Zuidelijke Nederlanden tussen 1780 en 1830,' *Tijdschrift voor Geschiedenis*, 1989, 102, pp. 422-450.

What Do We Know About the 'Rebels'?

It is impossible to go into the full complexity of the uprisings of Vendémiaire-Frimaire, VII (October-November 1798), more commonly presented as the 'Peasants' War.' Each word in the phrase 'Peasants' War' deserves careful attention. Was this an ideologically and politically unified movement or a series of disorganized local peasant uprisings or *Jacqueries*? Was it a war against a known enemy, or was it, if not spontaneous, at least a series of relatively unorganized explosions of anger? Was the revolt essentially peasant-led or was it actually carried out by impoverished craftsmen led by an elite established in towns or the countryside? To answer these questions, we must look at some of the most recent findings.

The chronology of the rebellion, as well as the location of its places of intense activity argue for the importance of a case-by-case interpretation of these uprisings. The 'war of the cockades' began in 1796 in the vicinity of Virton, against the French forest legislation. The peasants' war, 'Boerenkrijg,' developed in the departments of *Lys, Escaut, Deux-Nèthes and Meuse-Inférieure*, and especially Dyle. The 'Kleppelkrick' or ('Klöppelkrieg') broke out in the Walloon and German-speaking areas of the department of *Forêts*. Referring to the last case, G. Trausch has clearly shown how the objectives and the outcome of the rebellion differed, depending on whether the quarters of the new department were German or Walloon.[9]

---

9   Gilbert Trausch, 'Les soulèvements de 1798 dans la région de Neufchâteau et leurs répercussions dans le département des Forêts,' *Publications de la Section Historique de l'Institut Grand Ducal de Luxembourg*, 1962, 79, pp. 65-133; This hypothesis seems to be sustained by the analysis of the activity of a *tribunal de police correctionnelle* in the Walloon district of Habay-la-Neuve, by Josy Trodoux, *Le tribunal de police correctionnelle d'Habay-la-Neuve sous le Directoire (1795-1800). Une approche quantitative*, unpublished B.A. in History, Louvain-la-Neuve, 1997.

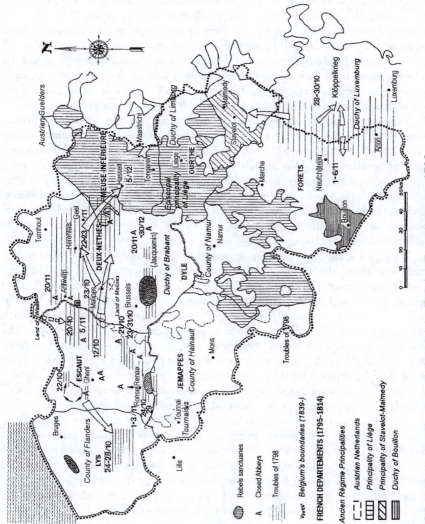

Map 10.1   The Peasants' War in the Belgian Departments, 1798

Were the characteristics of these revolts the same in all places? Often described in the Belgian, Flemish and Luxemburger nationalist hagiographies as uprisings organized with the aid of England, the rebellions sometimes presented a spontaneous character that was reflected in their short duration, their lack of objectives and organization, and the relative ease with which they were put down,[10] all of which would tend to make them look like the classic peasant uprisings or anti-government revolts of the *Ancien Régime*.[11] Nevertheless, in the departments of *Deux-Nèthes* and *Meuse-Inférieure*, where the large Catholic monasteries had played a strong role in rural economic and social development in the second half of the eighteenth century, opposition to the New Regime was more clear cut and involved broad sections of the rural population, notably landholders whose wealth was recently acquired.[12]

Two factors have been presented as driving the uprising against the French régime in the populations that were attached to their religious traditions and resistant to the idea of conscription: the conscription laws of 19 Fructidor VI and the religious policy of secularization (*police des cultes*). Although the two issues crystallized into a resistance against the invasion of rural communities by a State set on unification, they were not the only causes. In the forested departments the French forestry policy, which had broken with the traditional customary rules negotiated by rural communities under the *Ancien Régime*, no doubt sparked revolts such as the Neufchâteau uprisings.[13]

Do linguistic factors explain the geography of the revolts? While the 'Boerenkrijg' chiefly concerned the Flemish populations, and the 'Kleppelkrick,' the German-speaking regions, active though limited hotspots could also be found in the Walloon parts of Brabant and Luxembourg. It seems to me that the fact that the rebellions in the North and the East took place along the borders has been largely underrated. According to Trausch, the outbreaks in Luxembourg occurred in the part of the former Duchy recently detached from the department of *Forêts* and annexed to either *Ourthe* or *Sarre*. The imposition of new administrative boundaries exacerbated tensions among the inhabitants, whose traditional exchange circuits were disrupted by the new divisions. It is significant that the revolts remained endemic wherever, as in Brabant or Hainault, the changes made to the *Ancien Régime* boundaries were minor.

The rural character of these revolts, which almost never affected the large cities, should draw the researchers' attention. Along with religious problems and conscription, the geo-political re-organization of the departments, the interruption of traditional communication networks, as well as the burden of the requisitions and damages resulting from the war, weighed more heavily on the rural populations than on the large urban entrepreneurs. Would this not go further towards explaining the geography, the spontaneity and the lack of preparation of the revolts?

---

[10]   Gilbert Trausch, 'À propos du *Klepelkrich*. La répression des soulèvements paysans de 1798 dans le Département des Forêts (aspects et problèmes),' *Publications de la Section Historique de L'Institut Grand Ducal de Luxembourg*, 1967, 82, pp. 11-245 ; Gilbert Trausch, 'Die Luxemburger Baueraufstände aus dem Jahre 1798. Der 'Klöppelkrieg', seine Interpretation und sein Nachleben in der Geschichte des Grossherzogtums Luxemburg,' *Rheinische Vierteljahrblätter*, 1984, 48, pp. 161-237.

[11]   Dhondt, *Les processus...*

[12]   Stevens, *La résistance au Directoire dans les départements réunis...*

[13]   Trausch, *Les soulèvements de 1798 dans la région de Neufchâteau...*

Lastly, didn't the type of repression, legislation focused on the 'inhabitants of the countryside,' contribute to reinforcing the myth of the peasant-war? The 'criminalization' of the revolt, and therefore its repressive aspect, are indeed often cited as triggers or arguments, but they are rarely studied in depth. Some invoke it, often in passing, as a symbolic example of the occupiers' brutality and the rebels' courage. Others use repression as a good indicator of insecurity and of the State's response in terms of law and order. Still others attempt to make the phenomenon of 'revolt' a part of the new practices of collective action,[14] or of the clash between State-imposed modernization and traditional rural practices symbolized by banditry or smuggling.[15]

The Repression: Emergency Laws and Military Courts

It has already been mentioned that the measures taken to suppress the revolts fall into at least four categories:[16] (a) the repression by the army and the police, whose victims were essentially those killed in the fighting (some 5,000) and those arrested during the unrest (between 1,600 and 1,700 'peasants' and 648 priests who had refused to take the oath); (b) the repression carried out by the ordinary departmental criminal courts and the emergency courts, in this case military courts; (c) the repression by civil courts which imposed collective fines on the rebellious communities by virtue of the law of 10 Vendémiaire IV (2 October 1795);[17] and (d) the political repression which was carried out essentially by taking notables as hostages and deporting about 900 priests.

The analysis of criminal repression in this chapter is based on sources which have only recently been made available to the public in an accessible form: the decisions of the French military courts from 1795 to 1805.

---

14   Eric Hobsbawm, *Primitive rebels: studies in archaic forms of social movement in the 19th and 20th centuries*, Manchester, 1974.

15   Anton Blok, 'The Peasant and the brigand: social banditry reconsidered,' *Comparative Studies in Society and History*, 1972, 14, pp. 494-503; Anton Blok, *De Bokkerijders. Roversbenden en Geheime Genootschappen in de landen van Overmaas (1730-1774)*, Amsterdam, 1991; Florike Egmond, *Banditisme in de Franse Tijd. Profiel van de Grote Nederlandse Bende 1790-1799*, Soest, Amsterdam, 1986; Florike Egmond, *Underworlds. Organized Crime in the Netherlands 1650-1800*, Oxford-Cambridge, 1993.

16   Xavier Rousseaux, 'La révolution pénale, fondement de l'État national? Les modèles français de justice dans la formation de la Belgique, des Pays-Bas et du Luxembourg (1780-1850),' in Xavier Rousseaux, Marie-Sylvie Dupont-Bouchat and Christian Vael, (eds.), *Révolutions et Justice pénale en Europe (1780-1830). Modèles français et traditions nationales. Revolution and Criminal Justice in Europe, 1780-1830 French Models and National Traditions*, Paris, 1999, pp. 285-317.

17   A specific example is provided for the commune of Tielt dans in the department of Lys by J. Buyck, 'De Boerenkrijg in het kanton Tielt,' in François, *De Boerenkrijg...*, pp. 114-115.

An Arsenal of Laws

These military courts wielded a set of laws decreed under the Revolution. First, the law of 30 Prairial III (18 June 1795) defines the 'Rebel' and distinguishes 'leaders and instigators' from 'inhabitants of the countryside caught up and surprised in gatherings.'[18] Second, the law of 3 Brumaire, IV (25 October 1795), revising the 1791 Penal Code, recalls the existence of capital punishment for any act of conspiracy against the Republic.[19]

Along with these 'political' measures, the emergency legislation of 24 Floréal, year V (15 May 1797), and particularly that of 29 Nivôse, VI (18 January 1798) reinforced the fight against banditry.[20] The first punished by death those perpetrating armed aggression in groups (banditry in the strict sense of the term).[21] The second authorized trial before a military court for all acts of aggression against persons or property, in the home or on a public thoroughfare, committed by more than two persons. These two statutes explicitly introduced the concept of collective crimes into revolutionary legislation. Passed before the revolts, and extended until 29 Nivôse, VIII (19 January 1800), the law of 29 Nivôse, VI, was a powerful tool of repression in the hands of distressed authorities.[22]

Emergency Courts

Arrested suspects were not immediately brought before a military court. First they had to be handed over to the ordinary magistrate (*Directeur du Jury*) of their district (*arrondissement*), who would then decide whether the accused should appear before a military or a civilian court.[23]

These courts, comprised of seven military men and sitting without a jury but under the supervision of the executive branch, were organized by the law of 13 Brumaire, V (3 November 1795). A very rapid appeal process was instituted by the law of 18 Vendémiaire, V (9 October 1795).

---

18   Law of 30 prairial, year III, Article 1, 2 et 5.
19   Penal Code of 1791 revised in 1795, Art. 612 et 613 Pending the abolition of capital punishment and its replacement by 20 years in irons.
20   Bernard Schnapper, 'De Thermidor à Bonaparte,' in Philippe Boucher, (ed.), *La Révolution de la Justice. Des lois du roi au droit moderne*, Paris, 1989, pp. 216-271.
21   For more on banditry, see Florike Egmond, *Underworlds*, and Xavier Rousseaux, 'Espaces de désordres, espace d'ordre: le banditisme aux frontières Nord-Est de la France (1700-1810),' in Catherine Denys, (ed.), *Frontière et criminalité (1715-1815)*, Arras, 2000, pp. 131-174; Florike Egmond and Xavier Rousseaux, 'Brigandage, gendarmerie et justice. L'ordre républicain dans les départements du nord de la France et les départements "réunis" (Belgique, Rhénanie) entre Directoire et Consulat (1795-1804),' in Jean-Pierre Jessenne, *et al.*, (eds.), *Du Directoire au Consulat. 3. Brumaire dans l'histoire du lien politique et de l'État-Nation*, Rouen, 2001, pp. 91-123.
22   Article 22 of the law of 29 Nivôse VI stipulated that any procedure having begun before 'the end of the same year would be terminated in accordance with the previsions of the present law,' Vincennes, Service historique de l'Armée de Terre (SHAT) 2 J 311, 25th Division militaire, 2d *Conseil de Guerre*, n° 5533 (17bis), 25 frimaire an IX.
23   Howard G. Brown, 'From Organic Society to Security State: the war on Brigandage in France, 1797-1802,' *Journal of Modern History*, 1997, 69, p. 680.

This analysis is based on several large series of documents kept in the Vincennes military archives. These contain the copies of decisions of the military courts (*conseils de guerre*) and the military appeal courts (*conseils de révision*) sent to the War Minister by the military division commanders. The military courts which judged the 'Belgian' rebels were essentially the two divisions established in Brussels (24th *Division Militaire*) and in Liège (25th *Division Militaire*), respectively capitals of the former Austrian Netherlands and of the Principality of Liège.[24]

Profiles of Civilian Repression by the Military Courts

I will attempt to paint a general picture of the activity of the military courts of the 24th and 25th DM. Between years V and XII, the two divisions sent some 3,000 and 800 cases, respectively, before the military courts. Over 80 per cent these dealt with members of the military. Between 15 and 20 per cent of these, or some 700, dealt with civilians.

The Sentences

I have identified 693 sentences concerning civilians judged under the emergency laws passed between the years III and VI. These include decisions from Ventôse, V, to the beginning of the year XII (February 1797 to September 1803.) But nearly all of the sentences were meted out between Frimaire VII and Nivôse VIII, a period of 13 months running from November 1798 to December 1799.

Clearly these courts could pronounce only a certain number of sentences per month, 50 at best (including members of the military.) After the end of the uprising the number of prisoners judged per session therefore increased considerably between Frimaire VII and Nivôse VIII (Graph 10.1).

---

[24] The decisions are stored in some fifteen boxes, classified by alphabetical order. At the time of my first visit, in 1993, the boxes had not been inventoried. Since 1997, a typed list has been made. A detailed inventory was made in several stages – 1993, 1997 and completed in 2000-2001. For further information, see Service Historique de l'armée de Terre, *Guide des archives et sources complémentaires*, Vincennes, 1996.

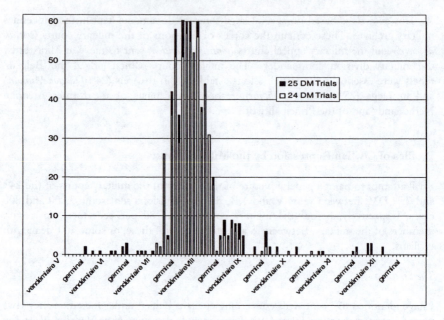

Graph 10.1 Monthly number of civilians tried by each military division
(Year V to Year XII)

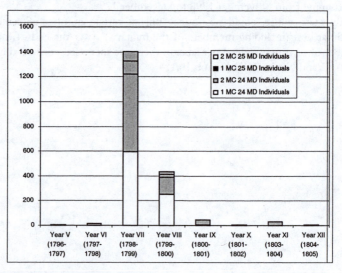

Graph 10.2 Civilians tried by military courts
(24th-25th Military Divisions)

These civilians were judged in one of four military courts (Graph 10.2). For the 24th DM, the first Military Court sat in Brussels or Ghent; the second sat in Tournai or Bruges; for the 25th DM, the first court sat in Luxembourg, the second in Liège. In reality, 85 per cent of the decisions (590 out of 693) were rendered by the courts of the 24th DM.

Those Tried

There are several categories of civilians: those tried for participation in the revolt of Vendémiaire VII; those tried for acts of banditry prior to the revolt; those arrested for emigration; those arrested out of precaution (Austrian deserters) or tried for military recruitment for the enemy (or with the Batavian Republic in the 25th DM); and, finally, a few recruits whose situations were unclear.

Table 10.1 Individuals tried by the military courts

		24th DM	25th DM	Total	%
Thieves and bandits		251	95	346	18
Rebels		1,350	178	1,528	79
Miscellaneous		15	50	65	3
Unspecified		0	5	5	0
	Total	**1,616**	**328**	**1,944**	**100**

Regrouping those tried into two broad categories: rebels (unrest and revolts), and thieves and bandits, we see that nearly 2,000 civilians came before the courts over this period: 80 per cent for rebellion and 18 per cent for theft with violence and banditry.

The vast majority were men. Nevertheless, we find 56 women, most of whom were tried for abetting banditry. Only 19 women were tried for taking part in a revolt.[25] All were acquitted except for Anne Philips Verdievelde, sentenced to four months in detention for having taken part in a rally of insurgents in Hooglede.[26]

Their treatment in the trial, as well as their symbolic place in the procedure, shows to no one's surprise that justice and, *a fortiori*, military justice, was a male justice. The women were usually questioned after the men and were usually suspected of having aided and abetted their husband or son. They were rarely given harsh penalties.

---

[25] 18 by the boards of the 24th DM, only one by the 25th DM.
[26] Vincennes, SHAT 2 J 298, 24th DM, decision of the 2nd CG, n°17221.

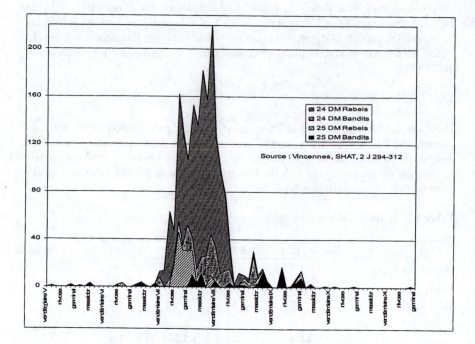

Graph 10.3 Rebels and bandits tried by military courts (24th-25th Military Divisions)

The Sentences

Of the 1,350 civilians tried for taking part in the revolt in the 24th DM, nearly 60 per cent were acquitted, 25 per cent were given detention and 15% were sentenced to death. In the 25th DM, 178 'rebels' were tried. Half of these were acquitted, 20 per cent were given detention and 25 per cent were sentenced to death. In both cases the majority of the sentences of detention or death were pronounced by the first military court, while the second pronounced the majority of the acquittals.

If we compare these rates with the decisions for thieves and bandits, we see that for the 25th DM the rates of acquittal, detention, and death sentences vary little. Alternatively, the judges were much harsher on bandits, who were rarely sentenced to detention (2 out of 10); but they acquitted in 4 out of 10 cases and sentenced to death in the other 4 cases.

Acquittals

Nearly 900 rebels were acquitted. Some received a conditional acquittal. Juveniles were sent home to their parents or to departmental prisons (*maisons de correction*), conscripts and Austrian deserters were sent to special centers for conscripts and deserters (*dépôts*).

Transfers

The military courts transferred some 50 accused to other courts, either because their cases were appropriate for ordinary rather than military courts, or because the initial procedure before the ordinary magistrate in the accused's judicial district was not respected. For example, three individuals suspected of having torn the national cockades off the hats of various persons, or of having shouted seditious slogans and having sung a song debasing the Republic, were transferred before the criminal court of Lys after summation by the executive agent by virtue of Articles 1 and 2 of the law of 1 Germinal.[27]

Convictions

The vast majority of the rebels were given a short jail sentence. 208 were sentenced to death. No rebel was given criminal confinement, as this was reserved for deserters or thieves.

413 men and one woman were sentenced, by virtue of Article 5 of the law of 30 Prairial III, to what was usually a four-month period of detention, starting from the date of their arrest.[28] This sentence was accompanied by a stiff fine of one half of a year's income.

Of the 1,874 civilians tried by the four military courts, 334 were sentenced to capital punishment, 80 of them in absentia. The judges cited various articles of the laws of 30 Prairial in 33 cases, but more particularly the law of 29 Nivôse (90) or the Penal Codes of 1791 (8) or 1795 (19). We can see that the distinction between 'rebels' and 'bandits' is linked not so much to the nature of the accusation as to the facts retained against the accused during the hearings.

From Rebels to Bandits: Changes in the System of Repression

Finally, a comparison between the figures generated by the judicial measures and those who died in combat or were arrested.

---

27   Vincennes, SHAT 2 J 298, 24 th DM, decision of the 2nd CG n° 12427, 17 Frimaire year 7.
28   351 in the 24th DM and 34 in the 25th DM.

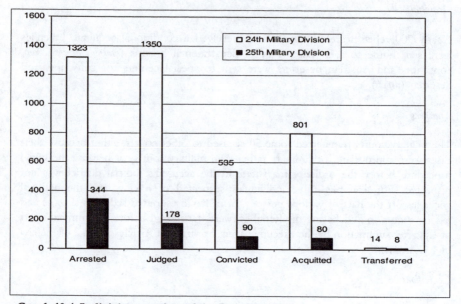

Graph 10.4 Judicial repression of the Revolts (1798)
(24th-25th Military Divisions)

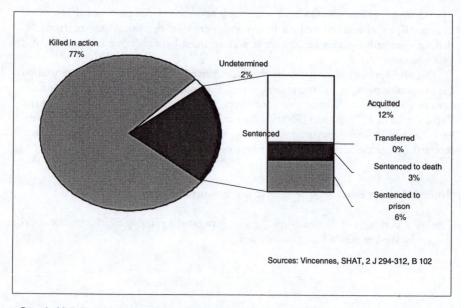

Graph 10.5 Judicial repression of the Revolts (Oct.-Nov. 1798)
(24th-25th Military Divisions)

The revolts that took place in Brumaire VII lasted less than a month and resulted in 5,638 insurgents killed, while an additional 1,667 were arrested. We know the decision of the military court for 1,528 civilians: 881 were acquitted, 174 were condemned to death (14 per cent), and 414 were sentenced to a maximum of 4 months in prison.

During the same period 346 'brigands,' including 30 women, were tried for banditry; 125, including three women, were given the death sentence; 20 others received several years of detention, comprising 40 per cent of the accused. The repression of banditry and revolt went hand in hand. Moreover, those sentenced to death for both banditry and revolt tended to come from overlapping geographic areas.

For instance, the region between Louvain, Wavre and Jodoigne was especially agitated. Henri Mouchat was sentenced to death for having been *'the principal leader of a seditious armed band, in different communes for felling the trees of liberty by shouting 'Long live the Emperor,' [having caused] the forest wardens [to be] disarmed, notably in Tourinnes-les-Ourdons, on the 15th Messidor and in Walhain Paul on the 15th Messidor last, he is also accused of theft committed with open violence (force ouverte) and violence on persons and by breaking and forcing entry (effraction tant intérieure qu'extérieure) during the months of Messidor and Thermidor last* [that is before the unrest]. *3° for having made an armed attack on the Namur mail-coach on 13 Thermidor and attempted murder on the person of Marie Albertine Strekx on the night of 25 Messidor, year 7 at her mother's farm in Latuy.'* This death sentence was therefore authorized by a complex charge. Some twenty others accused were sentenced to death or several years in irons for a series of acts of banditry that were committed in the year before the revolt, in addition to having attempted to assassinate a French light cavalryman, the local State tax-collector (*receveur des droits réunis*) and the president of the municipality of Jodoigne.[29] Not surprisingly, this region had been the home base of Charles of Loupoigne, a bandit whose image has received ambiguous treatment from the historiographers of the 'Peasants' War.' Several of his accomplices were acquitted by the criminal court in Dyle on 15 Fructidor, V,[30] and he himself finally died in an ambush led by the French troops in year V (1796-1797).

A systematic analysis of the correspondence held in the archives of the ordinary courts confirms the climate of insecurity that had reigned since the occupation in year III (1794). Considering this troubled context, the revolt could be said to have put the match to an already highly explosive situation.

Rebels or Bandits: A 'Peasants' War' or a War of Myths?

The quantitative analysis, the profile of the events, the vocabulary and the text invoked in support of the repression, produced a multi-facetted representation of crime and 'criminal' figures for the authorities.

---

29   Vincennes, SHAT, 2 J 299, 24th DM, n° 23058.
30   Brussels (State Archives), Archives du Tribunal criminel de la Dyle, 238, 15 Fructidor 5. Erik Martens and G. Janssens de Varebeke, *Cousin Charles de Loupoigne. Dernier défenseur de l'Ancien Régime. Commandant de l'Armée Belgique*, Leuven, 1994.

Representations in the Thick of Events

These mythic representations were constructed in the very thick of the 1798 revolt. One thinks in particular of the 1,400 acquitted or given short sentences who went home and diffused their linguistic and subjective – and thus cultural – interpretations of the 'trial.' One also thinks of the thousands of placards posted around the towns and villages of the departments affected by the uprising.

The myth was also transmitted through the language of the laws. The rapid merging of the rebels of 1798, the Vendeans of 1793 or the Chouans of 1793-1799 in legal discourse can be seen in Article 3 of the law of 30 Prairial III. The expression 'Belgian Vendée' is used in administrative correspondence as early as 10 Frimaire IV (1 December 1795), in a letter from General Songis, who specifies the source of the account and minimizes its importance:

> ... from what people say, a rather large band of well-armed bandits filled the forest and forbade all entry, it was a second Vendée, even worse than the first, in view of the present situation of our armies along the Rhine. (...) having seen everything and according to the report of the military commanders (officiers généraux), I am persuaded that the outcry and purported fears were but exaggerations created maliciously and by the aristocracy, athirst with the desire to see them come true in order to run down the government and cause an overly credulous people to rise up against it (...) I am convinced that these bandits who threatened the whole country with invasion were no more than men without an estate, accustomed by character to an idle do-nothing life, who were forced by extreme wretchedness first to steal grain and firewood, and when emboldened by success and impunity to take merchandise and to commit violent acts.[31]

By sentencing the majority of the participants on the basis of the law of 29 Nivôse rather than the law of 30 Prairial, the military judges reinforced the equation of 'the rebel as equal to the bandit.'

The controversial image of the bandit would fuel two centuries of historiographic debates. It fuses into a single character the figure of the rebel (peasant, Catholic, loyal to the Austrian Emperor, to his parish, 'a threat to the Republic'), and that of the bandit, an individual considered a threat to anyone who owns anything, especially rural landowners, and the (French) Republic.

A 'View of the Vanquished': The Fate of the Myth in Belgium (1830-2000)

The resurgence of the myth based on the repression of the revolt rests on several factors.

For Belgium and Luxembourg, recognized as independent nations in 1839, this was the first collective action and the first bloody uprising in a national context since the 16 sixteenth century.[32]

---

31 Paris, Archives Nationales (AN) BB 18 284 Dyle. Correspondance de la division criminelle du Ministère de la Justice, Letter from General Songis, 10 Frimaire IV (1st December 1795).

32 Gita Deneckere, 'De boerenkrijg in het internationaal perspectief. Een verkenning van collectieve actie op het platteland in de Franse tijd,' in François, *De Boerenkrijg...*, pp. 23-35.

With France acting as the strongest magnet for the new nation, the figure of the 1789 revolutionary and the 1795 Republican were highly evocative parallels for the élites to express themselves in French in reaction to the period of annexation by Holland (1815-1830). In this context a succession of competing historiographies emerged.

The first version appeared in the 1840s, as the witnesses were disappearing. Represented by the prominent novelist Henri Conscience (*De Boerenkrijg/ La guerre des paysans*), this historiography emphasized the uniqueness of 'Belgian' society after 1830, and within a context favorable to an independent State that was hard to 'sell' to the great powers, especially France. While there was a dominant, French-speaking, bourgeoisie, it was important to display, on the one hand, the solidity of the various components of the new nation (Flemish and Walloon populations) and, on the other, the model for the political modernization of Europe, as represented by the de facto alliance between the Catholics dominating the rural areas and the Liberals, masters of the cities with their industry and commerce within the framework of a Constitutional monarchy. The Peasants' Wars made it possible to exhibit the alliance between the bourgeoisie, the clergy, and the people under the discrete supervision of the invisible Throne.

A rival historiography developing in the context of the rise of the Flemish movement, emphasized the revolt in the Flemish countryside, accentuating the Catholic side, the role of the defiant clergy and, later, projecting onto the French occupier the role of the liberal French-speaking bourgeoisie which dominated Belgian political life until the end of the 19 nineteenth century. The 1898 Centennial saw a Flemish offensive led by the powerful cultural foundation, the *Davidsfonds*.

With the end of the Catholic-Liberal union (*Unionisme*)[33] after 1848 came a liberal historiography which stressed, on the contrary, the revolt for 'freedoms' that underscored the benefits of the model of the French State and pointed to the dangers of a return to the *Ancien Régime*.[34]

Luc François' recent book shows how, over the nineteenth century, historiography followed the twists and turns of the political debates between Catholics and Liberals, the two main components in the Belgian political elite. The events of 1798 were revisited first in the context of the School Struggle (the issue of God in the classroom). They were again revived under the Second French Empire (1852-1870), when, in light of the threat of another French 'Napoleonic' annexation, opponents to Napoleon III had taken refuge in Belgium. Additional revivals occurred: in the course of the conscription debate (1884 and 1887) and the resistance of the peasant society to militarization by the State; when the Flemish demanded that public life become more Flemish (especially the claim to a Dutch-speaking judicial system); and again in the course of social change following the industrialization of the Walloon basin that resulted in the opposition of Royalist Catholic Flemish peasants and 'Republican atheist' Walloon workers.

In the twentieth century, under German occupation (1914-1918 and 1940-1944), yet a fourth version of these events appeared; these had a nationalist, pan-Germanic

---

[33] This Catholic-Liberal alliance governed Belgium from 1830 to 1847, but was most effective before the official recognition of Belgium's independence in 1839.

[34] Hermann Pergameni, *Les guerres des paysans. Étude historique*, Brussels, 1880.

ring. Here the 'bandit' became the ethnic figure of the 'Germanic' peoples resisting the 'Latins.' The link was renewed between the Flemish peasants' 'Boerenkrijg' and the 'Kleppelkrick' of the German-speaking Luxembourg peasants.[35]

Conclusion

On 18 Brumaire in the year VIII, Bonaparte seized power. Less than two months later, the military tribunals of the 24th and 25th DM were trying the last of the 'bandits.' Seen from Paris, the pro-Bonaparte propaganda credited the Consulat, then the Empire, with restoring order. Repression of the revolt was consonant with the construction of a 'secure' society orchestrated by Bonaparte, one which depicted the General as the winner of the war on banditry. As of the 18th Brumaire, articles and books on the repression of banditry by the army, the *gendarmerie*, and the courts began appearing in the press and bookshops. Banditry justified the recourse to emergency courts and the development of the secret police and enabled the regime to speed the centralization and militarization of the populations via conscription.

Seen from the Belgian departments, the change of regime and the repression of the revolts above all signed the fate of a 'myth,' that of a return of the old regime, and signaled the advent of a new consciousness of a modern society structured by the State.

Together with the religious Pacification, the security myth perpetuated by the *gendarmerie* and the army especially enabled the regime to win the initial backing of two social groups most important to the transition from Revolution to an authoritarian regime: the urban bourgeoisie, major beneficiary of the sale of ecclesiastical property (*biens nationaux*), and the peasants newly enriched by the surge of agriculture at the end of the eighteenth century.

Alternatively, the lasting memory that grew up over the next two centuries among the descendants of the Revolution preferred a different myth: that of a 'peasant war.'

For the vanquished, this interpretation allowed them to transform a military defeat into a martyrdom. Thus supporters of the rebels chose to glorify the victims fallen in combat or shot to death, as in the case of the 'Martyrs of Mechelen (Malines)' or the deported priests. They were much less enthusiastic about those condemned by the military courts or the conscripts who left to fight in Napoleon's Europe.

For the victors, the alliance between the justice system and the army served to legitimize political repression by making the countryside safe.[36] Military justice cleverly mingled elements of liberty (temporary laws) and security (repression of violent assault), while playing down the political and cultural aspects of the revolts. The

---

[35] R. Van Roosbroeck, 'Die Bauern aufstände in den sudlichen Niederlände im Jahre 1798,' *Rheinische Vierteljahrblätter. Mitteilungen des Instituts für Geschichtliche Landeskunde der Rheinlande an der Universität Bonn*, 1937, 7, 1, pp. 328-340. F. Textor, 'Aufstansbewegung gegen die französische Fremdherrschaft (1792-1815) als Volksgeschichtliche Forschungsaufgabe,' *Zeitschrift der Deutsch-Vlämischen Arbeitsgemeinschaft*, 1938, 2, pp. 57-68.

[36] Marie-Sylvie Dupont-Bouchat, 'Les résistances à la révolution "la Vendée belge" (1798-1799): nationalisme ou religion?,' *Études sur le XVIIIème siècle, XVI: Deux aspects contestés de la politique révolutionnaire en Belgique: langue et culte*, Bruxelles, 1989, pp. 119-164.

bandit who strangled or tortured his victims, condemned for a series of violent and underhand aggressions, was a perfect candidate to stress the value of a return to law and order. By subsequently transferring the repression to the civil courts (albeit in the form of special criminal courts), the First Consul ensured the legitimacy of the new institutions – the *gendarmerie* and the public prosecutor's office, which would be major actors in the repression of collective crime in the nineteenth and twentieth centuries – in their role of maintaining order.[37]

Two centuries later, the 'view of the vanquished' has lost some of its emotional impact. The historians' bland discourse has little effect on the Rebels' descendants, and the local nature of the commemorations does little to forge mobilizing political identities. For the general public, all that remains of the myth are its commercialization and its media visibility: the 'Brigand' is a popular Belgian beer, and a famous bandit, Baekelant, has become a comic book character who is a mixture of fictional rebel and real highwayman.[38]

[37] Brown, *From Organic Society...*, pp. 661-695; H.G. Brown, 'Domestic State Violence: Repression from the Croquants to the Commune,' *The Historical Journal*, 1999, 42, pp. 597-622. Clive Emsley, *Gendarmes and the State in Nineteenth-Century Europe*, Oxford, 1999; Éric de Mari, 'Le parquet sous la Révolution. 1789-1799,' in J.M. Carbasse (ed.), *Histoire du parquet*, Paris, 2000, pp. 221-255.

[38] S. Top, *Lodewijk Bakelandt en zijn bende. Bijdrage tot de studie van de groepscriminaliteit rond 1800 voornamelijk in het Leiedepartement*, Kortemark-Handzame, 1983 (Louis Bakelandt and his band. Contribution to the study of collective crime around 1800, particularly in the Department of Lys).

Chapter 11

The Multiple Lives
of the Hungarian Highwayman

Mónika Mátay and György Csepeli

Why have Hungarians thought of highwaymen as national heroes for over two hundred years? How could they, at least at certain times and under peculiar political and social conditions, transform the negative figure of this criminal into a widely popular celebrity? This paper investigates how the Hungarian *betyár* (highwayman), a unique nineteenth-century criminal, was understood and even mystified in Hungarian culture and how he was represented in literature and the media. It attempts to show how ordinary, middle-class people, intellectuals, and journalists, constructed the figure of the *betyár*, how they infused him with emotions, and how he embodied the characteristics of a hero with different ideological ideas. We will also reconstitute the political and cultural milieus that constructed the Hungarian rural brigand as a cultural icon from the 1830s, the formative period of national revival, until the late twentieth century.

Unconscious Hero or Exploitive Brigand? Parallel Interpretations

The positive perception and interpretation of the character of the highwayman and his representation as a national hero is not only typical of Hungarian culture; it is international as well. Recently, historians have explored and contributed new interpretations, not only of the history of crime and deviant social behavior, but also of the underworld. In his pioneering and classic *Primitive Rebels* and *Bandits*, Eric Hobsbawm turned his attention to the highwayman or brigand, or, as he called him, the *'social bandit.'*[1] Brigands were vanguards of the peasantry for this Marxist British historian: they embodied, he argued, a rather primitive form of organized social protest against oppression. According to Hobsbawm, brigands did not have a consistent ideology, instead they adapted their programs in the defense or restoration of traditional order and the reestablishment of social justice. These bandits were, therefore, essentially reformers, but under specific circumstances they could be potential revolutionaries. Inspired by the values of brotherhood, equality, and

---

[1] Eric Hobsbawm, *Primitive Rebels. Studies in Archaic Forms of Social Movement in the 19th and 20th Centuries*, New York & London, 1959; see especially his chapter titled 'The Social Bandit,' pp. 13-29. See also Eric Hobsbawm, *Bandits*, London, 1969.

freedom, bandits could merge into a larger social movement and become a political force, which could, and sometimes did, change society.[2]

Hobsbawm made a sharp distinction between the peasant/social bandits and underworld criminals. Even though they were regarded by the state and state laws as simple criminals, *Social bandits* were peasant outlaws of a special kind. And within their own social environment, the peasant community, they were considered champions and heroes.[3] The peasants turned them into myth, and in return 'the bandit himself trie[d] to live up to his role, even when he (…) [was] not himself a conscious social rebel.'[4]

The career of social brigands seems to follow a fundamental pattern. They were rural outcasts, single, young, scions of peasant families, who incurred a minor infraction of the law, and ran off to the forest to avoid punishment; once there, they either joined or formed a band of outlaws. Myths about brigands, repeated over time, contain identical elements and are organized into a standard narrative: they were invulnerable, humorous, cunning and most importantly, supporters of the poor. For Hobsbawm, social banditry is the most universal and constant phenomenon of agrarian societies, the most 'amazingly uniform,' not only in the western tradition, but also in Asia and Australia.[5] Moreover, social bandits are typical representations of the pre-capitalist world and are powerless in the face of the forces of modern societies which they cannot understand; they only know how to fight modern society and seek its destruction.

Hobsbawm's image of the bandit is stereotyped, schematic and at times overly romantic. This is particularly so when it is compared to the view of the anthropologist Anton Blok, who favored a more socially based approach. In his review article of Hobsbawm, Blok claims that brigands were not champions of the poor; instead, he argues, they terrorized them, thereby contributing to their continued oppression.[6] By placing bandits into a larger and more complex social context and understanding their social relationships with their kinsmen and friends, and with peasants, lords, and the authorities, Blok asserts that highwaymen were not participants in social movements. Instead, seeking protection, they relied strongly on other people. In short, Blok rejects the idealized representation of the highwayman as an 'unconscious freedom fighter' and argues for understanding more about their living conditions and social networks, as well as the motivations of their behavior.

In her recent article on southern Italian brigandage, Marta Petrusewicz warns us against the reification of peasant brigands' political ideology.[7] In fact, she doubts if they ever had any coherent ideology or consistent political-social program. And although she criticizes Hobsbawm for overemphasizing the political and missionary roles of social bandits, Petrusewicz obscures the difference between her views and

---

2   Hobsbawm, *Bandits...*, p. 23.

3   *Ibid.*, p. 13.

4   Hobsbawm, *Primitive Rebels...*, p. 13.

5   *Ibid.*

6   Anton Blok, 'The Peasant and the Brigand: Social Banditry Reconsidered,' *Comparative Studies in Society and History*, 1972, 14, pp. 494-503.

7   Marta Petrusewicz, 'Society against the State: Peasant Brigandage in Southern Italy,' *Criminal Justice History*, 1987, VIII, pp. 1-2.

Hobsbawm's about the origins of brigandage. However, her arguments that bandits were politically and ideologically confused, that they were deeply religious, and that their rhetoric mixed republican and royalist components, are well taken. In Petrusewicz's sociological analysis, highwaymen are primarily created by poverty and ignorance, they defended traditional values, and opposed the regulative and interventionist aspects of the modern Italian state. Disillusioned peasants created and infused with legend a social bandit who was a champion and protector of the poor. 'The rise of brigandage during the nineteenth century was due not to the clash of two different ideologies,' she argues, 'but to an increase in *occasions* for conflicts between the peasant community – with its cherished values and rights, its modes of production and reproduction, and its notions of justice – and the encroaching state, which was eager to 'modernize' or transform these elements.'[8] And while brigands found the idea of the modern state alien and insignificant, they never attempted to formulate either an alternative ideology or to develop durable government institutions.

Undoubtedly, Eric Hobsbawm depicted an idealized version of the highwayman and he overemphasized his political and social role. But, if we scrutinize the ideal type of the Hungarian highwayman, the imagined *betyá*, and consider his representations, instead of attempting to establish his 'reality,' Hobsbawm's schematic model appears correct: The characteristics of the 'good bandit' he describes are congruent with the characteristics of the bandit in the universal myth.

The First Hungarian *Betyár* Celebrity

The 'true narratives,' the real stories of nineteenth-century Hungarian highwaymen, seem to be irretrievably lost. It is almost impossible to reconstruct the details of their lives, their criminal careers and miraculous deeds, and it seems foolish to search for them. Thus, attempting to apply Anton Blok's project of reconstructing the biographic elements of social bandits to the figure of the Hungarian *betyár* seems an almost futile endeavor. Available primary sources are fragmented and most of them are fictive. The existing biographies are hazy and the 'facts' of their lives are mingled with legendary details. Gamini Salgado's description of the life of the sixteenth-century British highwayman, Ratsey, is relevant here: 'His career is so thickly barnacled with legend that it is impossible to tell fact from fiction, but Ratsey appears to have been something of a Robin Hood character who robbed the well-to-do and often helped the needy.'[9] In the discussion that follows we will try to interpret the representations, not the historical 'facts.' First, however, we will provide an overview of the life of one such Hungarian figure, Sobri, based on what seems to be the most reliable biographical information.

Jóska Sobri was born József Pap in a small village, Baltavár, in Vas County, in the western part of Hungary. This son of a poor pastor was a shrewd young man, skilled at making decisions that would enable him to escape the miseries of the ordinary

---

[8]   *Ibid.*, p. 10-11.
[9]   Gamini Salgado, *The Elizabethan Underworld*, London, 1977, pp. 120-121.

pastor's life.[10] He abandoned his family in the early 1830s and shortly after he was arrested for stealing swine from a neighboring land and was imprisoned in Zirc, a small town in the Bakony Mountains. He struggled to escape and did so after two years, just before the end of his sentence. At this point Sobri began to pursue his short-lived career as a notorious *betyár.* In the mid-1830s he organized a small but well-disciplined and highly efficient group of highwaymen. Within a couple of months Sobri made a name for himself by directing the most awesome and daring plundering. The robberies that Sobri and his men carried out ended when they robbed and assaulted Antal Hunkár, the judge of the Court of Appeals. On 8 December, 1836 the band robbed the Hunkár castle; they stole precious arms and jewels, and locked up the indignant nobleman, his wife, and the servants in the cellar.

This was not the most scandalous enterprise of the band, but it had far more serious consequences than any of the previous ones. Hunkár, a pompous retired colonel, felt that the pillaging of his own house was a blow to his pride. Hunkár, of course, had both rank and reputation, and he was strong and wealthy enough to make an international scandal of the case. First, he left for Buda where he took his grievance to the Palatine of Hungary, Joseph. Not satisfied with the results of their meeting, he hastily drove to the court in Vienna where he met with Emperor Ferdinand V and attacked the authorities for being unable to cope with the exploits of a few criminals. As a former colonel of the Hungarian army during the Napoleonic wars who had rendered the Empire a service, he demanded punitive sanctions against Sobri and his men.

Thanks to this resolute gentleman, as well as to the newly emerging Hungarian national media of the 1830s, the case became national news within weeks.[11] Moreover, because of the Hunkár case, Sobri provoked the intense interest of the European public. Under the pressure of an excited and furious public, the army and the authorities wanted quick results. They placed a high price on Sobri's head and while most rural folk sympathized with the outlaws, some wanted the reward. The prosecutors followed clues provided by local residents and were soon hot on Sobri's trail. After a manhunt of just a few weeks, they easily found the highwaymen in the Lápafő woods in Tolna county. In February, 1837, a group of adventuresome noblemen led by the young and ambitious captain, Count Kesselstadt, surrounded and wounded the bandits. After a three-hour, bloody fight, most of the brigands were slaughtered. A few were captured alive while some managed to escape. Sobri's fate was later described by Mihály Kelemen, an eyewitness and the notary of Szakcsi, in his memoirs: 'When Sobri realized that he was going to be captured, he pointed his gun at

---

10   Imre Vahot, 'Sobricsalád Vasmegyében. Népismertetés' ('The Sobri family in Vas county'), in Imre Vahot, (ed.), *Magyarföld és népei eredeti képekben. Föld- és népismei, statisztikai és történeti folyóirat*, Pest, 1846, p. 14; István Békés, *Magyar ponyva Pitaval (Hungarian Pulp Fiction)*, Budapest, 1966.

11   Readers were hungry for rapid information, but contemporary journalists, and most likely, the authorities themselves, were at loss to piece together a coherent and reliable narrative. Wild rumors were fabricated about Sobri and his bandits and the Sobri myth was configured into endless narratives that incorporated magical as well as realistic components. See the reports of *Társalkodó, Hazai 's külföldi tudósítások, Erdélyi Híradó.*

the captain who was approaching him, but before firing at him, he turned it back on himself and shot himself through the heart and died instantly.'[12]

The Fabrication of the Panther of Bakony[13]

It is most likely that Jóska Pap, *alias* Jóska Sobri, died at Lápafő and his body was buried on the same evening together with other victims of the mêlée, including two gendarmes whom the bandits killed. But the only available record that actually supports this view is Kelemen's account. The highwaymen who were captured at the battle made contradictory confessions: Some of them reaffirmed that Sobri committed suicide while others suggested an alternative story line.[14] It is most likely Sobri's corpse was never identified. There are no records of the autopsy, a coroner's report was not made and the death was never officially registered. However, because of the ambiguities that surrounded his death, contemporaries as well as later authors of the Sobri myth, were hesitant to accept the report of his suicide.

Nobody wanted to believe that the star brigand was really dead. This was primarily because there were no reliable and satisfactory official reports about the confrontation and people were eager to believe fanciful rumors about Sobri's afterlife. A few years after the events in the Lápafő woods, in 1843, an enterprising publisher of dime novels found an unorthodox and clever way to keep Sobri's legend alive. He pretended that the author of the pulp fiction he circulated was Sobri himself. The title of the work was highly imaginative: 'Jozsi Sobri, the captain of brigands, a grocer, publisher, hatter and pharmacist, details about his present life in America included.' The work was actually written by Imre Vahot,[15] an illustrious journalist and editor of a faddish magazine in the 1840s who claimed to have tracked down Sobri and interviewed Sobri's father. 'Sobri the elder,' István Pap, by then seventy-five years old, tenaciously denied that he had recognized his son in the body of a brigand whom the authorities had shown to him in 1837. Later in 1848, commenting on the brigand's fate, Vahot declared: 'I think that the news about Sobri's death is a fairy tale and I believe those who say that after the collapse of his band he fled to Slavonia where he still passes as a swine-herd with a false name.'[16]

The desire to fantasize about Sobri's life after the Lápafő skirmish led to absurd fantasies. In the 1850s it was rumored among Hungarian revolutionary emigrants that he had fled Hungary and made his way to the New World where he became a pharmacist on Broadway in New York City. The poet Kálmán Tóth asserted that he

---

[12] Békés, *Magyar ponyva Pitaval* …, p. 99.

[13] Elek Vajdai, author of pulp fiction about Sobri's adventurous life applied the term, the 'panther of Bakony' to Sobri. See Elek Vajdai, *Sobri Jóska. A bakonyi betyár élete és kalandjai (Jóska Sobri. Life and Adventures of the Bakony's Highwayman)*, Budapest-Szeged, 1902.

[14] According to Béla Tóth, István Varga, a member of the *betyár* group, declared after the Lápafő fight that Sobri survived the battle (Béla Tóth, *Mendemondák. A világtörténet furcsaságai (Hearsay. Strange Stories from World History)*, Budapest, 1896, p. 130). His fellow, a certain Recze, proposed just the opposite. He stubbornly reiterated that he had seen Sobri shoot himself in the heart. *Hazai 's Külföldi Tudósítások*, 1837, 47, p. 372.

[15] *Sobri Jóska, Betyárok kapitánya…*, 1843.

[16] Vahot, 'Sobricsalád Vasmegyében…,' p. 16.

met General Kmetty, the illustrious national hero of the 1848-49 Hungarian war of independence, in London in 1862, where the general affirmed the 'American' version and provided details about the *betyár*-pharmacist's triumphant career.[17] Much later, at the end of the nineteenth century, the Sobri legend was still alive. In the late 1880s a peasant from a small village, Felsőpáty, told journalists that he had seen the legendary *betyár* in 1869, almost three decades earlier, and that he was in good health and in the company of a horse-dealer.[18]

The real and mythic components of Sobri's enigmatic story came to light in a confused amalgam during his lifetime. Sensational crime stories were a new element of the Hungarian press and the Sobri story was featured prominently. Even the international press found the story of the Hungarian brigand profitable; Sobri's exploits were splashed on the front pages of such prestigious newspapers as the *Köllner Zeitung* and the *Pennsylvania Inquirer and Daily Courier*. From the early 1840s, the Sobri myth was featured in underground literature as well as in folk plays and comedies[19] and additional details of his story were made popular in an 1858 ballet.[20] At the turn of the twentieth century, a genuine Sobri cult emerged and this legendary *betyár* became the main character of dozens of short stories, novels, plays, and even musicals, intended for both the Hungarian and foreign publics.

Presentations of Sobri's life varied greatly in terms of style and length, but all of the narratives about him contained the universal myth of the highwayman. Three versions of his origins dominated these tales. In one he was a child of a poor family; his father, Istvan Pap, was either a blacksmith, a swineherd, or a shepherd. The editor of a contemporary magazine who accepted this version also believed that István Pap was a deeply religious man who went to church daily in his native Baltavár and brought up his son accordingly.[21] A second version suggested that Sobri was a nobleman and an aristocrat, and either the son of a count or a lord lieutenant. The third suggested a romantic love story. According to this version Sobri's father was an affluent aristocrat who seduced a beautiful gypsy girl; Sobri was the illegitimate offspring of this illicit relationship.

The Noble Peasant

The various interpretations of Sobri's origins determined both the characteristics authors attributed to him, and also the motivations for his criminal career. All of the

---

17　Tóth, *Mendemondák...*, pp. 125-130. Sobri was only one of several pulp-fiction heroes who 'fled' to the New World. Transatlantic travel was a popular motif used by contemporary writers.
18　See 'Sobri él' ('Sobri is alive'), *Budapesti Hírlap*, 1887, 297, pp. 5-6.
19　See Ladislas Holics-Szekely, *Sobri, chef de brigands, d'après les Mémoires hongrois de son compatriote*, Paris and Leipzig, 1839.
20　*Vasárnapi Újság*, 1858, p. 257.
21　See *Hazai s' Külföldi Tudósítások*, 1836, 52, pp. 412-413.

narratives provided detailed physical descriptions and identified his main qualities.[22] Those who depicted Sobri as an ordinary peasant portrayed him as an astonishingly strong, astute, dauntless, cunning, and good-looking young man, a 'colossal fighter,' who was also a great rider and an excellent shooter. He was 'the hero of the woods' and 'the son of the Magyar *puszta*.'[23] Those who represented Sobri as a folk hero borrowed his character and many of his adventures from an eighteenth-nineteenth century genre, the satirical folk comedy, which was prevalent in contemporary European literature. Sobri's shrewdness, his playful behavior, and the way he cheated and ridiculed authority and the powerful sharply contrasted the feeble and helpless world of the nobility. 'The real Hungarian highwayman has always remained an authentic representative of our nation. (…) He had more noble characteristics than a coward tip-topper has these days.'[24]

The authors who depicted Sobri as a peasant provided their readers with thorough explanations of why and how their hero had given up his lawful life. The folk protagonist Sobri had always committed petty offences. Usually his friends provoked him, ridiculing him as a 'cowardly old woman' if he was reluctant to drive the herd of swine from the neighboring estate. Ultimately, in this tale he agreed to do so to show his sheer bravado and pride.[25] The other explanation for his choice of a criminal life, one that led him to violate social law, was his opposition to social injustice and poverty. Sándor Illés, in his juvenile novel, *The Youths of Bakony*, closed his eyes to Sobri's blunders: 'He is… wild and morose, but this is not his true nature, because he is filled with tenderness and love. He is gentle. He can gaze at a climbing ant, struggling butterfly, or twittering bird for hours. (…) Perhaps he would have become a painter, if he had been born somewhere else. Perhaps a poet or a writer. (…) But he turned into a bandit, because he stole a pig. He stole just because he wanted to get dressed as rich young men did.'[26]

All of these representations included repetitive elements of daring and humor. The Hungarian Robin Hood – like his foreign counterpart – was a firm friend of those who gave to the poor what they had seized from the privileged. In other words, he embodied social justice by punishing the rich and rewarding the poor. 'He considered poverty a true merit that deserved reward. (…) But he disliked the rich and abundant. (…) He tapped their fat, so that both Sobri himself and his fellow highwaymen benefited from the attacks.'[27] 'Jóska Sobri never assaulted the needy. He always robbed only priests and Jews. He was very popular among ordinary people.'[28] And

---

[22] To make it more reliable, the reporter of *Társalkodó* amused his readers with an exceptionally meticulous description: he said he was 5.7 feet tall, strong shouldered, gentle, quiet, sorrowful, and a serious young man. *Társalkodó*, 1837, 82, pp. 327-328.

[23] Lajos Reim, *Sobri Jóska a hires és rettegett bakonyi betyár élete és kalandjai (The Life and Adventures of Jóska Sobri, the Famous and Fearsome Betyár of the Bakony)*, Budapest, 1906, p. 1.

[24] Elek Patakfalvy, *Az úri betyár Sobri Jóska élete és merész kalandjai (The Life and Courageous Adventures of the Noble Highwayman, Jóska Sobri)*, Budapest, undated, pp. 4-5.

[25] Imre Sárosy, *Sobri Jóska a bakonyi rablóvezér (Jóska Sobri the Brigand Leader of the Bakony)*, Budapest, 1903.

[26] Sándor Illés, *Bakonyi legények. Sobri Jóska regényes élete (The Youths of the Bakony. Jóska Sobri's Adventurous Life)*, Budapest, 1975, p. 125.

[27] Vajdai, *Sobri Jóska...*, pp. 1-2.

[28] *Ibid.*, p. 51.

while other characters in these narratives varied, Sobri himself was always motivated by his eternal fight against social injustice. He was the tricky peasant who disguised himself and ridiculed his enemies, the privileged. He often appeared as a priest, a French nobleman, a quack, a prince, or an old peddler. Strangely, those biographers who represented him as the cunning offspring of ordinary people, often presented him as the reincarnation of the great medieval Hungarian king, Matthias. The ruler, nicknamed 'Matthias, the Just,' also liked to slip into other people's clothes to play tricks.

The Aristocratic Scion

In many bestsellers, the second depiction of Sobri made him the scion of an aristocratic family. Most authors claimed that he was the younger son of the Lord Lieutenant of Máramaros County, Ábrahám Vay. According to these representations, Sobri was either a deviant nobleman whose ennui led him to seek adventure, or whose gambling (or bankruptcy) had made him fall from his high social status and take up highway robbery. In this version he was an educated gentleman and distinct from ordinary criminals or even highwaymen. Most importantly, he was never cruel or heartless, but always genteel, elegant, eloquent and cultivated. The most preposterous tale was written by a German author[29] who claimed that Sobri was the gifted offspring of a Hungarian noble family who had been sent to study at German universities. He visited Gotha, Hannover, Holstein, and Lübeck where he devoted himself to poetry and science. Shortly, however, driven by misfortune, he broke with the law and escaped back to Hungary where he assembled his band of outlaws.[30]

The aristocratic outlaw was less concerned about social exploitation and oppression than the poor peasant Sobri. The 'noble' Sobri stories remind us of picaresque novels, where the main hero's moral calling leads him to follow principles of gentle behavior; in these tales the concept of the 'just' bandit was entirely absent.

What other components were typical of the Sobri stories? He played the role of a boorish pastor as well as an eloquent nobleman. Some biographers created a somewhat fashionable dictator, Jóska Sobri. At the beginning of these works (either in the introduction or on the first pages) the authors provided their readers with detailed and thorough descriptions of his appearance and his clothing. We have the impression that before he took any action, this handsome young man had preened for hours. But whether he was presented as the aristocrat or the swineherd, Sobri always paid particular attention to his outfit. In those tales where Sobri was the poor boy trying to flee poverty he was often tempted to evil by attractive clothes: with his first stolen money he acquired an appealing coat, endearing pants, or pretty arms. As one of the

---

29 Cited by *Társalkodó*, 1837, 82, pp. 234-236.
30 Interestingly, this story is almost identical to the biography of another national hero of the late nineteenth century, István Hatvani. Hatvani was a professor of chemistry in the famous Protestant college of Debrecen in the eighteenth century. Wild mysterious stories were fabricated about Hatvani during his lifetime and even more after his death. The funny, but at times rather bloody and brutal stories, earned him the famed nickname of the 'Hungarian Faust.'

authors, Elek Vajdai, has remarked: 'Jóska Sobri was a real Prince of Wales of contemporary fashion.'[31]

The highwayman's distinguished clothing served several functions in the stories. On the one hand, the leader of the group had to be better looking and more ostentatious than other bandits. On the other hand, the handsome outfit supported the image of the attractive and macho Sobri. These characteristics were fundamental elements of the story and were especially important because romantic love was an important aspect of the saga. The legendary brigand always found time and energy for romance, even in the midst of some daring activity or when he was about to be captured. Sobri, whether depicted as an ordinary peasant or as a distinguished aristocrat, was always represented as a 'ladies' man.' And whether as a faithful or faithless lover, his amorous relations were emphasized. With ladies and maids alike, he was gallant and polite, a real chevalier.

Jóska Sobri carried out his breath-taking adventures surrounded by faithful friends and evil opponents. And while his motivations varied and were largely determined by his origins, his supporters, persecutors, and victims remained the same. At this point the logic of the stories faltered somewhat; but he was always the 'noble brigand' who held off the 'blood-suckers of the Hungarian nation, the despotic landlords and the profiteering Jews' as well as the supporter of the poor.[32] Although it is hardly surprising that Sobri always robbed from the rich, from those he could acquire something, his enemies (regardless of his origin) were always the enemies of the people: 'parasitic' priests, Jews, and those who were outside of the feudal social structure, including 'idle' noblemen, and 'outlandish' and unreliable Germans. In contrast, Sobri's primary supporters were 'the people,' peasants as well as other ordinary men. And his main persecutor was the 'gendarme, the foolish and vile intimidator,' who had been an evergreen opponent of the brigand.

The authors of these legends frequently integrated miracles, or at least profound exaggeration, into their stories. They described Sobri as a mythic, invulnerable figure. As Vajdai remarked: 'None of the numerous bullets that were shot at him hit the captain (Sobri).'[33] Another author argued that he was able to become invisible, and that he had a gun that never missed its target.[34] After his release from the prison of Zirc he organized his *betyárs* within a week, an impossibly short period. And within a few days Sobri and his group were known as the most dreaded bandits in Hungary.[35] According to several descriptions, Sobri's group was more than a simple gang; it was an army of hundreds of well-disciplined soldiers whose leaders could even provide their men with medical care.[36]

In some of the short stories and novels, Sobri broke out of his traditional role as 'the people's friend' or the gallant aristocrat and became a hero of the Wild West. Elek

---

31 Vajdai, *Sobri Jóska...*, p. 55 .
32 Patakfalvy , *Az úri betyár...*, p. 5.
33 Vajdai, *Sobri Jóska...*, p. 106.
34 Elek Mihályi, *Sobri Jóska a híres rablóvezér élete és kalandjai (Jóska Sobri the Famous Brigand Leader's Life and Adventures)*, Vienna, undated, p. 62.
35 István Dienes, *A betyárbecsület vagy Sobri Jóska a Bakonyerdő királya (The Betyár's Honour or Jóska Sobri, the King of Bakonyerdő)*, Budapest, 1924.
36 See *Társalkodó*, 1837, 82, pp. 327-328.

Mihályi's gigantic work, a 1500 page long series of popular tales (similar to dime novels or stories), is exceptional in its flood of the more conventional Sobri legends. Mihályi attempted to fulfill the expectations of his contemporary reading public and his hero was a more complex figure than the ones created by his fellow authors. His Sobri, far from being the familiar, and generous gallant, was instead part merciless warrior, part romantic lover, and part Hungarian patriot who fashioned himself as an even more fantastic and dangerous adventurer; he was a late-nineteenth century James Bond. Mihályi delighted his readers with terrible images and scenes: we hear about a rotten corpse on the hanging tree, or a woman in labor who was beaten by a soldier. And horizons of the stories are broadened as Sobri makes forays into ever more exotic places. He traveled across the Carpathian basin, amused himself in the Prater of Vienna, then, with his lover and friends, he made his way to the New World, where he became alternately a planter, a slave liberator, and ultimately, a white hero in the war against native Americans.

The most enigmatic constituent of the Sobri legend was his mysterious death or 'disappearance.' Different authors invented different endings as solutions for their stories. Some tales suggested suicide since, their authors argued, only Sobri himself was capable of ending his life. They told of the dramatic defeat of his gang by the treasonous Lápafő, and in this context portrayed Sobri's suicide as a heroic and tragic act. Other writers tried to excite their readers' fantasy with tales of their leader's inscrutable disappearance. This version, in which Sobri was portrayed as an extraordinary adventurer, was plausible to readers who believed that because of his noble origins, Sobri could easily reintegrate himself into an upper-class world.

The Background of the Myth

Since Sobri adaptations were written over a long period of time – from the 1830s until the end of the twentieth century – the figure of *betyár* has served different ideological purposes. In the early period he primarily was embodied as a national hero who struggled against the institutions of the hostile and alien Hapsburg state. After the compromise of 1867, in the context of improved relations between Austria and Hungary, Sobri's anti-Hapsburg sentiments were emphasized less. At this point, writers turned Sobri into a symbol and champion of traditional ancient national values. Despite his fierce fights against the institutions of the state, Sobri was represented as one who had always been loyal to the king: 'He cheered the country, the king, and the people.'[37] He became the true Magyar *betyár*, who has endured as the representative of the Hungarian nation. These stories sought to establish Sobri's innocence by lacing the account of his life with permanent struggle against the enemies of Magyars. As time passed, the authors' rhetoric became more chauvinistic and at times, anti-Semitic. In this version, '(T)he true Hungarian *betyár* had never been persecuted by law or been driven by ignoble greed, but had taken up highwaymen's life because of an unhappy love or quarrels with his parents. Most importantly, he was driven by his ancient Hungarian warrior blood and adventurous nature. He robbed the traditional enemies

---

[37]   Mihályi, *Sobri Jóska...*, p. 194.

of Hungarians, especially the shark Jews.'[38] During the socialist period, writers for young people set Sobri's biography in historic times. Here the brigand was the son of exploited serfs and peasants, and despite his immoral actions, he was regarded as an active, although rather unconscious, participant in the class struggle. Undoubtedly, in the eyes of the socialist writer, this character had revolutionary potentials: 'What would happen, if this Sobri, supported by thousands and thousands of highwaymen… drove the Austrian dandies into the corner? What would happen if he broke the big mirrors of elegant palaces?'[39]

Writers avoided discussing Sobri's moral responsibilities. They admitted that his actions had been illegal, but they contended that in a country without sovereignty the laws were not legitimate either. The fact that most of Sobri's enemies were opponents of the Hungarian nation neutralized the immoral nature of his crimes. He was not an ordinary outlaw. He belonged in the Hungarian Pantheon, because in his own peculiar way, he advanced Hungary's freedom and independence. At the same time that he became a national hero, he was also a prominent figure in the class struggle against exploitation and oppression. Of course, even these Hungarian authors followed the rhetoric traditional to the international literature about highwaymen. Remarkably, these characteristics remained unchanged for over one hundred and fifty years. The writer of a conservative, if not anti-Semitic, dime novel used explanations like those of his militant-socialist colleagues.

What were the factors behind the emergence of the powerful *betyár* image in the 1830s? How could Jóska Sobri become the hero of the time? First, contemporary narratives turned him into a romantic figure. He embodied the natural subject for the romantic writer using hyperbolic language, strong emotions, and moral polarities that first appeared in Hungary in the new dramatic forms of the 1820s and 1830s. The *betyár*'s life was the typical subject matter of romantic literature. These were the decades of national revival in Hungary and Hungarian cultural nationalism, unlike its Western counterparts, put strong emphasis on national historic heroes. And, regardless of their social status, the emerging Hungarian public turned Sobri into a national champion. Second, he earned this stature because of his conflicts with the state and with the law, aspects considered alien by Hungarians still under Hapsburg control. And third, to those abroad, thanks primarily to the intense anti-Magyar propaganda of the Hapsburgs, the *betyár* was seen as the bloodthirsty descendent of Attila's barbarous Huns. In the European press it was even rumored that Hungarian highwaymen robbed and killed all foreign travelers; thus well informed journalists advised the public to avoid visiting the dangerous Hungarian provinces.

What makes Sobri's case unique is the fact that his scandalous affairs stirred up multiple discourses in both Hungarian and international media. He was the cruel brigand, the cavalier, the warrior of class struggle, and the rural hero, all at the same time. The Sobri stories had multiple functions since they both served and supported national as well as vulgar Marxist ideologies. As opposed to many heroes who lost their fame and prestige over time, Jóska Sobri maintained his lofty historical position. In addition, he paved the way for later heroes who identified with the highwaymen's role and who, in so doing, revived the legend of the *betyár*. In the following sections

---

[38] Sárosy, *Sobri Jóska…*, p. 42.
[39] Illés, *Bakonyi legények…*, p. 204.

we will examine why and how this was possible, even in late twentieth-century Hungary. As we shall see, many of the aspects of the original story were repeated. This reincarnation was possible because one young man consciously constructed a self-image that followed and copied the actions of his predecessor. Post-communist Hungary provided the perfect setting for the renewal of this ancient myth.

The Highwayman as 'Whisky Robber'

One hundred and sixty years later a series of undetected bank robberies stirred up public opinion in Hungary. Between 1993 and 1999, twenty-seven bank robberies were committed by an unknown man who came to be identified as the 'whisky robber.' His name referred to the story that he drank a shot of liquor before committing a crime. This was the only information the authorities (or the public) knew about him. Nevertheless, he was able to present himself as a real personality, a gentleman who robbed without any real motivation. His behavior was refined, he was elegant and gallant. When he completed his robbery, he presented bouquets of flowers to the women cashiers. Although he had weapons, he was never brutal or aggressive. His polite behavior and well spoken demeanor refuted the general assumptions about a bank robber. And while he acted alone at first, he eventually was joined by a friend. As it turned out, his friend was poorly chosen.

He was smart, with a good sense of humor. Once he masqueraded himself as the chief of the Department of Robberies for the Budapest Metropolitan Police. He committed robbery like an engineer building a bridge; his actions were always meticulously planned and every detail was anticipated with split-second accuracy. He knew that he must complete every act within three minutes; after the fourth, alarms would go off and police officers would arrive. Finally, in 1999 the events ended. On a murky afternoon, after a successful job, his accomplice was caught.

Reason should have led him to immediately flee abroad. He knew information traveled slowly through the communication network of the impoverished, post-socialist police. Passion, however, was stronger than reason. And before he attempted to flee across the border, he returned home to see his beloved dog, losing time that allowed him to be betrayed by his friend and accomplice. The police at the frontier were alerted, and he was caught. However, the robber's tale was not over yet.

In the next act of this drama, the robber presented himself as the inheritor of the noble *betyár* tradition. Using information about his eccentricity, the media transformed him into a popular hero. First they revealed his name, but more importantly, they told the story of his life, a story based on carefully selected facts. One commercial station even devoted a special program to him. He agreed to give interviews for a book to be written about his character and exploits. There were plans to produce a film about him. All was ready to create a new popular hero.

Who was the whisky robber? His name was Attila Ambrus. He had two personal characteristics that facilitated the myth about him. First, he was born in Transylvania on 6 October 1967, and 6 October is an important date in Hungarian history. Second, on that date in 1849 thirteen Hungarian generals were executed by the Austrians and turned into martyrs. Third, Transylvania itself is regarded as a holy land for Hungarians (like Kosovo for the Serbs). Fourth and finally, his first name, Attila conjured up associations with Attila, the Hun who is still considered a national hero by Hungarians.

Attila, the man identified as the 'whisky robber' was brought up by his grandmother and aunt. Before the Romanian revolution, Ambrus, an ice hockey player, moved to Hungary where he became one of the stars of the ice hockey team of the Újpest Sport Club, sponsored by the Ministry of Interior. He lived modestly at first, but soon bought an expensive flat and car, and rumors spread about his gambling habits.

After his arrest Attila Ambrus, eager to increase interest in himself, staged a successful prison escape. He climbed over a wall of four meters, despite the permanent monitoring of a security camera, and miraculously made his way to the third floor of the adjacent office building. There he broke down a door, blocked the entrance to the room, and removed the window bars. Then, dangling on a telephone cable, he reached the first floor and simply ran away.

The official response to the escape was no surprise. The Minister of Interior Home Affairs, Sándor Pintér stated: 'all I would ask of the media and the press is that they ask the people who were the victims of these robberies. Ask the people he threatened with his gun, the people who were present when he fired bullets into the walls shooting past their ears, the people whose money he took. He stole over 130 million Forints (approximately 650,000 US Dollars).'[40] Pintér's words, however, were not appreciated. Journalists as well as the public remembered that the minister himself had been involved in scandals; he had been accused of having connections with the Hungarian Mafia and had been connected to a series of bombing in 1998 that facilitated an election victory for his party.

There was an outburst of public sympathy for Attila Ambrus in Hungary. His lawyer became a celebrity. He argued that Attila Amburs had confessed to the robberies but that he had become depressed after learning that he would also be charged with attempted murder and illegal use of a gun. The lawyer also asserted that the police had initially offered the whisky robber better prison accommodations and the opportunity to write his autobiography, neither of which was actually granted.

The whiskey robber's fame grew in the summer of 1999. Opinion polls demonstrated that the robber's popularity was almost equal to that of the president of the republic. In addition, the police's efforts to catch Ambrus were ridiculed, and it was clear that the public sided with the fugitive (in a telephone poll conducted in August 1999, three quarters of the respondents said that they were rooting for Ambrus).

Vendors hawked mugs and T-shirts with his name, and fans set up a special Web site for him. While he was in prison, Ambrus published his memoirs which were an immediate success. During this time the government had established a special office to enhance and polish the international image of Hungary as a prosperous post-socialist country and to establish Hungary as the forerunner among post-socialist countries in the transition from state-socialism to a democratic, market economy. But it was the case of Attila Ambrus which drew the attention of the international press. One American media enterprise was even willing to buy the movie rights to his story; a German company even asked him to promote its new energy drink. A series about

---

[40] *Magyar Nemzet*, 22 July 1999.

the case and interviews in the *Budapest Sun* appeared in the *Christian Science Monitor, The Independent* and the *Deutsche Welle* in Cologne.[41]

Why did the Hungarian population continue to regard a bank robber accused of 28 crimes as a national hero? To understand this phenomenon, we would like to offer three explanations: 1) an historical explanation; 2) a social-psychological explanation; and 3) a socio-economic explanation.

1) No doubt the endurance of the *betyár* myth contributed to the popularity of Attila Ambrus. Earlier in this paper we argued that the myth of Jóska Sobri, the *betyár*, was a powerful means of delegitimizing political power. Attila Ambrus was able to exploit the legacy of this myth. He presented himself as a noble minded, generous, and courageous man who threatened only the state, not the people. There was no independent Hungarian state between 1526 and 1918. The interwar years and the subsequent state socialist period were characterized by authoritarianism and Hungarians were subjects rather than citizens. The post-socialist period was too recent to change this deep-seated, negative attitude about the state. Distrust of the state and of its institutions persisted.

2) According to Fritz Heider, who posits a social-psychological theory of cognitive balance, such a balanced cognitive state exists if P dislikes O, and their attitudes toward X are not in harmony.[42] Let us assume that in the case under review, P=Public, O=Police, and X=Attila Ambrus. During the socialist decades, the Hungarian police gained a reputation for stupidity and ruthlessness and they were simultaneously feared and ridiculed. Post-socialist police tried to change this attitude, and they declared that their function was to 'serve and defend.' Nevertheless, the gulf between this declaration and reality has persisted. The police hated Ambrus and according to this theory, the enemy of the police became highly sympathetic to the public.

3) After the police, the most despised institution in contemporary Hungary has been the banks. Banks and their directors collectively symbolize the worst aspects of the post-socialist transition. Sociological studies have shown that throughout Eastern European citizens are suspicious of the rich.[43] In these studies, hard work and intelligence were understood to be the least likely source of wealth; dishonesty and the use of networks were considered the most likely. Bank directors have been perceived as ex-members of the Communist *nomenklatura*. Before 1989 many of these networks were still important to the country's economy, but after privatization in 1999, they were increasingly perceived as a special form of theft. In 1999, with the support of the new government, the police launched criminal proceedings against Gábor Princz, the former president of *Postabank*, the second largest bank in Hungary. The government alleged that his abuse of power cost the state 158 billion Forints (approximately 754 million US Dollars). Earlier in 1999, a Hungarian weekly revealed that *Postabank* had given some politicians cut-rate loans and interest above market rates on deposits. The widespread belief that most members of the political, economic, and cultural elite are little more than licensed criminals only boosted the popularity of Ambrus. In

---

[41]　At the time, one of the authors of this paper, a social psychologist, received many inquiries about the case from the international press.

[42]　Fritz Heider, 'Attitudes and cognitive organization,' *Journal of Social Psychology*, 1946, 21, pp. 107-112.

[43]　Antal Örkény, *Hétköznapok igazsága (Everyday Truth)*, Budapest, 1996.

Brechtian terms, the whiskey robber's popularity in post-socialist Hungary could be explained by the ironic suggestion that founding a bank is far worse than robbing one.

Epilogue

On 28 October, 1999 the police finally caught the 'whisky robber,' ending his three months of freedom following his escape from prison. He had continued to rob banks during this period, with the last robbery of 47 million Forints occurring on 18 October. He lost his temper during this final event and, regressing into the traditional behavior of a bank robber, shot a policeman and also injured himself. The police, who had established a hot line and offered a reward of five million Forints to anyone who could provide a clue to the 'whiskey robber's' whereabouts, were informed and sent special commando units to surprise the modern *betyár* that evening in a friend's apartment. He had been betrayed again.

Because of the increasingly brutal style of his final robberies, Ambrus's popularity had already declined. Once he became an 'ordinary' robber he lost his fame and prestige and was no longer regarded as the 'new Sobri.' In May, 2000 he was sentenced to 15 years' imprisonment.

The reincarnation of Jóska Sobri in the person of Attila Ambrus proves the endurance of the *betyár* myth in Hungary. As long as this myth survives, it demonstrates the continuing tension between the Hungarian state and its citizens. Moreover, it exemplifies the persistence of historical patterns in a political culture which has not yet come to terms with the conflicts and tensions of the present. Both Sobri and Ambrus are our contemporaries; it was difficult to live without such figures in the past and it would be difficult to live without them today.

Chapter 12

From Old Cap Collier to Nick Carter; Or, Images of Crime and Criminal Justice in American Dime Novel Detective Stories, 1880-1920

Wilbur R. Miller

Dime novels, paperback thrillers first published in 1860, were one of the first forms of American mass-circulation literature. Descendants of serialized story papers dating back to the 1840s, their first mass audience was Civil War soldiers. The plots of the dime novels were familiar to readers of higher-priced fiction, thrown into bolder relief and stripped of all dilemmas of the soul. Their cheap price (originally a dime, later a nickel) reflected the concern of their writers and publishers to sell as many copies as possible and also made them readily available to segments of the population who might not have the means or time to do much reading. Content, which was often drawn from newspaper crime reporting and other contemporary accounts,[1] was selected for its popular appeal and its resonance with popular attitudes and imagery. And since they reflected popular attitudes, the novels in turn reinforced them in the minds of readers already prepared by earlier reading experiences with gothic novels, and penny newspaper sensational crime stories, as well as with 'blood and thunder' theatrical productions.

The tales of adventure in dime novels emphasized action and danger in settings colored by romanticism and sensationalism. Reading one carried the reader along with the sweep of the action; mental pictures emerged uncomplicated by subtle meanings or complex characterization.[2] 'I was absolutely unable to stop reading,' one reader wrote a publisher, 'until I had finished it. I expected to read for an hour or so, but the situations were so dramatic and exciting at the end of each chapter, that before I knew it I had started the next one. I have read it three times, once while practicing exercises on the piano, and shall read it again.'[3] Not surprisingly, dime novels faded in

---

[1]   Michael Denning, *Mechanic Accents: Dime Novels and Working-Class Culture in America*, London-New York, 1987, pp. 17 and 22.

[2]   Charles N. Harvey, 'The Dime Novel in American Life,' *The Atlantic*, July 1907, p. 44.

[3]   Ad for *Macon Moore, the Southern Detective* on back cover of *Old Sleuth, Life in New York; or, Thrilling Detective Tales*, Old Sleuth's Own series 83, c. 1897. Since a new title came out each week, this response was perfect for the publishers who wanted the reader to read quickly and buy the next title. Also, of course, the drama at the end of each chapter reflects the technique of serialized novels.

popularity as movies gained during the 1920s, although they left direct descendants in the form of 'pulp' westerns and detective stories.

Although they could not keep up with the appeal of movies, dime novels changed with changing times. The earliest ones were tales of pioneers, revolutionary heroes, and cowboys and Indians or bandits. During the 1870s they shifted their focus to confrontations between detectives and criminals. Probably an immediate impetus for this change was the publication of Allen Pinkerton's memoirs of detective adventures, which first appeared at this time. Instead of purveying an agrarian ideal as the earlier dime novels had,[4] these new works became part of the literature of revelation and criticism of urban life. The transition from Indians and bandits to urban criminals was smooth, as the action – violence and the chase – remained the same. The West continued to be used as a setting for dime novels, but it became merely a stage for the activities of detectives, sometimes from New York, who fought miscellaneous criminals.[5] Just as Eastern urban ways were reaching into the real West, so they came to dominate the dime novels. As such, they embodied a composite of the urban literature that became significant at the end of the 1860s: One form was the documentary of city life, 'Sunshine and Shadow' or 'Daylight and Gaslight' descriptions of the pleasures and pitfalls of the metropolis; the other, which often echoed these same themes, was the Horatio Alger success story based on the hero's 'luck, pluck, and decency' in struggling to escape poverty, degradation and deceit.

Readership

Who were the readers of dime novels? Contemporaries sometimes described readers of the 'lower classes,' but they worried most about the thrillers' impact on children or adolescents of all classes, fearing that the sensational stories would corrupt the nation's youth.[6] One publisher, Frank Tousey, decided to orient his dime novels exclusively toward adolescents in 1878.[7] Indeed, in 1883 the Postmaster General forced Tousey to stop publishing stories featuring outlaw heroes, Deadwood Dick and Jesse James, in series priced at five cents and explicitly aimed at boys.[8] On the other hand, Michael Denning has argued that 'the bulk of the dime novel audience were young workers, often of Irish or German ethnicity, in the cities and mill towns of the North and West, and (...) dime novels and story papers made up most of their reading.' He argues that many novels featuring 'honest mechanic' heroes expressed the virtues of the 'producing classes': self-respect, independence, dignity of labor, mutual aid through organization.[9] This is not surprising, considering that young working men were the eager readers of the penny press, probably the *Police Gazette*

---

[4] Henry Nash Smith, *Virgin Land: the American West as Symbol and Myth*, Cambridge (Mass.), 1950, chs. IX, p. X.

[5] Denning, *Mechanic Accents*, p. 204.

[6] E.g. William McCormick, 'The Dime Novel Nuisance,' *Lend a Hand*, V, April, 1890, p. 253; W.H. Bishop, 'Story-Paper Literature,' *The Atlantic*, XLIV, September, 1872, p. 385; Anna L. Dawes, 'The New Dangers of Sensational Fiction,' *The Critic*, XIII, Dec. 8, 1888, p. 281.

[7] Charles Bragin, *Dime Novels; Bibliography, 1860-1928*, Brooklyn (NY), 1938, pp. 8-9.

[8] Denning, *Mechanic Accents*, pp. 159-160.

[9] *Ibid.*, p. 45, and chs., pp. 7-10.

without which no saloon was complete, as well as the major audience for 'blood and thunder' melodramas. Denning does not say that workers were the only readers. It could be possible that adolescents of both classes shared an interest in dime novels, but middle-class boys grew up to move on to 'serious' reading, or at least considerably more expensive hard-cover novels, while workers retained their taste for inexpensive forms of sensationalism. Since manual workers began their occupations during adolescence, the overlap could also reflect the fact that adolescence is the phase in the life cycle in which middle-class and working-class people have the most in common.[10] Dime novel 'libraries' or series aimed at youths and adults coexisted throughout the later nineteenth century. Denning does say, that with the 1891 advent of Nick Carter, 'The Young Detective,' (at age twenty-four a young adult) and Frank Merriwell, a college football player, both youthful, clearly Anglo-Saxon heroes, working-class readership declined in favor of middle-class youths.[11]

Whatever the class base of dime novel readership, readers of the detective genre seem to have been overwhelmingly masculine. Occasionally there are female heroes, as in 'Lady Kate, The Dashing Female Detective,' or 'The Girl Detective,' though women are more common as partners or assistants. A story of a 'lady detective,' published in 1885, describes the heroine as 'placed in an essentially unfeminine position (…) and more than holding her own with desperate law-breakers without any sacrifice of her womanly attributes.'[12] Such a heroine could easily have been one of the horse-wrangling, pistol-packing ladies of the western stories. Women also often appeared as villains, such as the evil Kate Davis in a story featuring Old Sleuth, the first of the professional dime novel detectives, supposedly modeled on the famous Allan Pinkerton.[13] Generally though, the world of dime detectives was overwhelmingly male.

A Dubious Hero

Whether they were fictional characters intended for adolescents and young men, or real life operatives, many people considered detectives very dubious heroes. Because their profession necessitated close association with the underworld, some critics believed that the detective's character would inevitably be tarnished (If he sometimes has to dress and acts like a criminal, how can we tell if he is really honest?). The detective was a quintessential urban figure, stalking amid the confidence men and painted women in a world where nothing was what it seemed. If police detectives were suspected of colluding with criminals (as some did), private detectives, like other entrepreneurs, sometimes cared more about making money than securing the triumph

---

10 This generalization is based purely on my own observation that middle-class teenagers readily adopt 'lower class' culture of dress and music, such as ragtime, rock and roll, and rap.

11 Denning, *Mechanic Accents*, pp. 204-206; Gary Hoppenstand, *The Dime Novel Detective*, Bowling Green (Oh.), 1982, p. 182.

12 *Ibid, p.* 194, quoting an 1890 ad for *The Lady Detective.*

13 In his war with Kate and assorted other villains, Sleuth employs his assistant Maggie. *Old Sleuth, Badger & Co.*, OSL 59, Dec. 17, 1891. Sigmund A. Lavine, *Allan Pinkerton, America's First Private Eye*, New York, 1963, p. 23.

of virtue and justice. One shady practice, which the famous Pinkerton Agency vowed it never condoned, was spying on people to gather evidence of infidelity for divorce cases. And some detectives engaged in outright fraud. One individual swindled from $10 to $200 from gullible people by pretending to appoint them private detectives and presenting them with elaborately engraved certificates (a New York Police detective arrested him).[14] An explorer of the New York underworld who expressed contemporary attitudes was critical of detectives in general, but most of all of private detectives.

> The word detective, taken by itself, implies one who must descend to questionable shifts to attain justifiable ends; but with the prefix of private, it means one using a machine permitted to the exigencies of justice for the purpose of surreptitious personal gain...
> It is difficult to deny that as an institution they are wholly unnecessary and evil in their influence.[15]

The dime novel heroes were always private detectives, establishing the dominant trend in American detective fiction until 'police procedurals' became popular in the mid-twentieth century. In the context of these views about private detectives, dime heroes were, almost by definition, dubious moral influences on their readers.

Were the dime novel detective stories really immoral? Did they glorify deceit and violence? My reading of a sample of fifty-six stories from each year between 1880 and 1920,[16] suggests that although they operated on the margins of respectable society and donned disguises routinely as part of their profession, the detective characters emerge not as defiers of conventional morality but rather as purveyors of a pessimistic view of city life. They were liminal figures, moving freely between the normally impenetrable boundaries of social class. They knew the underside of all class experiences, from the highest to the lowest.[17] The image of the city as a place of danger and guile is a familiar nineteenth-century middle-class view of urban life. Images of the city where the surface always hid dangers and gentlemanly men and ladylike women could not be judged by appearance alone permeate literature of warning and advice, from police officials' memoirs to sermons.[18] If school readers like the famous McGuffey's (and later improved versions) expressed certainty about the universal victory of good and the simple need to embody moral traits to succeed, then the dime novels presented a

[14]   Augustine E. Costello, *Our Police Protectors: History of the New York Police from the Earliest Period to the Present Time*, New York, Published for the Police Pension Fund, 1885, p. 426.

[15]   Edward Crapsey, *The Netherside of New York; or, the Vice, Crime, and Poverty of the Great Metropolis*, Hartford (Conn.), 1872, pp. 56 and 66-67.

[16]   The fifty-six dime novels are from the New York Public Library's Beadle Collection, which holds hundreds of titles. The sample includes at least one title from every year. The author will provide a full list on request, or it is available in his M.A. thesis, 'The Dime Novel Nuisance,' M.A. Thesis, Columbia University History Department, 1966, available at the Columbia University library.

[17]   Amy Gilman Srebnick suggested this idea of the detective's liminality (comments on version of this paper presented at the Social Sciences History Association conference, November 16, 2001).

[18]   For the danger of appearances, see Karen Halttunen, *Confidence Men and Painted Women: a Study of Middle-Class Culture in America, 1830-1870*, New Haven (Ct), 1982. Inspector Thomas Byrnes' *Professional Criminals of America*, New York, 1886, is full of mug shots of well-dressed sharpers and thieves.

more complex reality suitable to a changing society and also reflected middle-class doubts about that society. They did not endorse evil, but reflected how difficult the fight against it could be. Though the hero always won in the end, final victory over the villainous hordes society produced was never certain.

Crime as Conspiracy

Dime novels pictured a society pervaded with crime that, because of its conspiratorial nature and widespread occurrence, was understood to be a threat to social stability. The writers of the novels expressed the doubt that crime could ever be eradicated. Although the individual criminal was invariably done in, crime continued. 'I know this world is full of crime and criminals; indeed the true state of society is appalling to one who knows all that I do,' says Old Sleuth. Continuing, he says, 'I can not stop the great tide of evil that sweeps onward, but here and there I can snatch some poor innocent victim from the black, whirling current.' Less dramatically, but with similar resignation, Nick Carter observed that an honest man is 'a rather unusual sight these days.'[19]

Although the writers considered crime a social malady, the stories do not probe its causes in the social environment. Although one author observed, '[C]rime consorts with poverty and rags, not with wealth and costly garments,' in most of the novels crime spans the whole class structure and it is the result of personal plotting and villainy.[20] Criminals are evil individuals drawn from all classes and are usually white and Anglo-Saxon. The critic, Michael Denning, has demonstrated that many dime novel heroes embody virtues of the 'producing classes,' including some who are detectives; however, those I have read do not display class consciousness. They do not expect working-class readers to sympathize with either working-class criminals or with proletarian detectives who battle bourgeois villains. They do not include the social criticism often found in their British equivalents, the 'penny dreadfuls.'[21] In this respect they follow conventional American social views.

While the detectives may be conventional, without either a working-class or even a reform perspective, the stories do not describe an unequivocal 'triumph of the wealth-based upper class over the lower class, triumph of the conservative capitalist over the radical socialist'; or even 'ultimately (...) the triumph of the utopia-evolving city over the forces of chaos.'[22] Many, if not most of the criminals are drawn from the upper classes, and the hero defeats only elements of the forces of chaos, without ever conquering them completely. The city is always able to produce more villains, and moral triumph meant winning only a battle in an eternal war.

---

19 Harlan P. Halsey, *Old Sleuth's Luck; or, Day and Night in New York*, OSL 46, Sept. 28, 1889, p. 2; *Nick Carter's Human Weapon; or, the Woman with the Branded Face* NNCW 455, Sept. 16, 1905, p. 1.

20 Albert W. Aiken, *The Spotter Detective; or, the Girls of New York*, Beadle's New York Dime Library [hereafter BNYDL] No. 27, Feb. 19, 1878, p. 18.

21 Louis James, *Fiction for the Working Class, 1830-1850, a Study of the Literature Produced for the Working Classes in Early Victorian Urban England*, London, 1963, pp. 168-169.

22 Hoppenstand, *Dime Detective*, p. 6.

In speaking of their productions as 'social and criminal revelation,' dime novels meant to describe and reveal rather than analyze and criticize.[23] Rarely did they step back to assess the significance of their narratives, but one writer's digression neatly summarizes the underlying attitude of the whole genre:

> During the last fifty years many mysterious assassinations have occurred in the great city of New York, and these mysterious murders have rarely been traced.
> The chances are that, were the truth known, it would be discovered that a large percentage of these assassinations were the outcome of some well-arranged conspiracy, deeds of blood carried out in the most ingenious manner, while seeming to be the result of some immediate incident. And again, some dramatic history may have been associated with these crimes.
> It is well known how men have led double lives through a score or more of years, and their secrets have only been disclosed when some tragic deed has crowned their misdeeds.[24]

This image of crime as pervasive conspiracy could be the prescription for the plots of thousands of dime novels; indeed it is the premise of most mystery stories. Men lead double lives. Things are never as they seem. The surface of urban life is particularly deceptive. It is by no means clear that the stories imply 'a 'good' or moral communal structure where the criminal is a hideous aberration from the norm.'[25] Instead, the criminal is inherently part of urban life.

Deception was most forcefully illustrated in a Nick Carter story. Returning from an adventure in the Orient, the hero is happy to return home to his familiar city. It is a lovely spring day; even the carriage horses seem to nod a welcome to him. He reaches his house, however, only to discover that his wife has been murdered in a particularly nasty fashion as part of a carefully engineered plot of revenge against him. Just when Carter felt at one with the city, its lurking underworld strikes most cruelly. After this personal tragedy he still has not apprehended the mastermind, and must face 'a most gigantic scheme for banding all classes of criminals together in the form of a trust.'[26]

The Individual Against the Organization

The dime novel detective is a classic American figure of the late nineteenth century: the individual battling the organization. Before the turn of the century criminal organizations were hierarchical, serving the complex purposes of upper-class villains who recruited members of the lower classes to do their dirty work. The organization itself is formed around the personal aims of its leaders and simply does their bidding.

23 Aiken, *The Wolves of New York: or, Joe Phenix's Greatest Hunt*, BNYDL 161, Nov. 29, 1881, p. 2.
24 Harlan P. Halsey, *Mephisto; or, the Razzle-Dazzle Detective*, Old Sleuth Library [hereafter OSL] 84, March 18, 1899, p. 3.
25 Hoppenstand, *Dime Detective*, p. 4.
26 *The Little Giant's Double; or, the World's Two Strongest Men*, New Nick Carter Weekly [hereafter NNCW], p. 384, May 7, 1904, throughout and p. 28 (ad for no. 385, which was not available to me). Carter's wife was killed by the villains who tied her to a dining room chair and forced a tube connected to the gas chandelier into her throat; they then left the lamp on but not lit.

Often the leaders were involved in swindling plots, frequently adopting the classic gothic novel motif of disinheriting rightful heirs. Around the turn of the century the criminal organization in these works becomes more professional and crime becomes a full-time business rather than merely the plotting of individuals for strictly personal goals. The distance between the organization's leaders and followers is narrowed; it becomes like an actual urban gang, engaged in more prosaic activities like forgery, safe cracking or burglary. One might argue that this change parallels the development of American industry from entrepreneurial, personal organizations to impersonal managerial corporations.

Criminal organizations in dime novels were remarkably large. Nick Carter once had to combat a gang, which had enlisted 250 men to rescue one of their members, on his way to prison. On another occasion he had to face a gang of 100 members known as the 'Coyotes,' made up of all types of criminals, sort of a vertical trust as suggested above. This gang had a complete apparatus of secret codes, oaths, and underground passageways.[27] When Old King Brady faced a plot against his life, he was told: 'The smartest crooks in this country are at the bottom of it.'[28] The criminals were organized, all-pervasive, and clever.

Although more realistic in their image of the criminal organization, the later novels, like the earlier ones, did not usually reproduce the contemporary identification of crime with specific ethnic groups. The critic Gary Hoppenstand defines the detectives as representing 'the triumph of the frontier-bred American hero over the dirty immigrant'; however, that is not the dominant theme of the tales I read. Although detectives sometimes battled Chinese gangs like the 'Tong Kings,' and the ethnic slur 'Chink' might be freely used, villains usually had Anglo Saxon names, including the worst villain in the Tong story.[29] Like their opponents, most detectives also had Anglo-Saxon names, and were the literary descendents of the western heroes. Some minor characters were drawn from various ethnic groups. Among these were 'Old Opium, the Mongol Detective,' an Irish and a Dago detective, as well as a couple of 'Negro' or 'Colored' detectives. But even ethnic identification was part of the uncertainty and mystery that surrounded the detective, since sometimes ethnicity is a disguise.[30]

---

27 *The Millionaire's Nemesis; or, Paul Rogers' Oath of Vengeance*, NNCW 390, June 18, 1904, p. 2; *Nick Carter's Wonderful Nerve; or, the Little Giant's Task*, Nick Carter Weekly [hereafter NCW], 303, Nov. 18, 1902, p. 6.

28 Francis W. Doughty, *The Bradys in a Snare; or, the Worst Case of All*, Secret Service Weekly [hereafter SSW], 819, Oct. 2, 1914, p. 1.

29 *The Bradys After the Tong Kings*, SSW 565, Nov. 19, 1909, reprinted in Hoppenstand.

30 Hoppenstand, *Dime Detective*, 16 (quotation); various titles are from a list of 434 titles on the back cover of Old Cap Collier Library [OCCL] 379, Aug. 4, 1890. For black detectives, one of whom was a white man in disguise, see Denning, *Mechanic Accents*, p. 210.

Luck, Pluck, Decency and Poetic Justice

Unlike actual private detectives in agencies like the Pinkertons, or the most sophisticated police detective branches, the fictional dime detectives did not meet criminal organizations with increasingly complex counter-organizations. While they often formed firms or partnerships, they did not run scientific, professionalized operations. There is a certain democracy in the world of dime novels; they suggest that anybody can become a detective, whatever their occupation, class, or ethnicity. The dime novel titles often identify the descriptive traits, professions, and even affiliations of detectives and they include: descriptions like self-made, tramp, athlete, lady, female and girl, Amazon and pedagogue; occupations like reporter, lawyer, blacksmith, fireman, and baseball player; and affiliations like Quaker, Mormon, and G.A.R. (organization of Union Civil War Veterans).[31] A 1926 advertisement appearing in a dime novel story weekly invited amateurs to become detectives:

> BE A DETECTIVE
> Make secret investigations. Earn big money.
> Work home or travel. Fascinating work.
> Excellent opportunity. Experience unnecessary.
> Particulars free.[32]

If not written by one of the swindlers mentioned earlier, this ad emphatically affirms faith in individual success, even if the detective stories themselves require their readers to have considerable imagination to make the hero's triumphs believable. Even if the odds are great, and to overcome them the detective must be drawn in fantastic shape, go ahead, they urged, be a detective!

One police critic described fictional detectives as 'endowed with such prescience, fitted out with such a wonderful brain and gifted with so many more senses than the average man.'[33] The heroes do indeed display such virtuosity, but they relied most often on Horatio Alger's combination of 'luck, pluck and decency.' Luck appears in the form of miraculous rescues or fortuitous circumstances. Dime detectives are rarely theorizers, like their English counterpart Sherlock Holmes, but are rather impulsive individuals who narrowly avoid death or capture and whose hunches luckily turn out to be correct. The average hero is incautious, and gets into troubles he could have avoided with a little prudence; pluck is usually what saves the detective from his own impulsiveness. He fights his way out of the scrapes he did not have the foresight to avoid. In fact, the detective's strength was sometimes superhuman. The average hero could cope with four or five, sometimes even ten, murderously inclined ruffians. Old Sleuth and Badger were able to handle attacks by thugs with the greatest of ease. Nick Carter, 'The Little Giant,' was as strong as Sandow the strong man, and showed tremendous fortitude in enduring the tortures he suffered as a result of blundering into the lair of a gang. Dime detectives were wonderfully able to get from one place to another with amazing speed; often they resemble Superman more than any real

---

31   From same list, above.

32   Ad from 'George R. Wagner, former government detective', in *Fame and Fortune Weekly*, 1099, Oct. 22, 1926, p. 28.

33   George W. Walling, *Recollections of a New York Chief of Police*, New York, 1887, p. 517.

detectives. We think of the Horatio Alger heroes' exploits as unrealistic, but they are prosaic compared to those of Nick Carter. Both forms affirm faith in success against great odds, but detectives operate in the fantastic realm of schoolboy's daydreams.

Decency, of course, is essential. The hero in these novels is always moral. He never drinks, smokes, or engages in sexual adventures; he 'represented the best the culture had to offer.'[34] The dime novels do not reflect contemporary fears that detectives became corrupt because of their association with the underworld. Occasionally the existence of selfish detectives is recognized, but dime novel detectives undertake investigations from only the highest motives. They are always ready to assist those who have no other redress, and often do so free of charge. Our heroes are not anti-heroes like Dashiell Hammett's Sam Spade. The creators of dime detectives turned the image of the confidence man on his head: donning disguises, spying, misleading criminals into revealing secrets, they nevertheless were always on the side of justice. The means did not corrupt the ends.

Dime detectives from the 1880-1920 period embodied the highest forms of justice. Old Cap Collier expressed the ideal of all the detectives when he said: 'To the good he was a mysterious guardian; to the evil he was mysterious and terrible.' Continuing, he warns a villain, '[B]ut look to yourself, the avenger is on your track.' Indeed, Gary Hoppenstand appropriately characterizes the dime hero as 'the avenger detective.' A police officer, who wrote during this period, spoke of the real-life detective in similar idealized terms; he was 'the silent, secret, and effective avenger of the outraged majesty of the law.'[35] The dime detective, however, seems more concerned about the actual achievement of justice than he is about either the law's majesty or legal procedure.

Novel writers generally considered it wiser to trust an avenger like Old Cap than the police, who did things in an unimaginative way. A friend of Kent Keen, the Crook-Crusher, informs a prospective client in one novel, that if he wishes to locate a missing person, '[Y]ou don't want to see the Police. I can do better than that for you... I can take you to Kent Keen, the best man-taker in this city.' Even a young boy doing amateur detective work for the first time proves more sagacious than a public official – the local sheriff. Sometimes the police doubt the hero's competence, and he must prove himself. Old Cap Collier chose the dramatic method of demonstrating his physical strength to a skeptical police chief by harmlessly throwing him across the room. The officer was impressed. As well as being more skilled, the dime detectives are more devoted to duty. In one novel about a murder case, the police considered Old King Brady foolhardy because he rushed into a burning building to prevent the destruction of evidence. Generally, the principal role of the detective is to show, as did Old Cap Collier, that the police had all the time been 'barking up the wrong tree.'[36] Indeed, the notion of the private detective's superior ability is a classic theme,

---

34 Hoppenstand, *Dime Detective*, p. 4.

35 W.I. James, *Old Cap Collier; or, 'Piping' the New Haven Mystery*, OCCL 1, c. 1883, pp. 4 and 14; McWatters, *Knots Untied*, pp. 643-644. Hoppenstand, *Dime Detectives*, p. 4.

36 T.C. Harbaugh, *Kent Keen, the Crook-Crusher; or, the Man from Spokane in New York*, BNYDL 896, Dec. 25, 1895, p. 1; *Dauntless Dan, the Boy Detective; or, the Mysterious House in the Hollow*, New York Detective Library [NYDL], p. 476, Jan. 9, 1892, throughout; James, *Old Cap*,

whether it refers to Sherlock Holmes or Sam Spade, and this view was first developed by American dime novelists. In these works the police are not criticized as corrupt or obstructionist, just narrow-minded and stubborn.

Though he invariably outshines the police, the dime detective is not hostile to them and does not scorn their authority. Such scorn is a product of later fictional 'tough-guy' private detectives. Though dime detectives do not work against the police, neither the police, nor their procedures, control the dime hero. Even if he is ostensibly connected to the police or U.S. Secret Service (the Bradys), the dime detective does not present the image of a public official. The trappings of officialdom, reports and orders from higher up, are scarcely present and the detectives' relation to the police is always presented vaguely. The heroes' contact with officials may lend an air of legitimacy – Old Cap Collier is rewarded by commendations from the police chief and Nick Carter is 'great friends' with the chief – but credit for their successes is theirs alone.

When 'barking up the wrong tree' the police sometimes obstructed justice by their arrest or even suspicion of an innocent person. They do not seem to be able to penetrate beneath the surface of things, and that is the detective hero's special ability. They [the police] are too often satisfied with superficial evidence of guilt, even when it is planted by the true villain as part of his plot. The police never recognize the fundamental principle of the dime novels that things are never as they seem.

It is up to the dime detective to place guilt where it really belongs. Rescuing innocent people from false charges is a theme that appears in works most frequently published before the turn of the century, reflecting the general gothic plot complexity of the earlier novels. Before 1900 twelve of thirty-four novels studied carried this theme; after 1900 only one out of twenty-two. The prosecuted innocent appears particularly in novels where the villain works for limited personal ends, unlike the professional gangs that characterize the twentieth century. Anybody can be accused of embezzlement, but not of safe cracking. Although it was never dominant in the novels before 1900, the representation of the prosecuted innocent underscored the belief that when public authorities actually take action in a case, they have charged and arrested the wrong person. In other words, when the authorities do place guilt, they are mistaken.

Often (nine out of the thirteen prosecuted characters) the wrongly accused person is a young man who has risen according to the principles of the Alger success stories, only to find himself the victim of some villain's conniving.[37] The detective emerges from an interview with the young man in prison convinced of his innocence, often because of his intuitive ability to detect sincerity. The detective is very paternal and convinces him that justice will be done.[38]

The ultimate fate of the true criminal, once apprehended, is not of great concern to dime novel writers. It is sufficient that the detective has caught him (or her) and proven guilt. Nick Carter, for example, never bothered his head about a prisoner after

---

p. 2; Francis W. Doughty, *The Bradys' Race for Life; or, Rounding up a Tough Trio*, SSW 809, July 24, 1914, p. 2; James, *Old Cap*, p. 41.

[37] The remaining four prosecuted innocents are the detectives themselves, arrested as suspects while in disguise.

[38] As in the case of Albert Gray in *Old Sleuth, Badger & Co.*, OSL 59, Dec. 17, 1891.

he had turned him over to the proper authorities. In over half the novels I read, there is expressed indifference about the publicly authorized punishment that the criminal receives. The villains are always punished, but in the majority (thirty) of the novels their punishment takes the form of poetic or unofficial justice (*e.g.* going insane, committing suicide, death in a gun battle). In the remaining twenty-six stories criminals are punished according to the due process of the law (execution or imprisonment), but trial scenes, the climax of many modern mysteries, are not a plot element. Although Gary Hoppenstand characterized the dime hero as a 'vigilante crime fighter,'[39] that designation would apply only to about half the tales. And while vigilantes usually carry out the punishment themselves, in 'poetic justice' novels that is not always the case. The kind of justice meted, whether unofficial or not, is not influenced by any specific plot requirements. It is not associated with particular writers, by the plot requirements of a particular series, or even by the degree of evil attributed to the criminal's character.[40] And there is only slight suggestion of a shift from this pattern of indifference with the emerging theme of the professionalization of crime.[41] And while indifference towards the form of punishment did not necessarily reflect hostility toward authority, the power of the state to mandate punishment is hardly affirmed in dime novels.

The indifference with which dime novel writers regarded both official and unofficial punishment appears in the Nick Carter series. On the back cover of one of the magazines the stories are represented as showing 'how impossible it is for any man to transgress the law without being punished (...) Nick (...) seldom fails to land his man behind the bars.' Yet, when he does fail, even lynch law can be a valid form of justice. 'Try to remember that you have laws in the East and we have laws in the big West,' one of Carter's assistants is told, 'Some of ours may be unwritten but they are effective. Let it go at that.' Jail and lynching are both forms of justice, and it is with justice, not the niceties of the law, that the detective stories are concerned. Significantly, a student of lynching, writing at the time the Carter tales were published, noted that among Americans '[T]he value of laws as rules of conduct is not minimized but there is no sense of sanctity pertaining to them.' Outwitting, avoiding, defying, or forgetting the law 'is not a serious offense so long as an appeal can be made to the individual sense of justice in support of such courses of action.'[42] In short, the dime novels reflected a major cultural theme about justice, but not one that adults necessarily wanted children to learn or that moral reformers wanted working-class people to see in print, but one deeply rooted nevertheless.

The dime novel detective of this period transcends the limitations of the organized system of criminal justice. The reader's hero is free-wheeling, the only person capable of getting at the truth, and of going beneath the surface to see things as they really are.

---

[39] Hoppenstand, *Dime Detectives*, p. 4.

[40] Kate Davis, a scheming and desperate woman, is let off completely after providing evidence of Albert Gray's innocence, in *Old Sleuth, Badger & Co.*

[41] In novels published before 1900, nine of thirty-four leading villains received poetic justice; after 1900, eleven out of twenty-two.

[42] *Human Weapon*, back cover; *Kid Curry's Last Stand: or, Nick Carter in Dangerous Surroundings*, NNCW 558, Sept. 7, 1907, p. 28. For a good example of the genre of detective story in western setting see James E. Cutler, *Lynch-Law: an Investigation into the History of Lynching in the United States*, New York, 1905, p. 268.

There is no direct challenge to authority, only the creation of a world in which justice can be achieved through the efforts of individual imagination and physical strength. The detective does not need elaborate official machinery or resources to triumph. His or her battle may be one on one or one against a hundred, but in each case it expresses a form of individual combat. Without rejecting social authority, the dime novels find the truest source of justice in the heroic individual.

Detective heroes who operate outside the official norms of the criminal justice system and function as agents of higher justice are conventions of detective fiction, English and French as well as American. Yet dime detective stories were written to appeal to Americans, and they expressed the deeply rooted fears and values of American society.

Index